QUICK & CLEVER Drawing

Michael Sanders

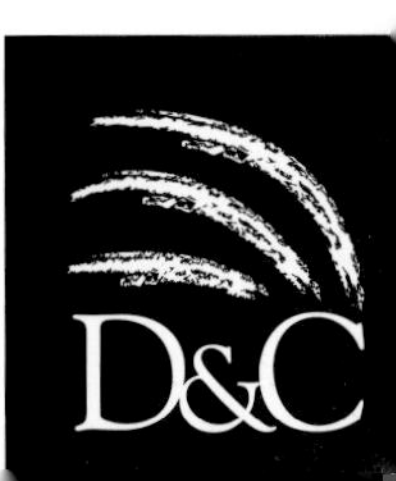

A DAVID & CHARLES BOOK
Copyright © David & Charles Limited 2009

David & Charles is an F+W Media Inc. company
4700 East Galbraith Road
Cincinnati, OH 45236

First published in the UK in 2009

Text and illustrations copyright © Michael Sanders 2009
Michael Sanders has asserted his right to be identified as author of this work in accordance with the Copyright, Designs and Patents Act, 1988.

All rights reserved. No part of this publication may be reproduced, stored in a retrieval system, or transmitted, in any form or by any means, electronic or mechanical, by photocopying, recording or otherwise, without prior permission in writing from the publisher.

A catalogue record for this book is available from the British Library.

ISBN-13: 978-0-7153-2943-6 paperback
ISBN-10: 0-7153-2943-6 paperback

Printed in China by Shenzhen Donnelley Printing Co. Ltd
for David & Charles
Brunel House Newton Abbot Devon

Senior Commissioning Editor: Freya Dangerfield
Editorial Manager: Emily Pitcher
Editor: Verity Muir
Art Editor: Sarah Clark
Designer: Joanna Ley
Production Controller: Kelly Smith
Photographer: Kim Sayer

Visit our website at www.davidandcharles.co.uk

David & Charles books are available from all good bookshops; alternatively you can contact our Orderline on 0870 9908222 or write to us at FREEPOST EX2 110, D&C Direct, Newton Abbot, TQ12 4ZZ (no stamp required UK only); US customers call 800-289-0963 and Canadian customers call 800-840-5220.

CONTENTS

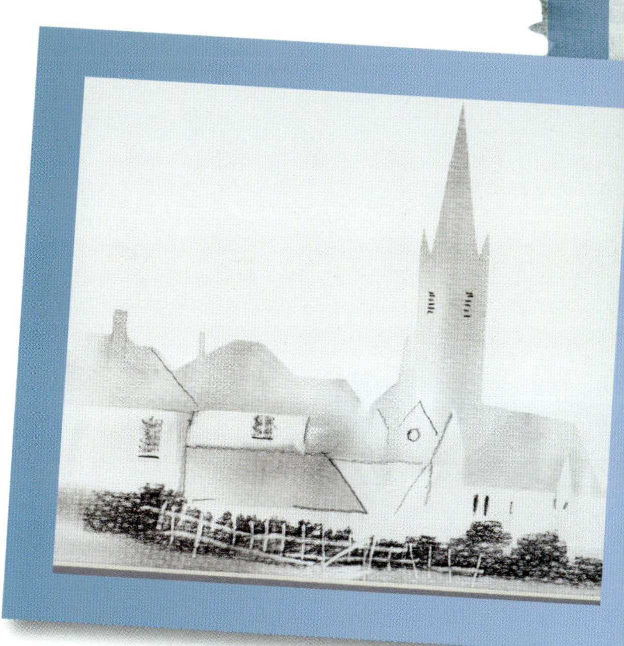

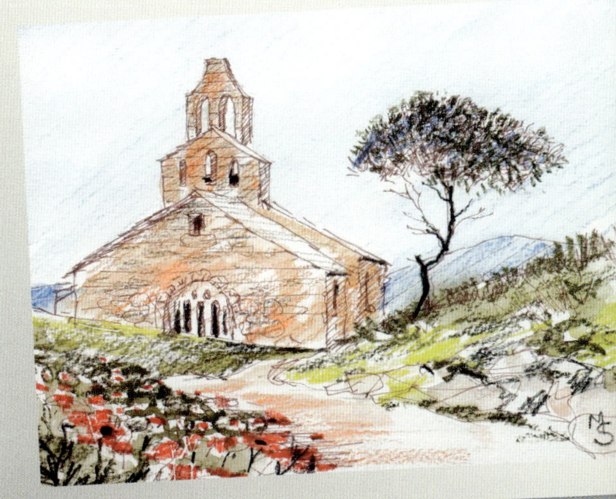

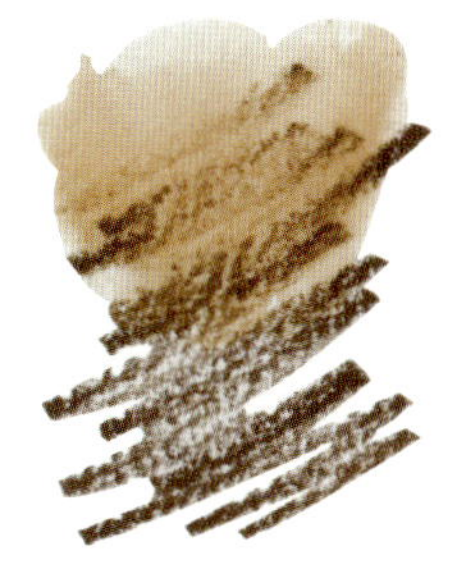

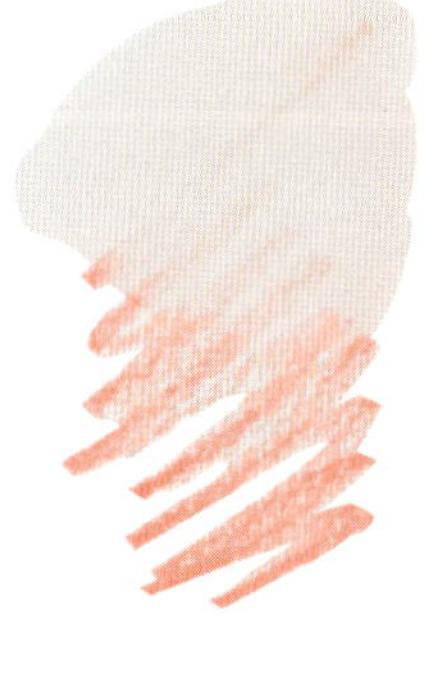

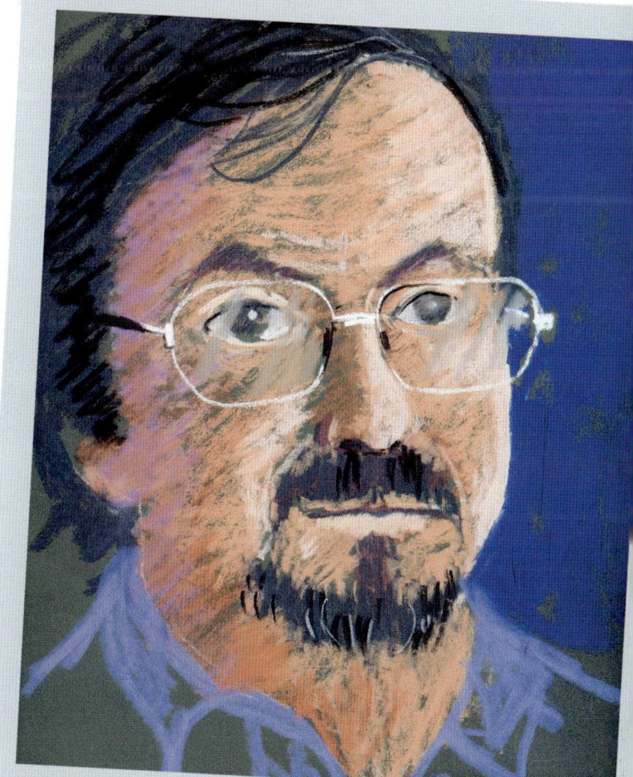

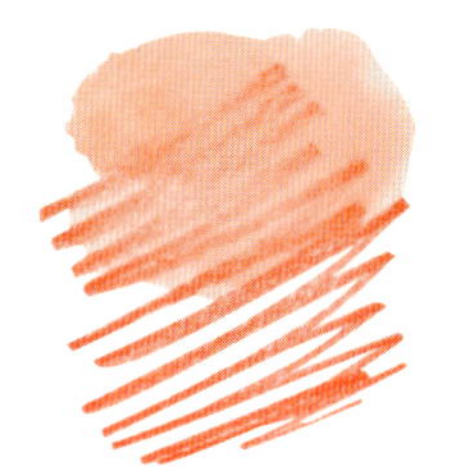

STARTING TO DRAW

Do you remember when you were a child? I bet that some of your memories are of making drawings, being excited by coloured crayons, scribbling and smudging. Children love drawing, so why do we stop doing it when we get older? Kids love to draw because they know it's fun, and one of the reasons they stop is that they start to believe it's difficult. We also get told that we mustn't smudge or make a mess; that our lines should be straight; and that only clever or talented people can draw well. My aim in this book is to prove that you can draw, and that it can be fun; that smudging, scribbling and making marks is not only acceptable – it's very useful!

MAKING MARKS: A BIT OF HISTORY

The urge to make marks is a primeval instinct. The cave art in such places as Altamira, El Castillo and Las Monedas in Cantabria, northern Spain, and Lascaux, Rouffignac, Saint Cirq and Peche-Merle in the Dordogne and Lot areas of France, as well as that found in caves in many other parts of the world, are vibrant reminders that our ancestors, 15,000 years ago, produced some fine drawings. These drawings, made with bits of burnt stick and powdered rock, evoke the movement of horses and bison. And the cave artists didn't have an art shop to get materials from! Where there was nothing to make charcoal from, or maybe before the discovery of fire, they scratched their drawings in rock with hard flint points.

So you could say it's innate in humans to want to make marks on things. There is something very rewarding about being able to turn ideas into visible things so that others can see them. Throughout the ages, people have used drawing as a means of communicating ideas, such as plans, designs and maps; but drawings have also always been works of art in their own right. Over the centuries, drawing materials have improved. Burnt stick developed into fine charcoal; dark stones evolved into pencils; powdered rock pigment with animal fat developed into ink and paint; and twigs dipped in mud developed into quill pens, then metal nibs, ballpoint pens… And now we are in the digital age, where art can be created with the click of a mouse. Where next? Who knows. What I'm sure of, though, is that traditional drawing tools are just as exciting to use as they always have been. Learning a new skill is rewarding; drawing is fun!

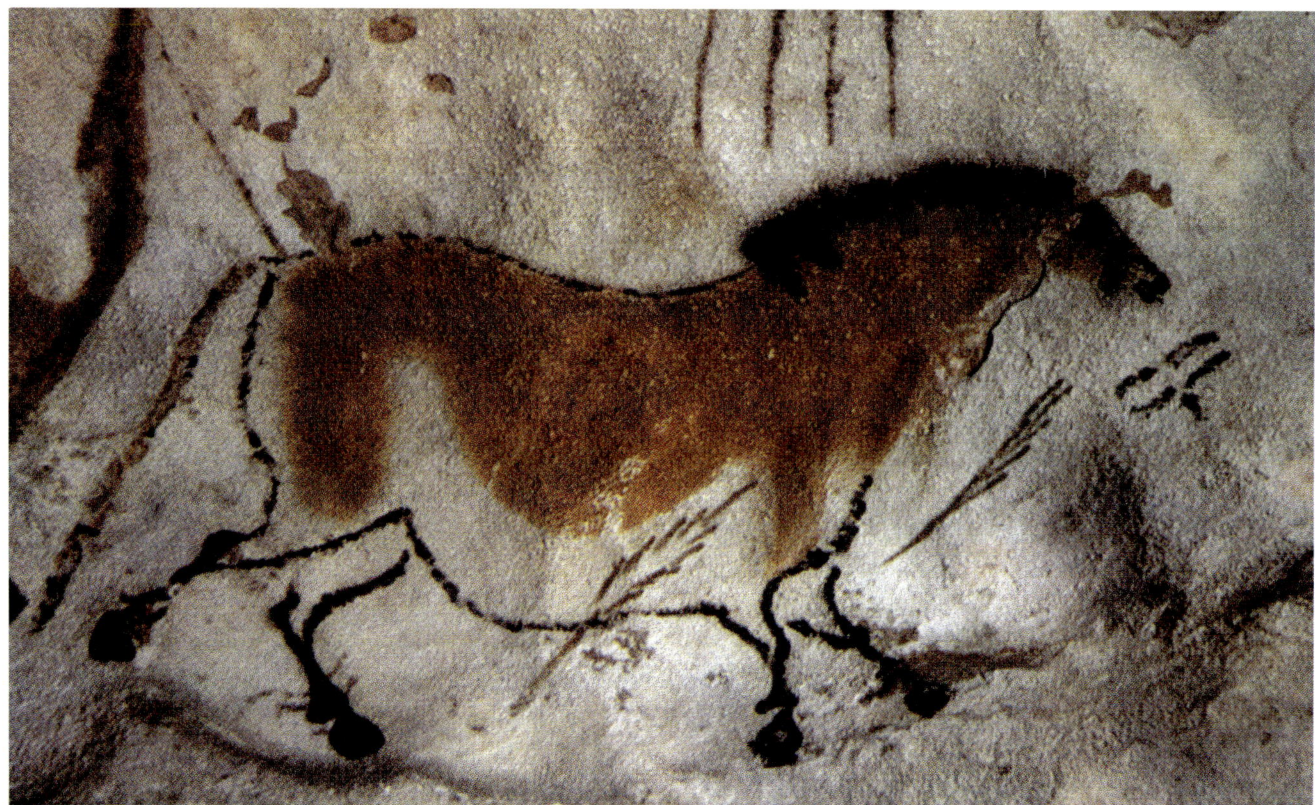

▲ *This cave painting from Lascaux Cave, Dordogne, France, is a vibrant reminder of how our ancestors loved to draw.*

DRAW YOUR VACATION!

Drawing can give a new dimension to many areas of your life. Imagine coming back from holiday, and rather than just showing off the usual photos, getting out your sketchbook and explaining to your friends where you sat and how the light cast shadows, the way the sun shone and the scent of the flowers. A nice drawing, well framed, can evoke memories in a way that a photograph simply can't. When you sketch you become more observant and more aware of your surroundings. Everything is imprinted in your memory.

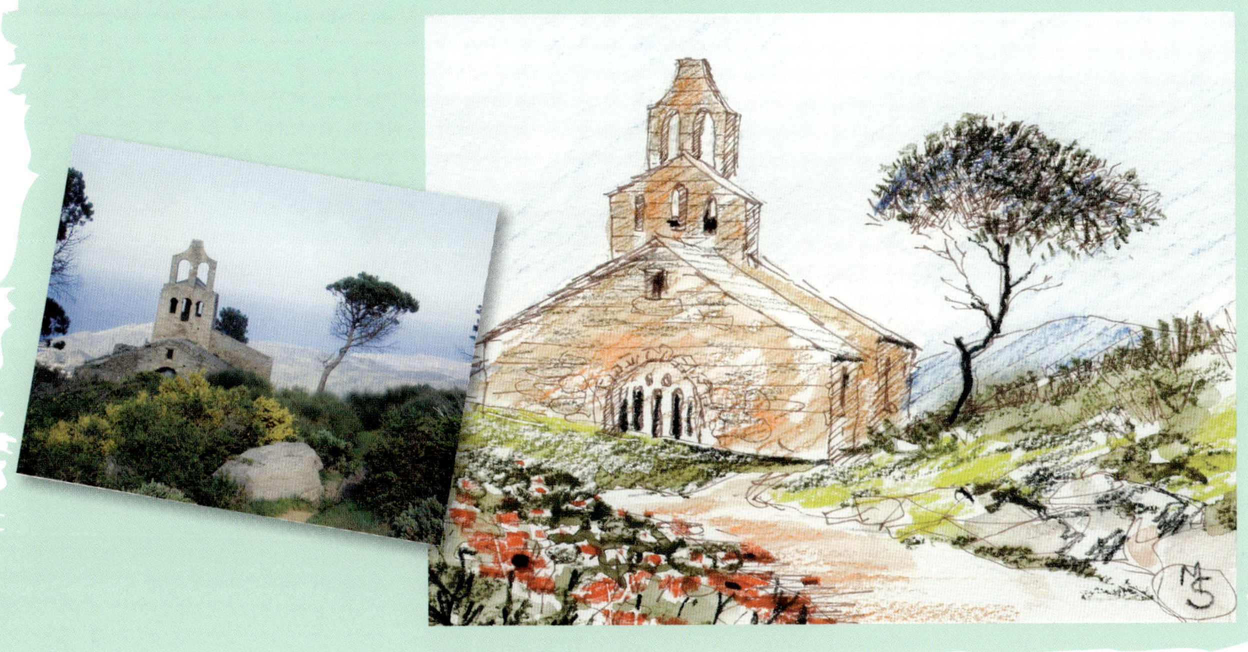

STARTING TO DRAW

WHAT EXACTLY IS DRAWING?

Drawing is simply making marks on paper or some other surface. It can be done with lines or smudges; it can be done using grey and black, or with any colour you like. Drawing is about expressing yourself in the most basic and straightforward way. To learn to draw, all you need are two items and two attitudes: you need something to draw on and something to draw with; and you need the desire to learn and the persistence to practise.

People sometimes say to me, 'I can't draw'. My reply usually is, 'Well, I can't play the bagpipes.' I leave a short pause and add, 'Of course, no one has shown me how to, and I've never really tried.' The point is, if you want to draw and you are prepared to practise (and make mistakes, like all of us), then you will succeed. Before you continue reading, I want you to do me a favour. Somewhere, in the back of your mind, is a negative voice, telling you that you can't draw. We've all got a voice like that. What I want you to do is repeat to yourself several times, before picking up a pencil, 'I can learn to draw.' Not 'I ***can*** draw', but 'I can ***learn*** to draw'.

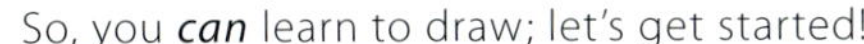

So, you ***can*** learn to draw; let's get started!

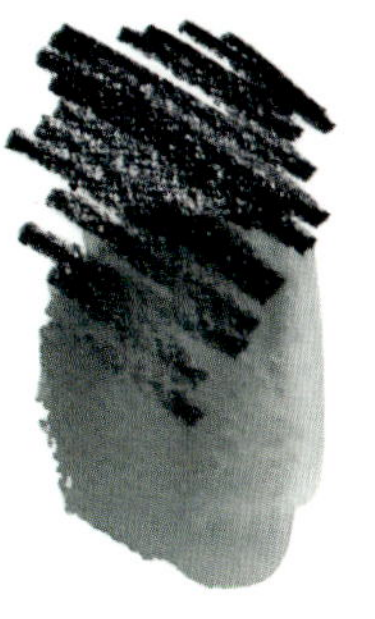

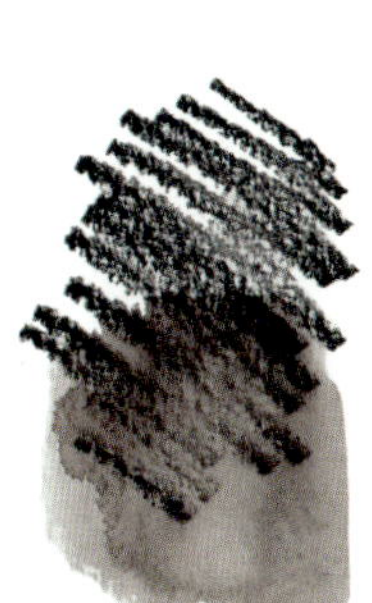

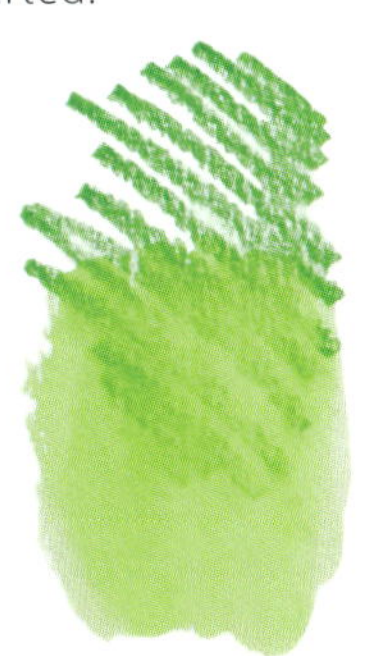

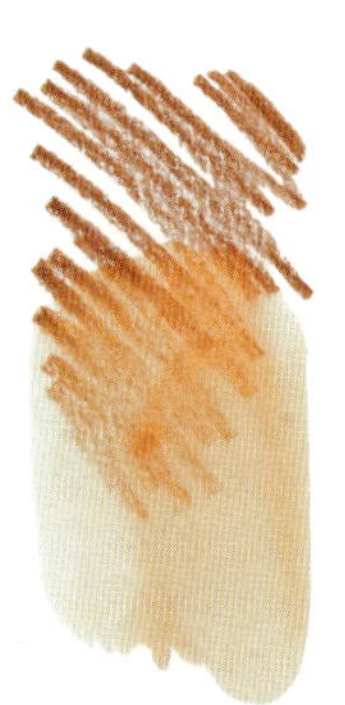

USING THIS BOOK

Throughout this book I'll be showing you drawing techniques, with simple exercises to enable you to practise these before using them in your drawings. You can learn at your own pace, gradually developing confidence as you progress. The first techniques are very straightforward – you don't even need to draw a line to produce an image! The book is a progressive learning experience: it is very simple to start off; then, as your skills develop (and they will, if you practise), you will make drawings using a variety of methods and materials. None of the tools or equipment used is complex or very expensive; that's the joy of drawing.

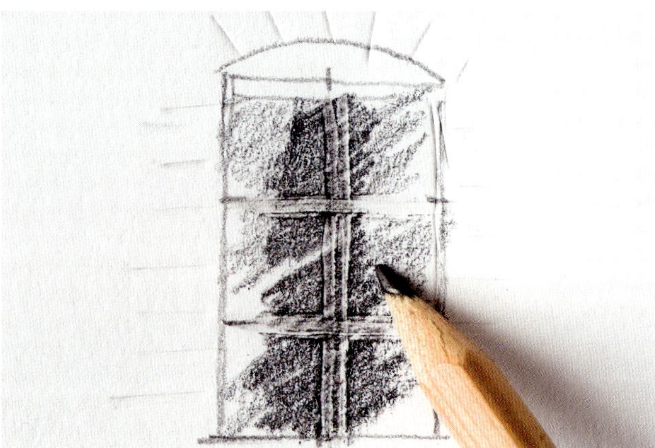

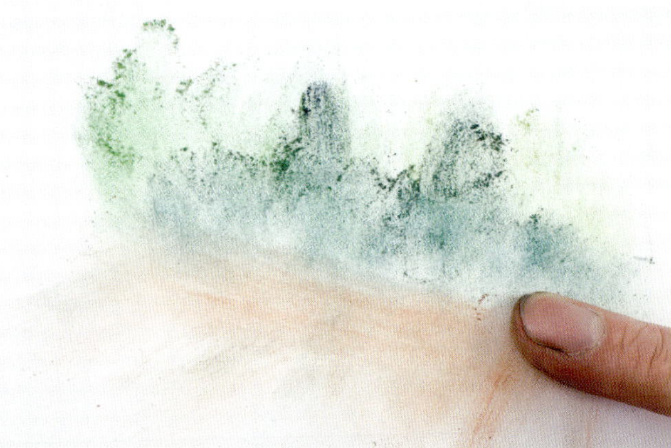

▲ *You can start by practising various techniques that are simple to pick up before you move on to the main project.*

The major part of the book (pages 46–119) consists of drawing projects. These six projects are designed to show you how to put the techniques you're learning into practice. Before each project there's a section on the methods needed to create that drawing and related subjects. The idea is that you practise these methods separately, before starting on the project itself. That way, you don't go into the exercise unprepared. It's important to do these exercises before each project; you'll be more confident, and will learn more. This is the most important thing in learning to draw – guided practice is essential. Please don't skip these bits! Each project builds on the skills learned from the session before, so your confidence will improve.

Scattered throughout the book you will find plenty of tips; these are ways of working that I've found useful over the years. I want you to succeed. So, will you promise me now that you are going to practise the exercises? C'mon, it's fun! OK, we have a deal. Let's get started by looking at the materials available.

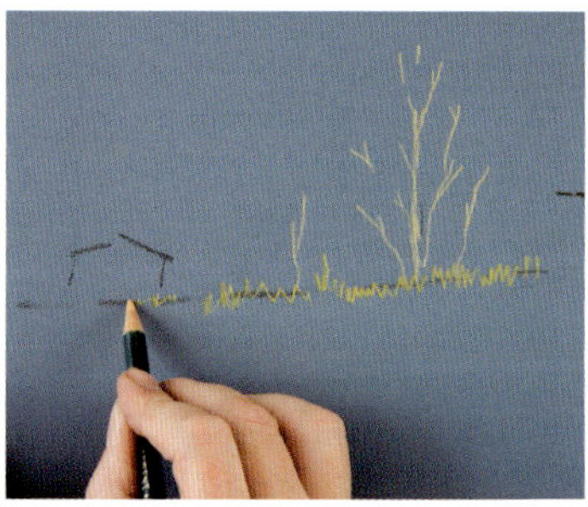

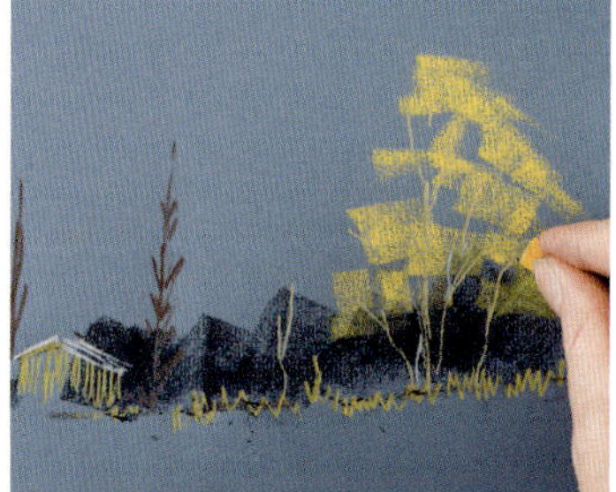

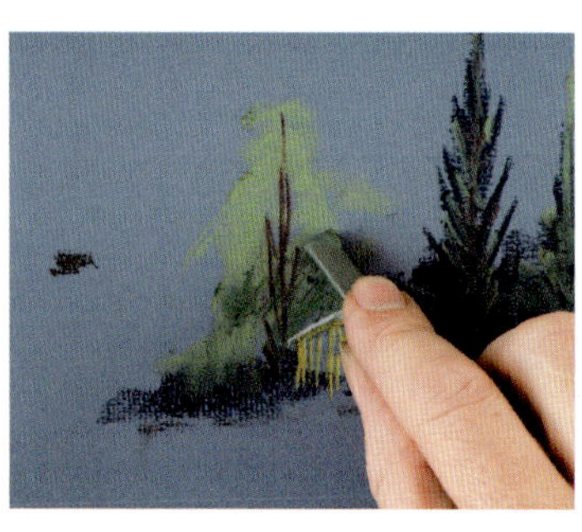

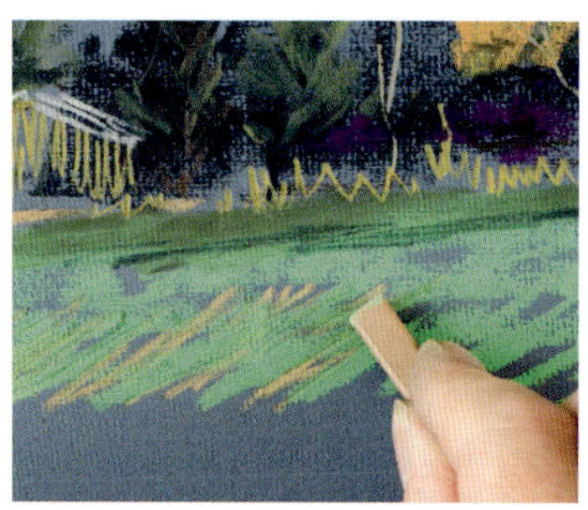

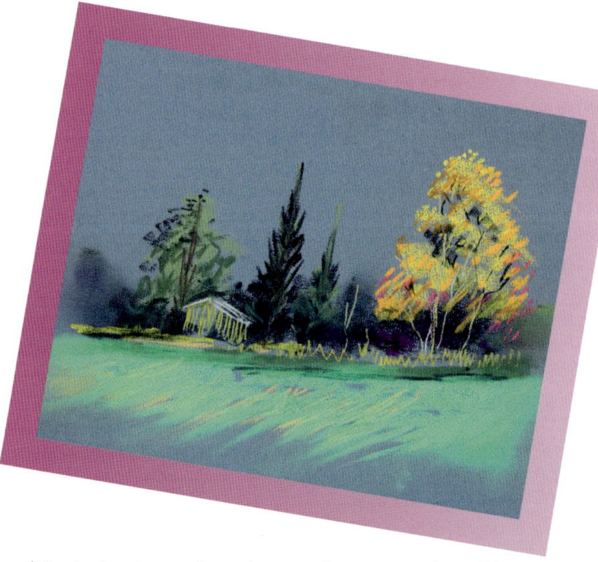

◀ *Each chapter explores how to draw a popular subject, starting with technique-focused exercises before moving on to a step-by-step drawing.*

EXPLORE THE SUBJECT...

Each project covers a different subject, giving you a wide range of skills.

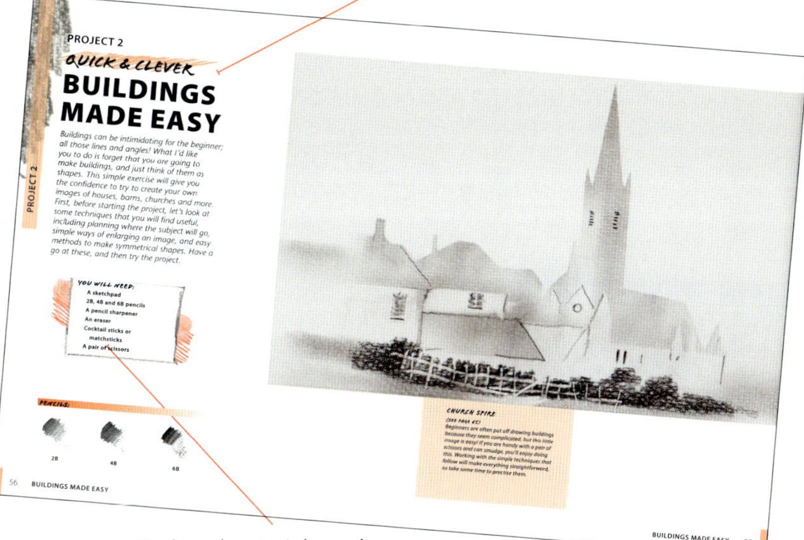

Tools and materials used are fully described, including colour swatches for matching.

PRACTISE THE TECHNIQUES...

TECHNIQUE – PLANNING

TECHNIQUE – ENLARGING

Start with technique-focused exercises.

Each technique is clearly demonstrated with examples of how it is used.

Quick and clever tips offer advice and shortcuts throughout the book.

COMPLETE THE DRAWING...

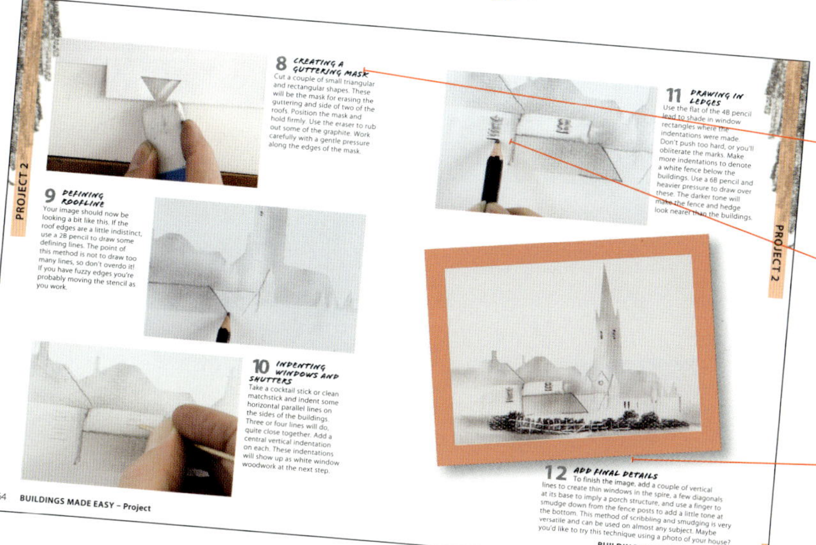

Each step is carefully described in the text and shown close up for clarity.

Close-up detail allows you to see how the drawing tools are used and how the marks are made.

Step by step, you can follow each drawing right from the first line through to its completion.

MATERIALS

DRAWING MATERIALS ARE WIDELY AVAILABLE, FROM SIMPLE BALLPOINT PENS TO EXTENSIVE SETS OF WATERCOLOUR PENCILS. TO START WITH, A SET OF SKETCHING PENCILS AND SOME CARTRIDGE PAPER WILL BE ALL THAT YOU NEED, BUT AS YOU PROGRESS THROUGH THE BOOK YOU WILL FIND IT ESSENTIAL TO HAVE SMALL SETS OF WATERCOLOUR PENCILS, PASTEL PENCILS, HARD PASTELS AND ASSORTED PENS, AS WELL AS A RANGE OF COLOURED PAPERS.

TOOLS OF THE TRADE

All manufacturers of drawing equipment have large ranges available. To begin with, it's best to buy small sets until you know what you prefer; this knowledge comes with experience. It's best to get a starter pack of, for instance, watercolour pencils, and add to it as necessary. Alternatively, get your Christmas present list in early!

The two essential items that you need to start drawing are drawing materials (such as pencils, pens and pastels) and paper. You need very little extra gear in order to get started, but there are a few things that you can buy to make life easier.

▶ *One useful item is a board to rest on. If you're using sheets of paper rather than pads, a board is essential; even with pads a board helps to keep things steady. If you would like to try standing up to draw, then fixing your board to a sketching easel could be useful.*

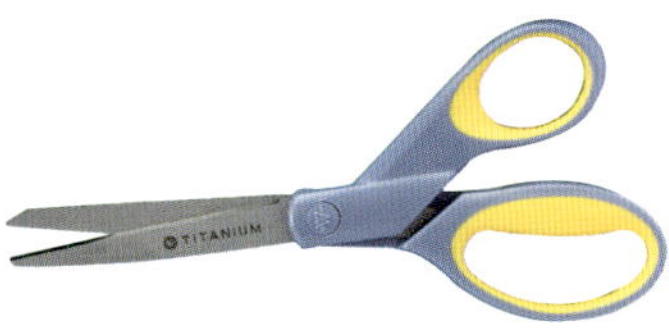

▲ *Scissors are useful for trimming sheets of paper, cutting out masks and so on.*

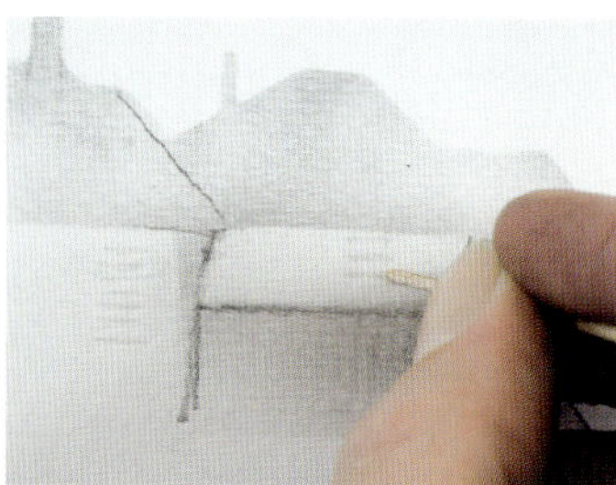

▲ *A few cocktail sticks might be useful for indenting into paper.*

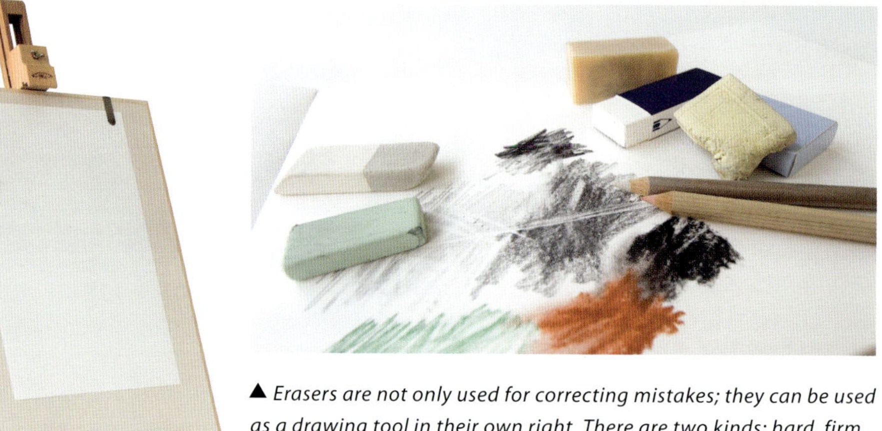

▲ *Erasers are not only used for correcting mistakes; they can be used as a drawing tool in their own right. There are two kinds: hard, firm 'traditional' ones, and soft, kneadable 'putty' types.*

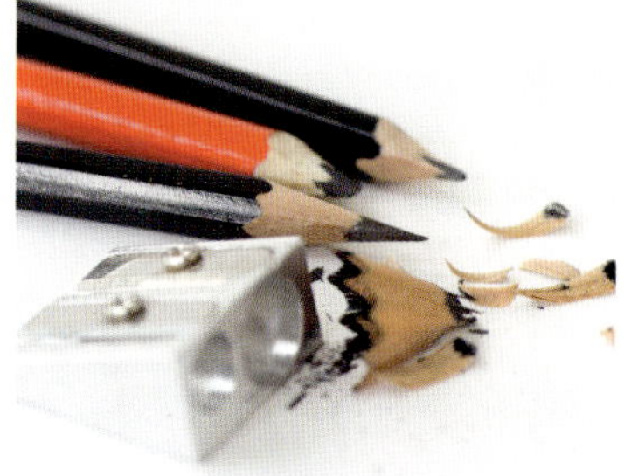

▲ *Pencil sharpeners are often overlooked on a sketching trip; make sure that you carry a spare one!*

PENCILS, PAPERS AND SURFACES

The humble lead pencil is perhaps the most overlooked of all art materials. The 'lead' was originally made from graphite mined in Cumbria, northern England, in the sixteenth century. These days, powdered graphite is mixed with clay and fired to produce the 'lead' for pencils. Used sensitively, pencils can produce attractive drawings that are works of art in their own right. One of the delightful things about drawing is that you can work on almost anything, including brown paper, DIY lining paper and cartridge paper.

Pencils come in two basic grades: hard or soft. The prefix 'H' denotes that the pencil is hard, whereas 'B' means it's soft. ('B' stands for 'black', because soft pencils make darker marks.) 'HB' is in the middle. The higher the number on the pencil, the softer or harder it is. This means that a 5B pencil is softer and darker than a 2B, and a 4H is harder than an H.

For art purposes, we want an expressive line that can be blended or smudged, and easily erased if needed, so we use 'B' grade pencils. These are often sold in sets, from B to 6B, as 'sketching pencils'. Propelling or clutch pencils are available that contain the lead strip in the body of the pencil. These can be useful if you can obtain a range of grades for the lead. The best paper to use with pencils is good-quality cartridge paper or light-coloured pastel paper.

Pads come in various sizes. Typical sizes are A5 (15 x 21cm/5¾ x 8¼in); A4 (21 x 29.5cm/8¼ x 11½in); and A3 (29.5 x 42cm x 11½ x 16½in). You don't have to commit yourself to working in any particular size; just choose a pad that seems comfortable.

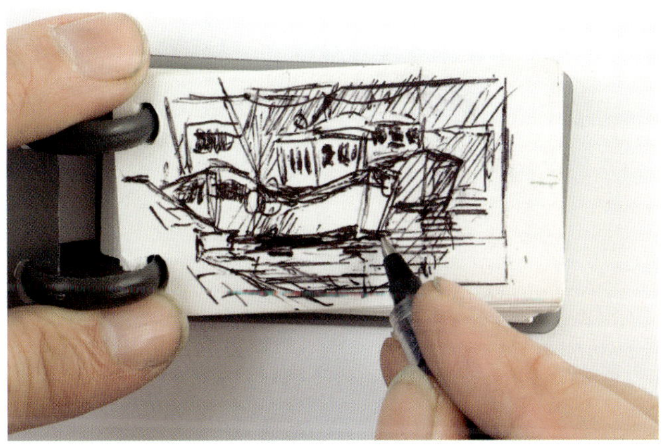

▲ *Look closely at the size of this pad compared to my fingers! Yet this tiny pad is still big enough to record a scene for reference.*

QUICK & CLEVER EFFECTS!

Pencils can be used to make a wide variety of interesting marks.

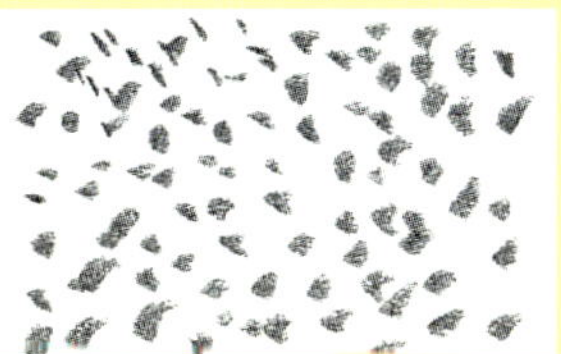

Dots look like small stones, rough surfaces, distant pebbles or leaves.

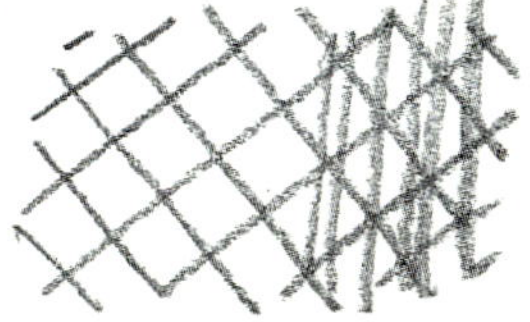

Cross-hatching adds more tone with every additional line.

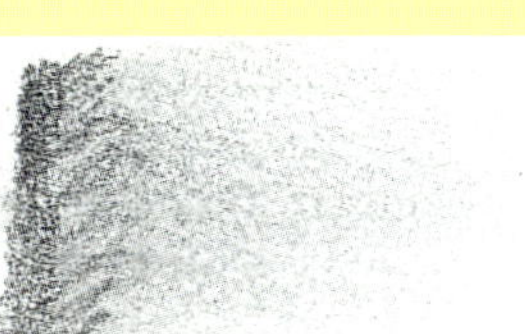

Smudging is useful for softening, and builds into a useful technique.

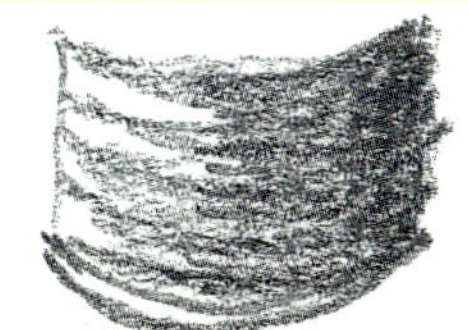

Form shading is where the lines follow the shape of the subject; this is very useful.

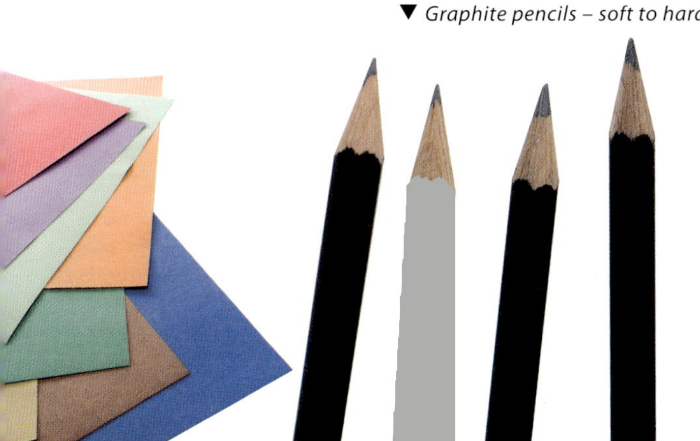

▼ *Graphite pencils – soft to hard.*

◀ *Carpenter's pencil.*

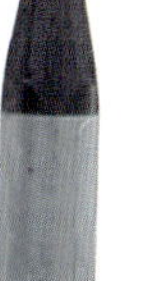

◀ *Water-soluble graphite pencils.*

COLOURED PENCILS

Coloured pencils come in a huge variety of colours. The 'lead', which is technically known as a 'strip', is made from pigment and a binding material such as cellulose gum to hold it together. Before being put into the wooden casing, the strips of colour are dipped in molten wax to improve their drawing properties. Most of the colours contain a filler such as chalk. The cheaper ranges have lots of chalk compared to pigment. The more expensive coloured pencils have higher levels of pigment, and give better results. You get what you pay for!

Coloured pencil gives a slightly waxy line, and is not easy to rub out or smudge. Because of the slight waxiness, these pencils often resist being worked over by softer materials such as pastels. This can be a useful technique. It is possible, using a light pressure, to gently apply one colour onto another and achieve very subtle and interesting results.

QUICK & CLEVER EFFECTS!

Use coloured pencils on multiple surfaces to achieve different effects.

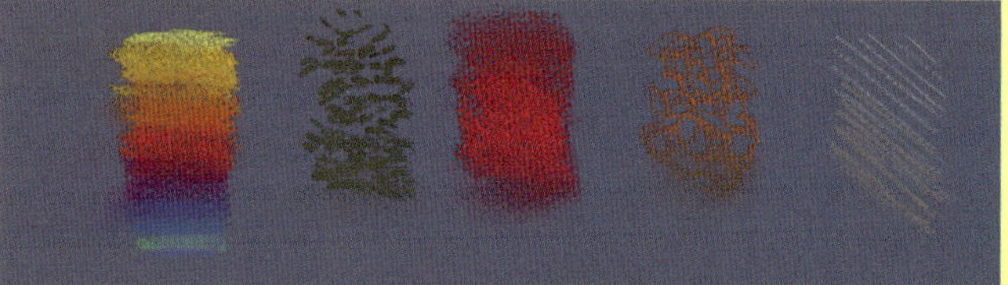

Pastel paper has a characteristic fine-line texture that is ideal for these versatile pencils.

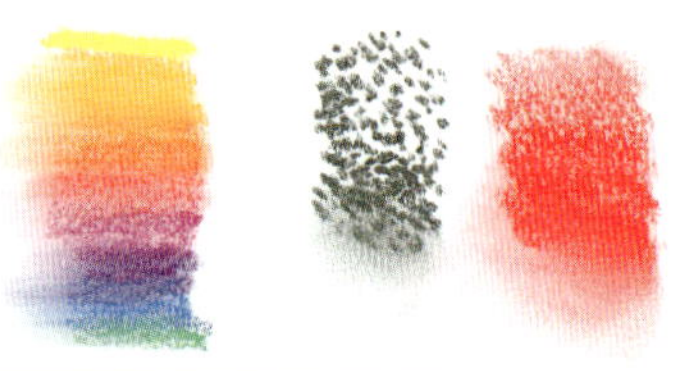

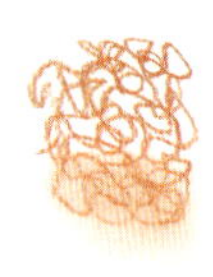

Varying the pressure produces light to dark tones. Using the tip or the side gives different effects, as shown on this cartridge paper.

QUICK & CLEVER!

When taking pencils on holiday don't forget a pencil sharpener! Good pencil sharpeners should have two holes: one for normal-size pencils, and one for thicker ones. If your pencil sharpener tears the wood and breaks the lead rather than sharpening it, the blade has become too blunt and needs replacing.

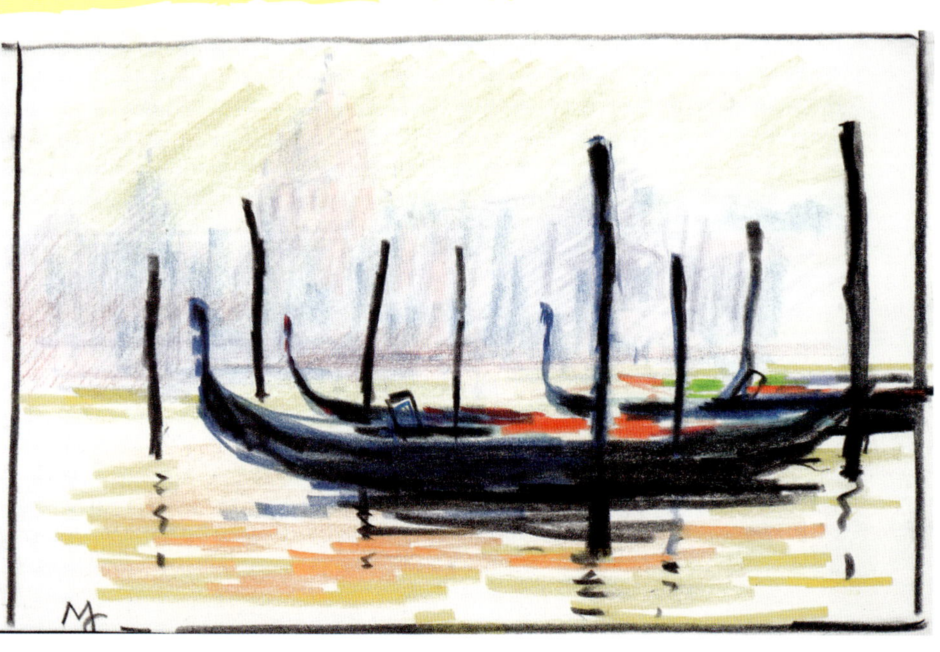

◀ One benefit of coloured pencils is their portability; I always take a small pocket-size set with me on holiday. They can produce charming little images, and are quick and precise to use.

COLOURED PENCILS

WATERCOLOUR PENCILS

These can be used as traditional coloured drawing pencils, where line and other marks are used, or they can be used in combination with water, when they give a watercolour effect similar to washes. They are made from a pigment similar to coloured pencils, but no wax is added: the binder that sticks the pigment together is a water-soluble gum.

Watercolour pencils are primarily a drawing medium, because the water is usually applied after the pencil has been used, but good effects can be achieved by dipping the pencil into water before use, or lifting the pigment off the tip with a wet brush. It is also possible to abrade the end of the pencil onto sandpaper and use the coloured dust. These pencils add another dimension to a drawing. If used alone they give exactly the same effects as ordinary coloured pencils, but adding water enables them to be blended to create softer mixed colours.

QUICK & CLEVER EFFECTS!

This medium can be used in the same way as normal coloured pencils, but if you add water the colour dissolves and can be blended.

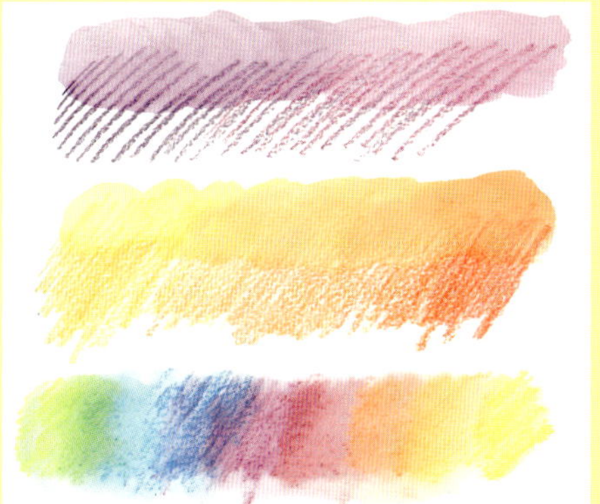

HATCHING AND WASH

If washed over with not much water and a gentle brushstroke, the colour will wash out but the lines will still be slightly visible.

LIGHT SCRIBBLE AND WASH

If there are no defined lines, washing water over will produce a softer effect.

WETTED PAPER

This softens the lines as soon as the pencil touches the paper. Good-quality heavy watercolour paper works best for this.

QUICK & CLEVER!

Watercolour pencils work best on watercolour paper, especially rough paper. Cartridge paper is too smooth and won't give such vibrant results.

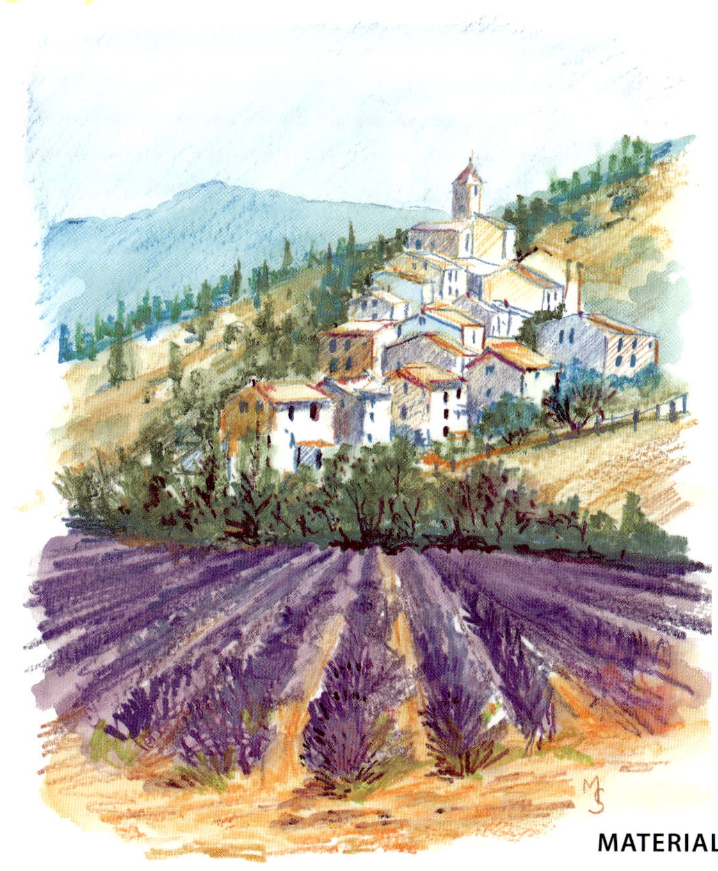

▶ *This image of Provence in France, uses strong, vibrant colours. Some of the lavender was drawn with watercolour pencils onto wet paper, which adds to the strength of colour. Hatching lines are still visible on the buildings, adding shading.*

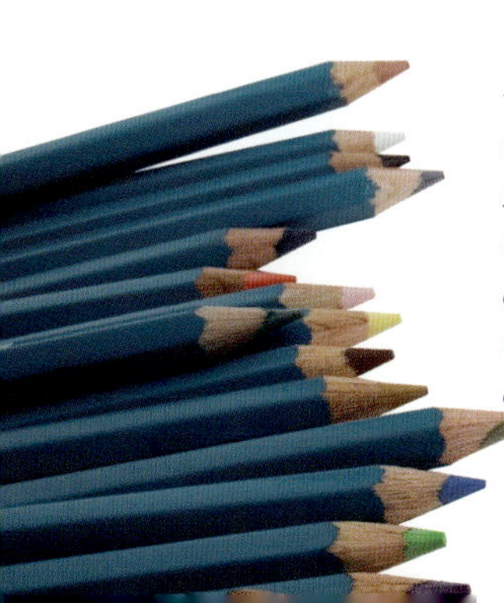

◀ *There are two grades of watercolour pencils: the softer pencils give a good wash, whereas the harder ones dissolve with a paler wash, often with the original drawing lines still visible.*

WATERCOLOUR PENCILS

PASTEL PENCILS

Not to be confused with coloured pencils, pastel pencils are like thin pastels in a wooden case. Although similar to soft pastel sticks, they are manufactured slightly harder. Made from pigment and a binder such as gum tragacanth or methyl cellulose, they impart a soft velvety look and can be easily blended with fingers or a special rolled paper cylinder called a torchon or stump.

Pastel pencils avoid the drawbacks of pastel sticks: they are clean; colour doesn't come off on your hands; and they don't break easily. Pastel pencils need pastel paper, or fine sandpaper, for best results, and work better on coloured backgrounds.

When storing drawings, take care not to rub the surface, or the work could be spoiled. A fixative is available for pastels and this can be used for pastel pencils too, although there will be some colour change. Alternatively, get your drawings mounted and behind glass as soon as possible. Then you can start selling them!

QUICK & CLEVER EFFECTS!

A wide variety of marks can be produced with pastel pencils, from areas of solid colour, to fine individual lines, to soft blends of one colour into another.

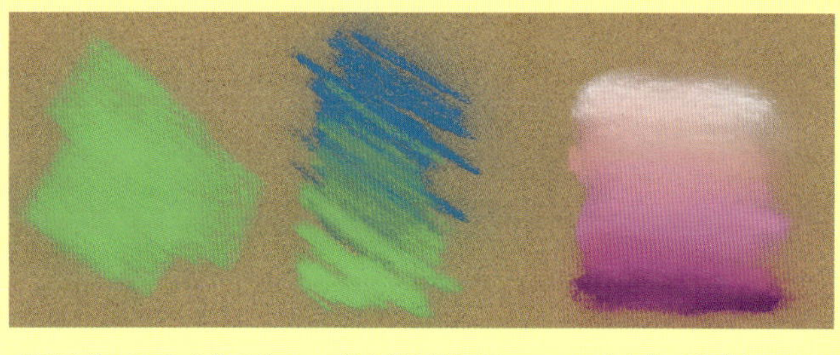

USED ON EDGE HATCHING BLENDED

QUICK & CLEVER!

Make sure you have the right type of pencil sharpener (most manufacturers make ones specifically for pastel pencils); otherwise you will find it difficult to sharpen these pencils. Alternatively, use a sharp craft knife with a retractable blade.

▼ *This quick sketch of Cortona in Spain was completed on the spot; blending was used afterwards to soften some of the edges. I've brushed water on here and there to soften the edges still further, especially in the sky. The individual strokes of the pastel pencil can be seen clearly in places.*

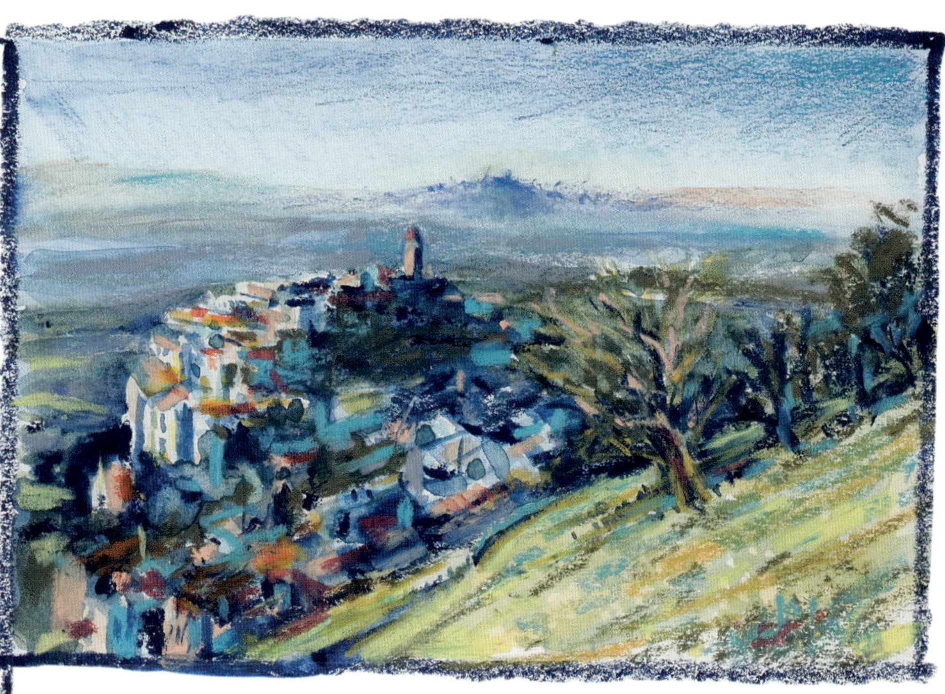

▼ *These wood-cased pencils with a pastel lead are ideal for beginners as they are less crumbly than pastels and are easier to control.*

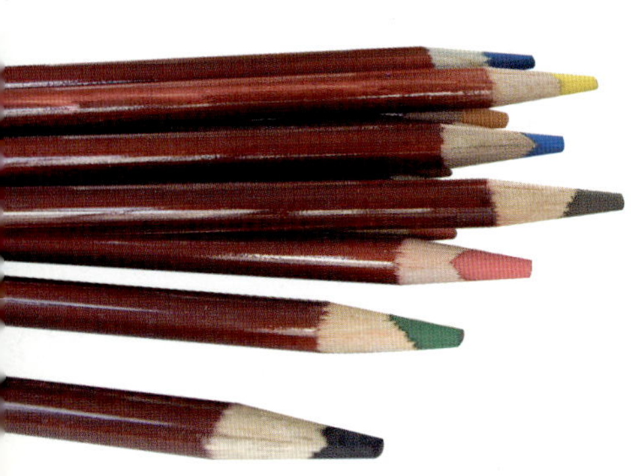

SOFT AND HARD PASTELS

Soft pastels are sticks of pigment and binder, usually wrapped in paper. They are available in a huge range of colours, and are easily blended. Line is variable with pressure and can be smudged. Like the pencil variant, they are capable of producing a soft velvety quality that is quite distinctive. Pastels are particularly suitable where a degree of blending between tones is concerned – for instance, in portraits or for soft atmospheric effects or distance in landscapes.

Hard pastels are usually square in cross-section rather than round, come in a more restricted range of colours and are capable of producing finer lines than soft pastels. It is useful to have some of each kind, and they can be intermixed in a drawing quite usefully. Conté crayons are hard pastels that are restricted to sepia, browns, ochre and white, and are traditionally favoured for portraits and figures.

QUICK & CLEVER!

Soft pastels, kept together in a box, tend to rub together. This causes colours to be contaminated by other colours, and eventually the pastels look 'dirty'. To clean them, take a large, lidded jar and half fill it with dry rice. Put the pastels in, close the lid, shake for a few minutes, and the pastels will come up clean again!

QUICK & CLEVER EFFECTS!

Strong, vibrant strokes can be modified and blended to give a whole range of attractive effects.

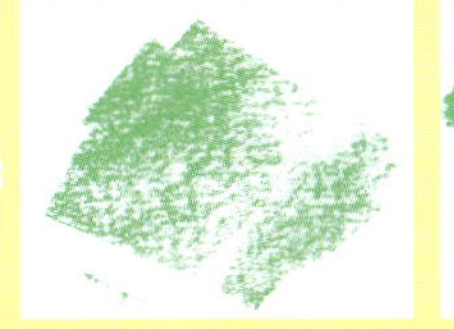

USED ON EDGE

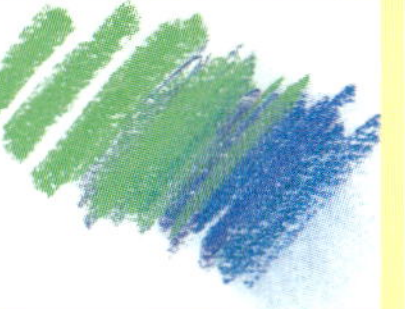

HATCHING

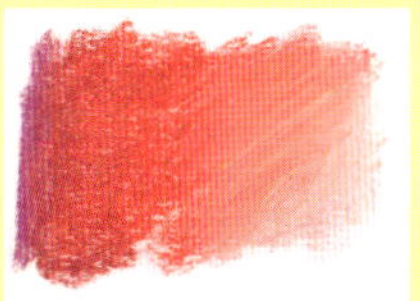

BLENDED WITH FINGER

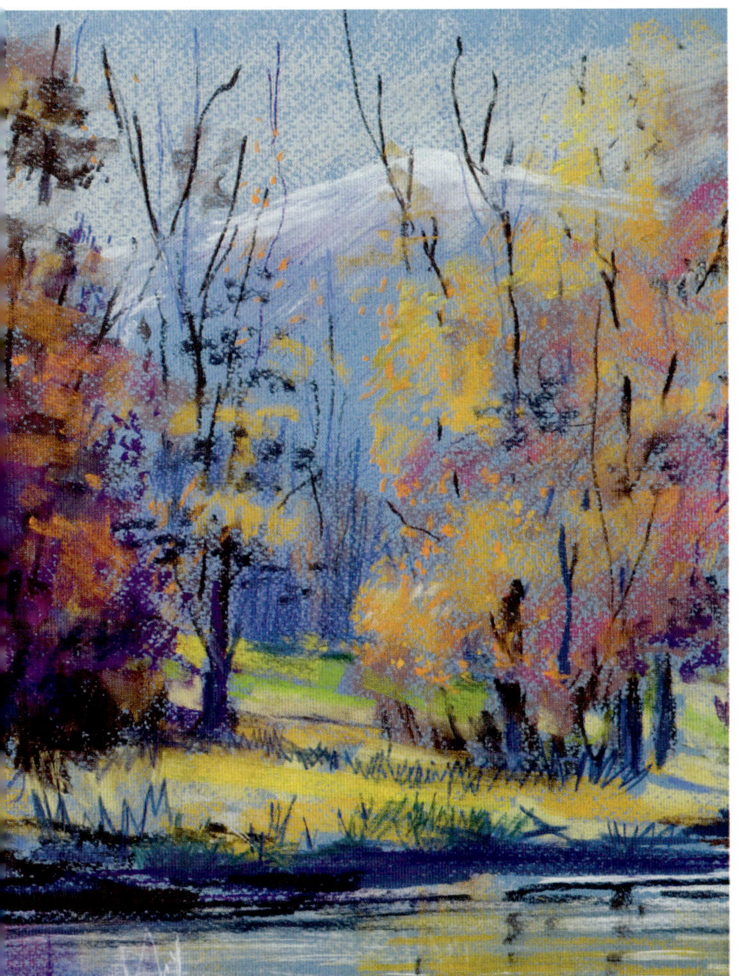

◀ *This evocative image was drawn on blue pastel paper with a mix of hard and soft pastels. It was worked up in stages. The bright colours of the autumn trees contrast with the cool background. Blending the background produces a distant effect when compared to the harder unblended strokes of the nearer trees and water.*

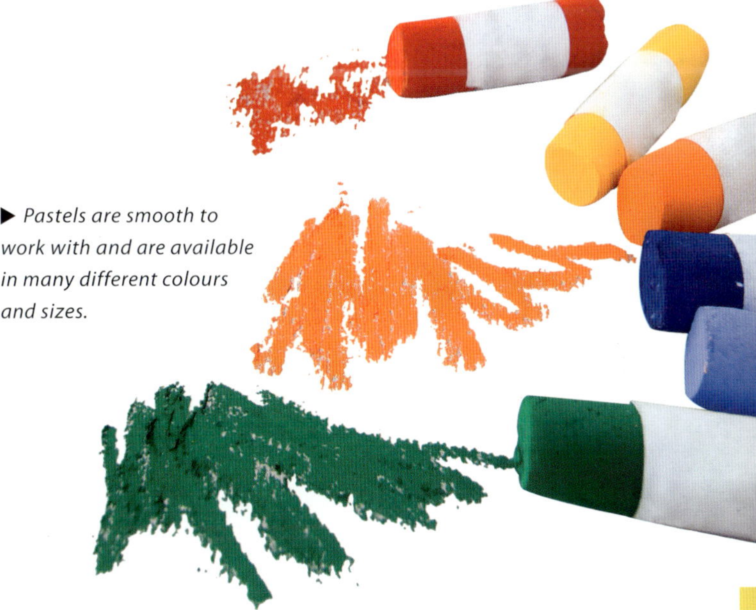

▶ *Pastels are smooth to work with and are available in many different colours and sizes.*

OIL PASTELS

The term 'pastel' when used in this context can cause confusion. These are oil-based pigments, rather like lipstick in consistency, and shouldn't be mixed with dry mediums such as soft or hard pastels or charcoal. Some manufacturers call them oil sticks or oil bars, which is less confusing! They are made from a mix of pigment and an oily binder such as a hydrocarbon-based wax, or sometimes animal fat. They are similar, in feel and use, to children's wax crayons.

Unlike oil paints, which eventually dry quite hard, oil pastels never completely dry, so need to be mounted and put behind glass or stored where they can't come into contact with anything else. They can be blended with each other, and softened with mineral spirit or turpentine.

QUICK & CLEVER EFFECTS!

Oil pastels can be used in several ways, from building layers to cross-hatching and scraping back with a pointed instrument.

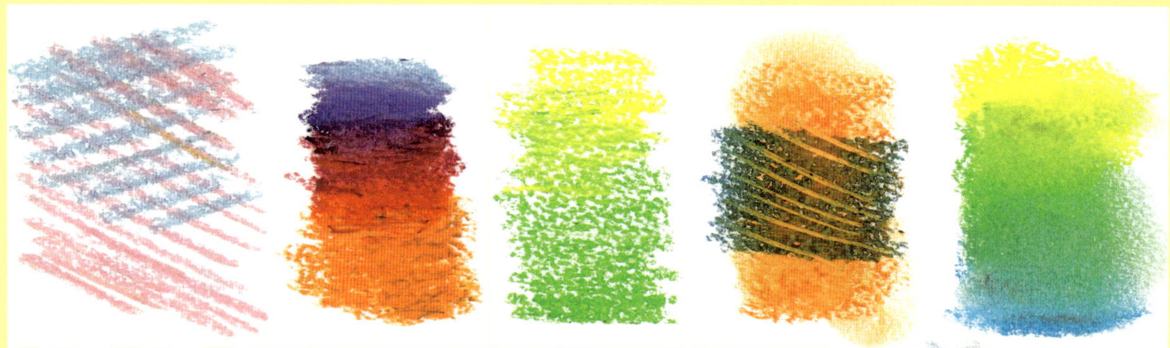

HATCHING AND CROSS-HATCHING | BLENDED WITH HEAVY PRESSURE | BLENDED WITH LIGHT PRESSURE | SCRAPING TO SHOW COLOUR | BLENDED WITH WHITE SPIRIT

QUICK & CLEVER!

If using pencils or pastels out of doors, spread them on a handkerchief or piece of cloth on the ground so you don't lose them in scrub or long grass.

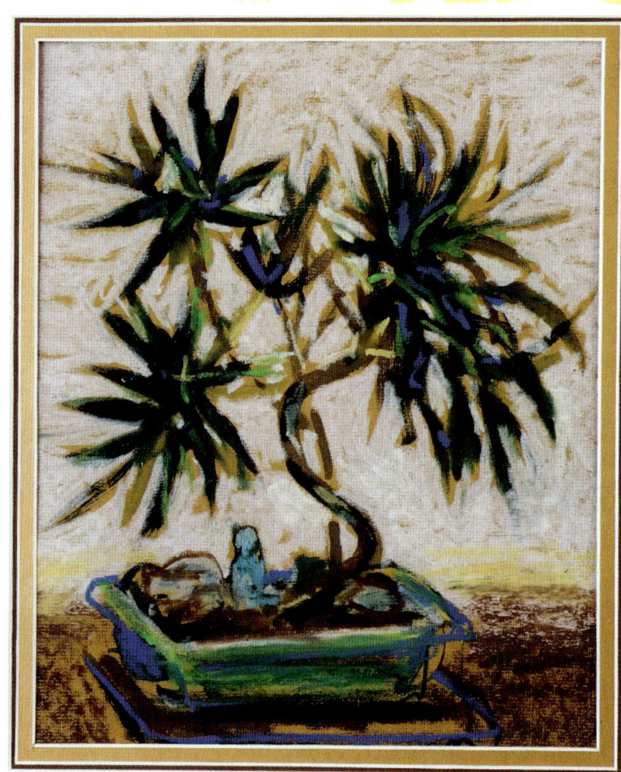

▶ *This drawing of a bonsai tree was made on smooth, heavy brown parcel paper lightly toned with oil pastel diluted with mineral spirit. The image was drawn on in thin layers and built up with thicker ones. In some places, where the paper was still damp with mineral spirit, the oil pastel has run slightly into the surrounding area of the stroke, giving a softer look.*

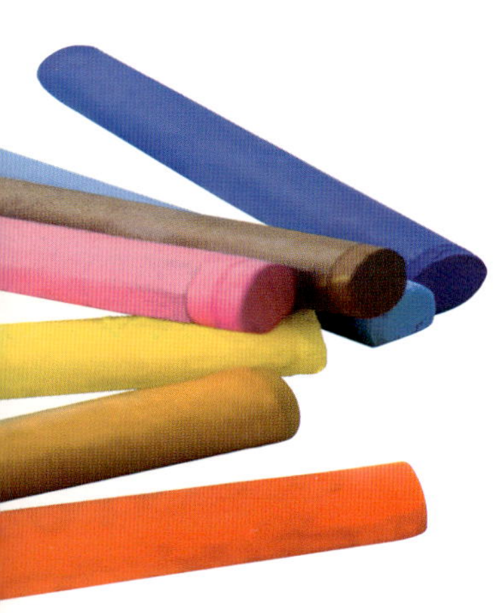

◀ *Oil pastels are soft and smudge or blend easily. They are easier to use with the wrapper left on.*

CHARCOAL

Probably the oldest of all drawing mediums, charcoal is made by burning willow twigs at high temperatures in an almost air-tight environment. This burns away the oxygen, leaving a carbon-rich stick suitable for drawing with. For centuries this was the medium for starting almost every piece of art; all the old-master oil paintings from the sixteenth century onwards were first sketched with charcoal. Artists liked it because they could make changes by erasing lines with a feather duster. Today, charcoal is often used in its own right because of its bold, expressive qualities of tone and deep, velvety texture. Charcoal comes in sticks or pencil form.

There have been some exciting developments in charcoal-based products recently. Tinted or coloured compressed charcoal is now available in a range of subtle greys, browns, oranges, greens and blues. These are available in pencil form, encased in wood, and are very useful used in conjunction with pastels. Because charcoal is relatively soft, fixative is useful to bond it to the paper.

Charcoal is best used on rougher paper. A cheap paper much used by art colleges for charcoal life drawing in the past was sugar paper. This is still available in sheets, and comes in a variety of pale colours or white. Even lining paper from DIY shops can be used.

QUICK & CLEVER EFFECTS!

Charcoal has a range of expressive line, from dense and strong to hesitant and fluffy. As it is a soft material, it is easy to blend to produce grey tones.

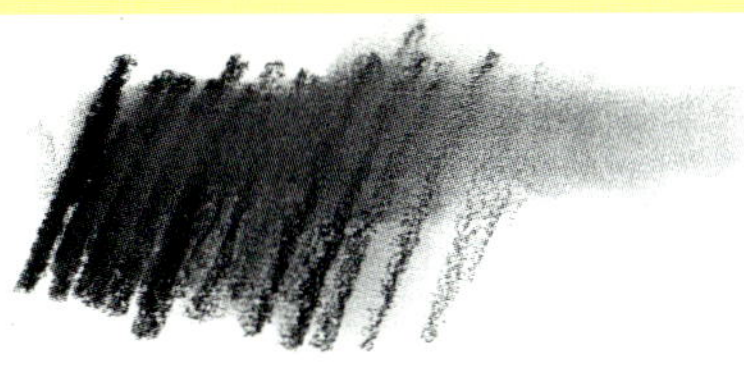

SCRIBBLING AND BLENDING

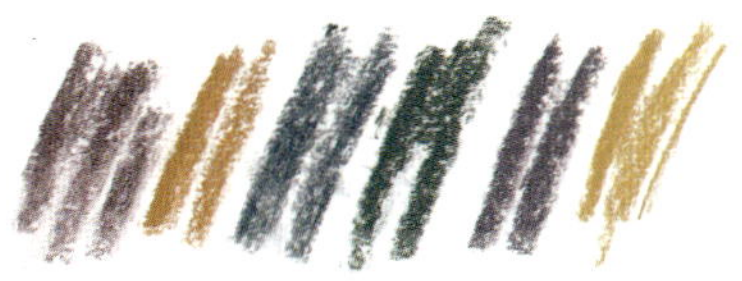

TINTED CHARCOAL

QUICK & CLEVER!

Charcoal is too crumbly and soft for fine, delicate work. For best results while you are practising, use large sheets of paper and big, expressive movements. If smudging, remember to wipe your fingers afterwards!

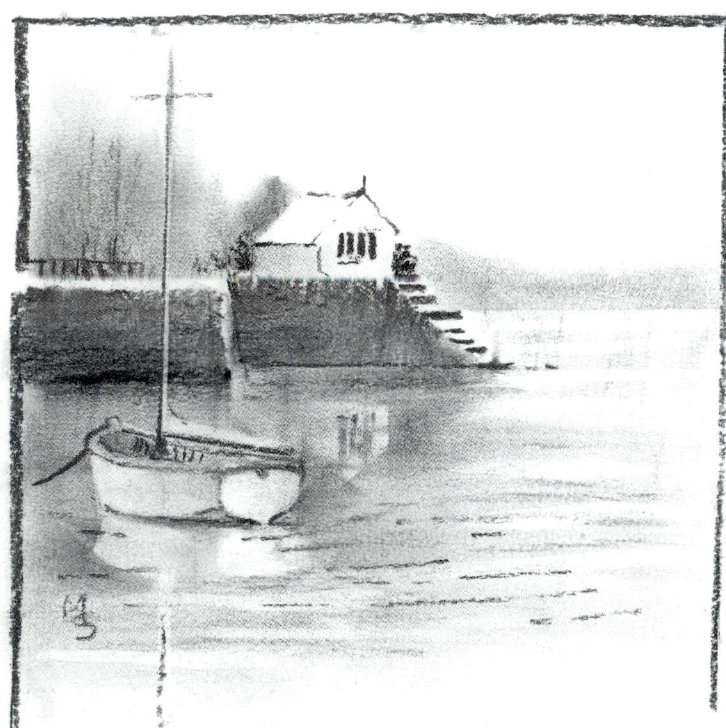

▲ Areas of charcoal can be lifted out with a soft putty eraser to allow lighter tones from the paper to show through; in this image this is where the boat and reflections are. Dark areas can be stroked in on top of lighter ones, as in the wall in the background. Softer impressions, for distance or still water, can be smudged on. The mast was rubbed out using the edge of a harder eraser.

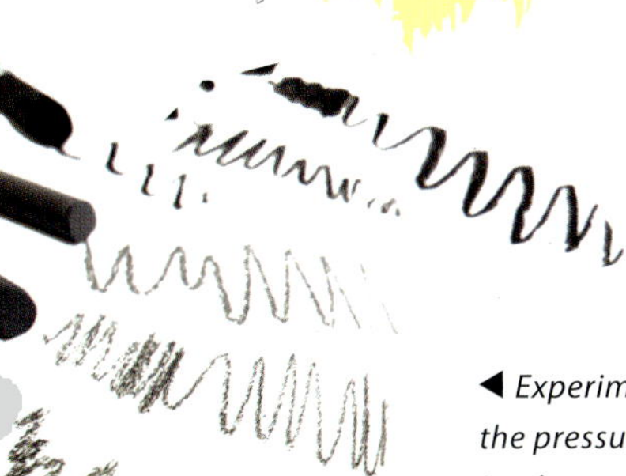

◀ Experiment by changing the pressure on the charcoal to give marks that vary from light, feathery strokes to bold, intense darks.

PENS

There is a huge choice of pens available to the artist. In fact, almost every pen produced is suitable for drawing with! Beginners find ballpoints or fibre-tip pens best to start with, as they are easy to control, don't leak or spatter, and are available almost everywhere. It's best to test each pen before you use it on a 'serious' drawing, to see whether it's waterproof or not. Some of the techniques available include adding washes of paint to the pen drawing (line and wash), and you will be disappointed if your drawing runs.

Some inks when washed with water produce colours that are quite unexpected. For example, some blacks produce a violet-grey, whereas others have a brownish tinge. Brown and sepia are good colours for sketching; brown imparts a nostalgic, soft look to a drawing. Dip pens, where you need a separate bottle of ink and dip the nib in, are not as common as they used to be, but have a charm and are worth trying. Never push a nib pen; always pull it, or you'll break it. Felt pens can also be used; bold and bright, they can be great fun.

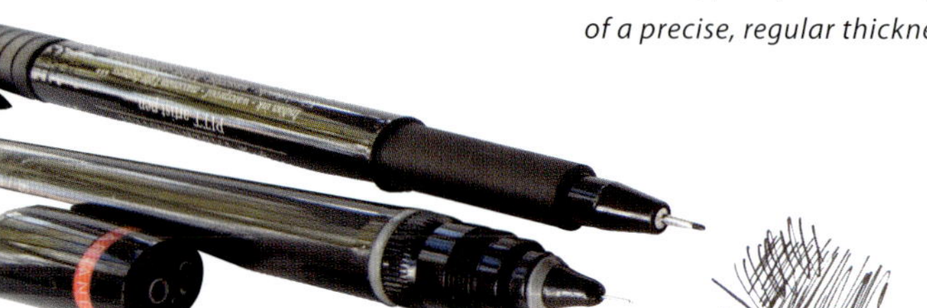

▼ *Technical pens produce lines of a precise, regular thickness.*

QUICK & CLEVER EFFECTS!

You can use pens to make bold, expressive marks or controlled and delicate ones, depending on the subject and your style of drawing.

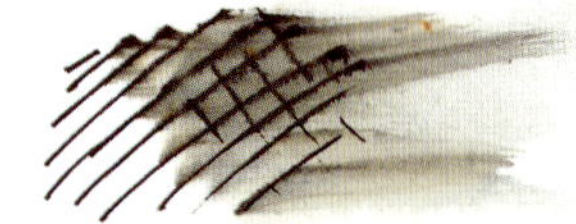
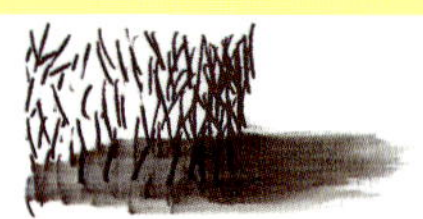

Use a water-soluble pen to blend or soften when water is added; the more lines there are, the darker the blend will be.

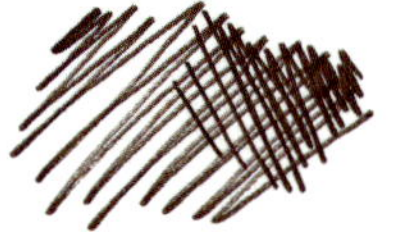
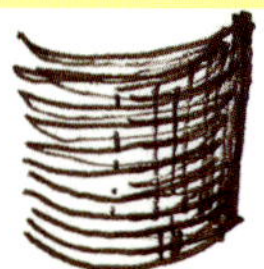

Fibre-tip pens are easy to use, and the ink is usually dense. The fibre 'nib' is enclosed in a thin metal tube.

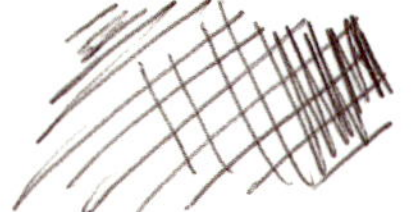
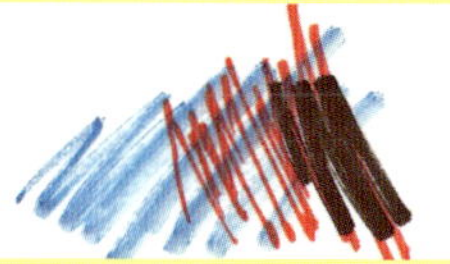

Ballpoint pens are the most common of all. Free-rolling and easy to handle, they are capable of expressive marks. Felt pens are big, vibrant and can cover a lot of paper quickly. Best used in larger drawings, they can impart a bold, expressive look.

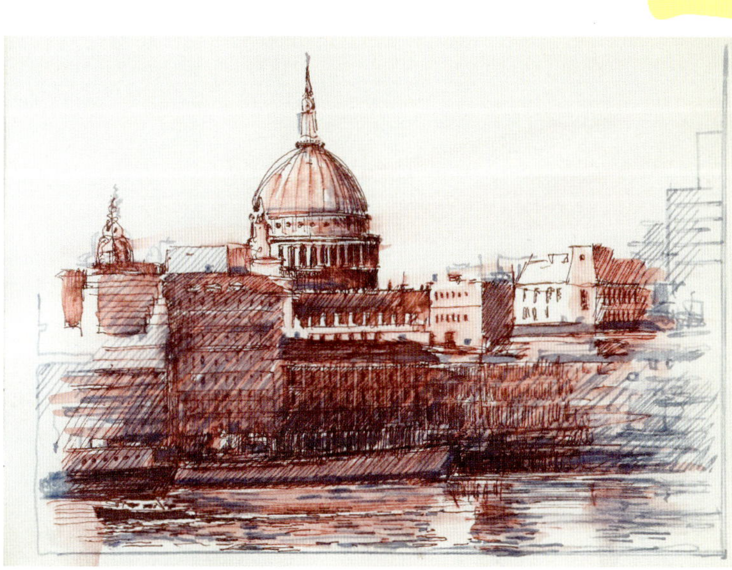

QUICK & CLEVER!

You can often find large sets of pens on market stalls and in discount shops. These aren't always as much a bargain as they seem; they often run out of ink quickly and so don't last long. It's better to get a few good pens from an art shop, stationery store or art catalogue.

◀ *This drawing uses two colours. The initial sketch was made with a fountain pen and blue ink. This was then drawn over with a dip pen and brown water-soluble ink. Blue and brown work well together in a drawing.*

WATERCOLOUR AND BRUSHES

Watercolour is a great addition to line drawings, and although this is a drawing book, I felt it would be a shame if I didn't include some watercolour advice. When using watercolour to add to a drawing, the main thing to remember is that the drawing should be understandable. If the drawing is vague or looks somehow wrong, adding colour won't make it right. Colour should be washed on sparingly, so as not to detract from the drawing.

A few pans of watercolour in a little pocket box will be all you need. I use these six colours, but you may find your own favourites: Lemon Yellow, Cadmium Red Light, Winsor Blue, Quinacridone Magenta, Burnt Sienna and Raw Sienna. These can be mixed to produce many other colours.

QUICK & CLEVER EFFECTS!

The thickness of a brushstroke partly depends on the force with which you apply the brush. A light touch makes a thin line that becomes thicker as you press harder.

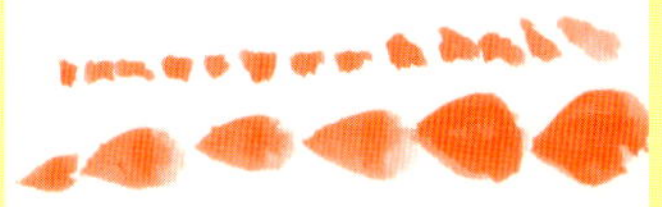

Marks made with round synthetic bristle brushes.

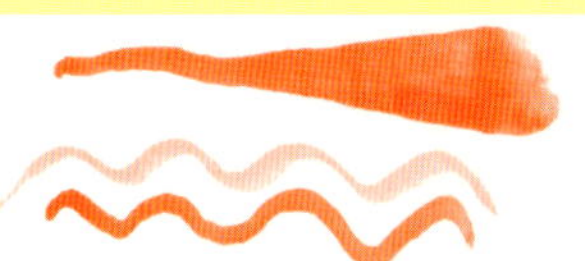

Thin lines can be made with the point of a synthetic sable.

A filbert can produce a stroke with a soft edge.

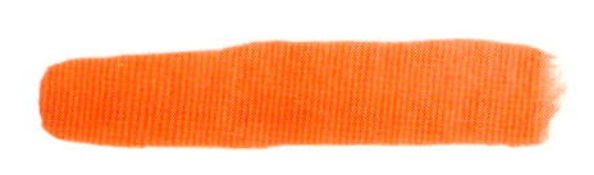

A flat brush gives a hard edge.

QUICK & CLEVER!

When cleaning brushes, paint gently onto a bar of soap, then continue the painting motion in the palm of your hand. When no more colour comes from the brush, rinse it under the tap, then paint onto the soap one more time. Leave the brush to dry, hair up, in a jar, with the soap left in it. When almost dry, gently pull the hair carefully to a point, then let it dry. It will keep its point forever!

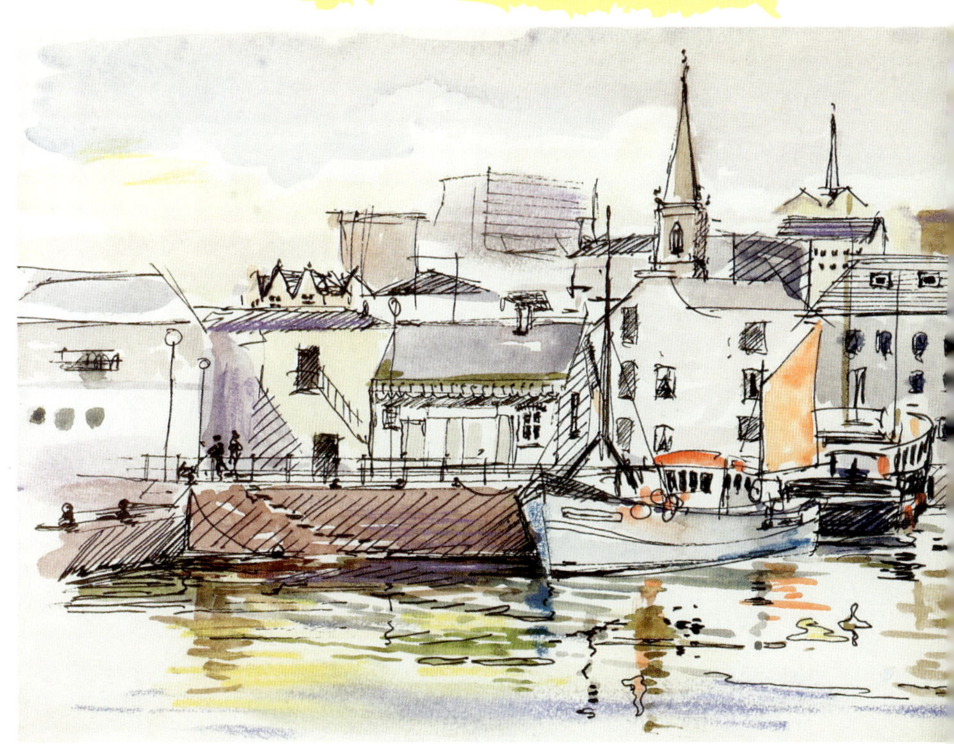

▶ *This little sketch of Plymouth, England, from the historic Mayflower Steps, is quite simple. The colours are used to enhance the drawing, although without colour the sketch would still be recognizable.*

▼ *Bushes can be expensive. I prefer to use synthetic sable brushes; they are reasonably priced and last a long time. A No. 8 is a good all-round brush.*

TECHNIQUES

ON THE FOLLOWING PAGES YOU WILL FIND MANY DRAWING TECHNIQUES, SOME WITH SAMPLES OF HOW I'VE USED THEM IN MY OWN DRAWINGS. MOST OF THE DRAWINGS HERE ARE FROM VARIOUS SKETCHES I HAVE MADE TO REMIND ME OF DIFFERENT PLACES OR EVENTS I'VE BEEN TO. WHY NOT TRY OUT THE TECHNIQUES THAT YOU LIKE THE LOOK OF; THEY ARE NOT DIFFICULT, AND THEY ALL HELP BUILD INTO INTERESTING IMAGES. PRACTISING TECHNIQUES, WITHOUT MAKING A DRAWING FROM THEM, IS NEVER A WASTE OF TIME; IT ENABLES YOU TO LEARN HOW TO MANIPULATE THE TOOLS. THIS IS MUCH LIKE A MUSICIAN PRACTISING THE SCALES ON AN INSTRUMENT; NOT PLAYING A TUNE, JUST PRACTISING THE NOTES.

HOLDING THE PENCIL

It always surprises me, when I see a book on drawing, that no one pays any attention to the grip on the pencil. Your hand, and how it moves, is the motive power of the drawing, transmitted to the paper by the pencil, which then leaves a mark. Yet most people hold a pencil as if they were writing; that's the only grip they know. Practise the following grips, and try some movements with the pencil on paper: see how different each one feels.

FLEXIBLE GRIP

This is the grip you will be familiar with from writing, except that it's a bit further back from the tip than usual. This means you have more flexibility in the fingers, and also (importantly) you can see what you're drawing because your hand isn't in the way! Use this technique to shade in large areas of colour.

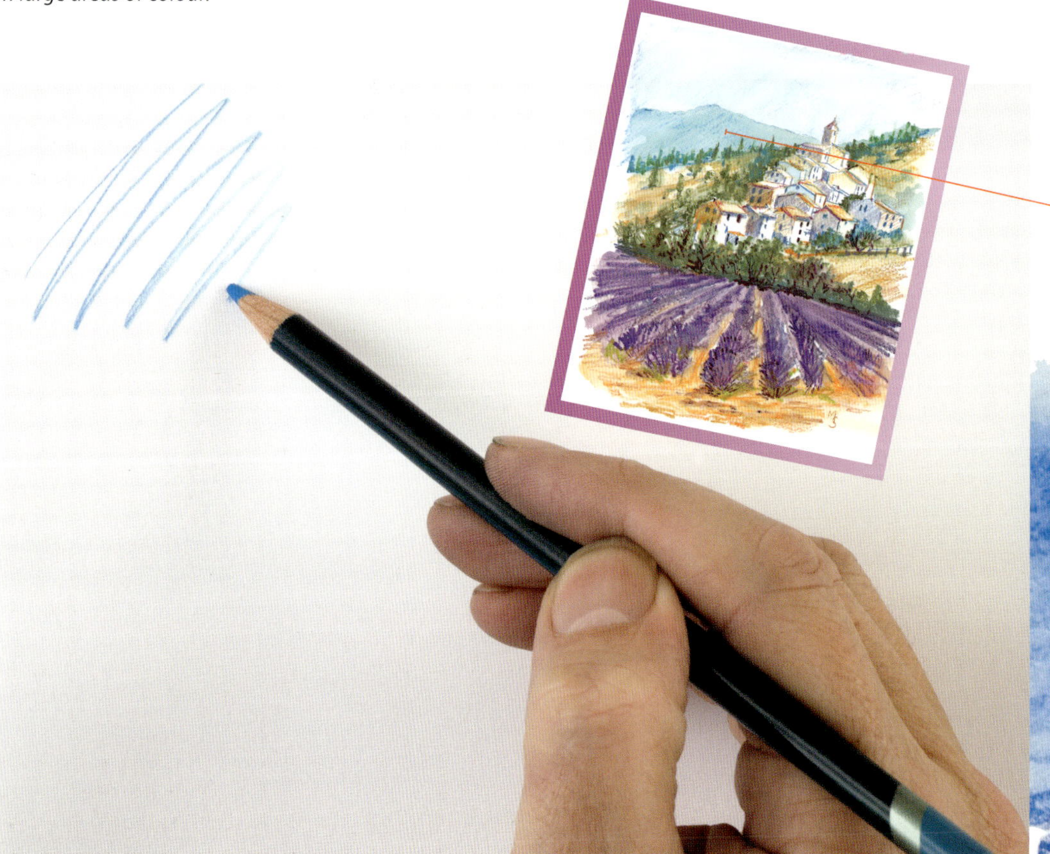

In this image of Provence in France, you can just see the fine lines on the distant hill. They were carefully applied close together, using a flexible grip on the pencil.

LIGHT GRIP

Now, move your hand further back the pencil, holding it very lightly. This grip needs hardly any pressure. Just let the weight of the pencil do the drawing. This will produce light, delicate lines. Move the wrist and the fingers and you'll make longer lines. If you overlap the strokes you will achieve continuous tones rather than lines.

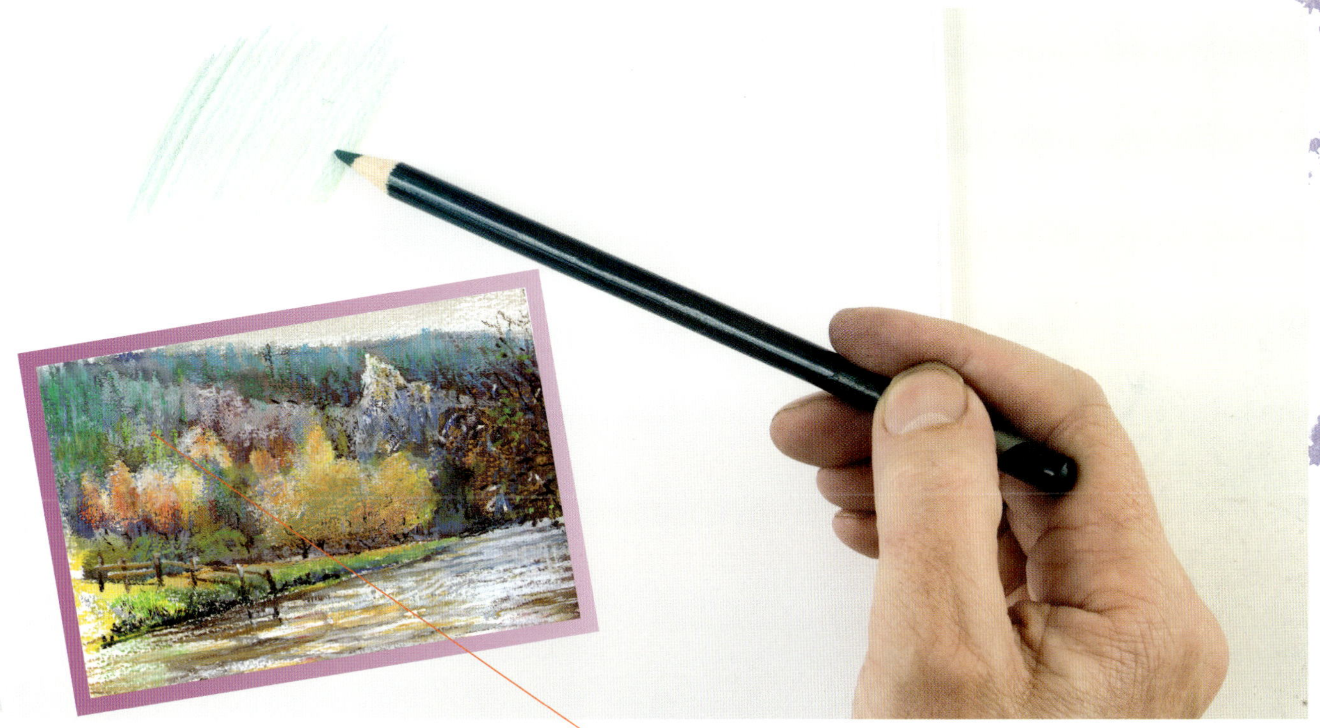

In this vibrant autumnal image, I used the light grip to add the texture and depict the pine forest.

SIDEWAYS GRIP

To pick the pencil up, place it on a flat surface. Then push gently on the tip, where the lead is, with your index finger. As you do so, the other end of the pencil will rise slightly. Grip the pencil with your other fingers and thumb, and then sketch with sideways movements. This means you can cover a larger area with pigment rather than using the point in the usual way. Always keep the pencil sharp when using this method.

QUICK & CLEVER!

If you find you get cramp after a few minutes' drawing, force yourself to relax; cramp is nature's way of telling you that you're gripping too tightly!

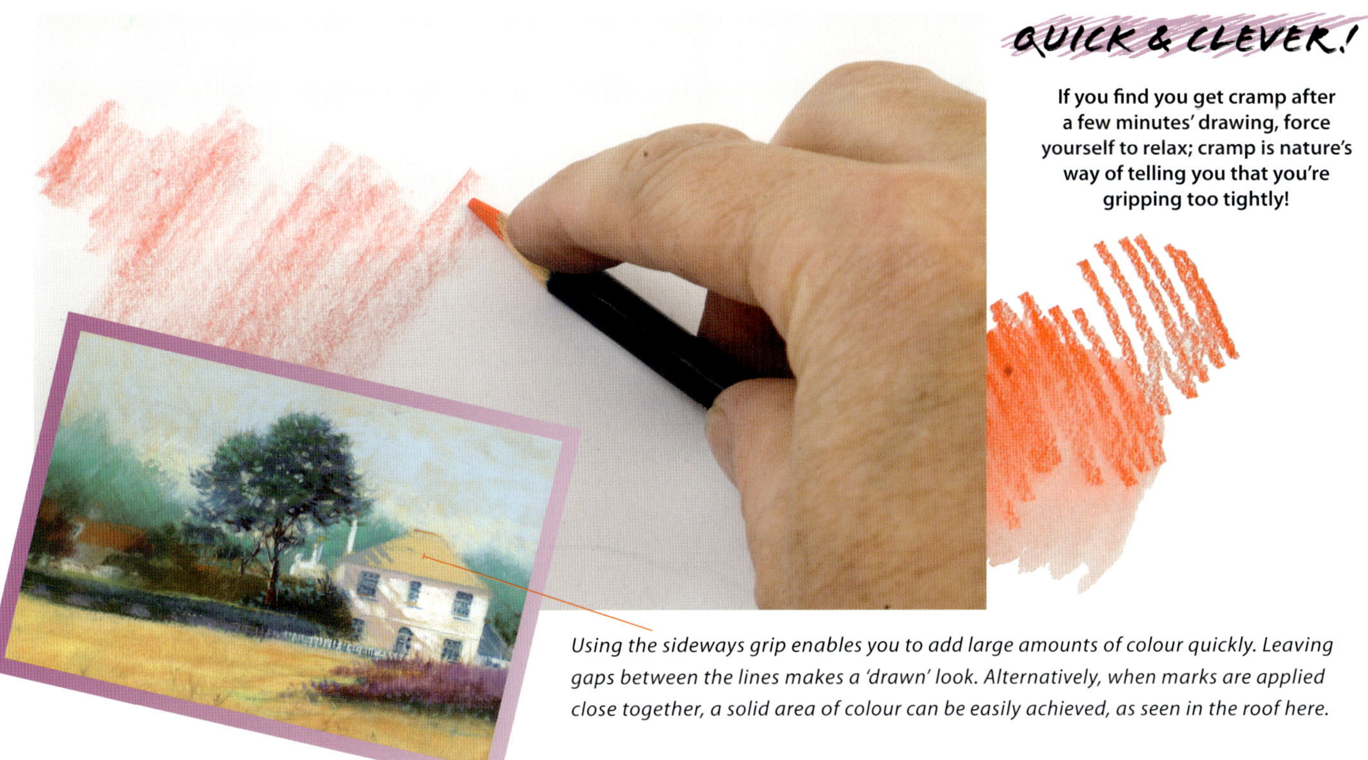

Using the sideways grip enables you to add large amounts of colour quickly. Leaving gaps between the lines makes a 'drawn' look. Alternatively, when marks are applied close together, a solid area of colour can be easily achieved, as seen in the roof here.

LINES, CROSS-HATCHING AND SHADING

Drawing with lines can be very expressive. Lines can be thick or thin, sloping or horizontal, straight or curved. Each one looks subtly different. With a pencil, simply increasing the pressure will change the line from a light one to a darker one. Lines often need to be able to create tone – the difference between light and dark. In addition to this, lines are capable of showing 'form' – the illusion of the shape of objects.

▼ *Each of these shaded areas looks subtly different; most look flat but one has the illusion of being cylindrical – can you see why? Also, can you see which side the light appears to be coming from? Have a go at copying these, with a 2B pencil.*

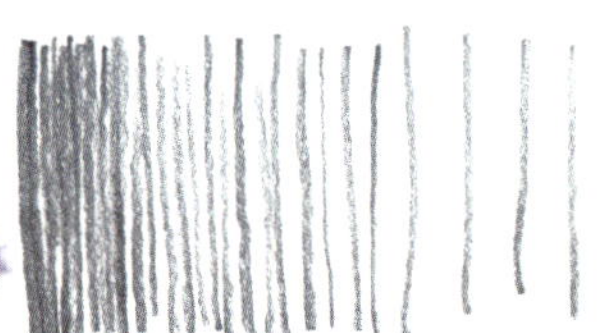

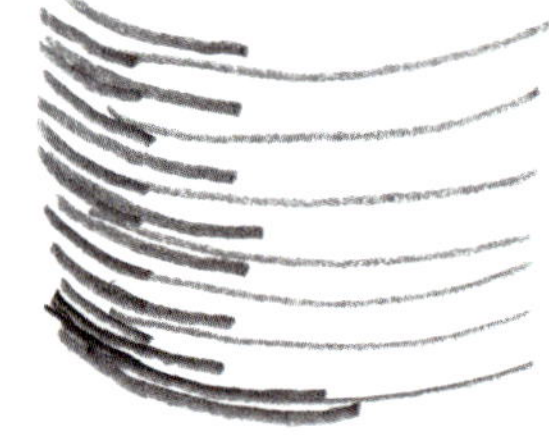

EXPERIMENTING WITH SHADING

▼ *Each of these rectangles contains lines drawn with the same black ballpoint pen, yet they all create different effects. Draw some rectangular boxes (no need for a ruler; draw them freehand, it's good practice). Now, copy the marks in the first, left-hand box. As you move across to the right, on the same row, add more lines or squiggles, making the rectangles darker each time. The right-hand box should be darkest, almost black.*

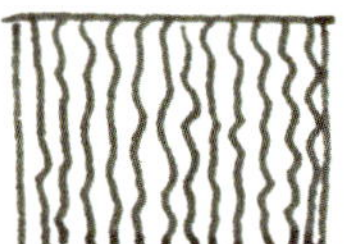
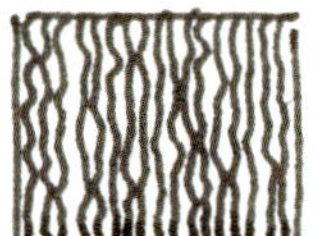
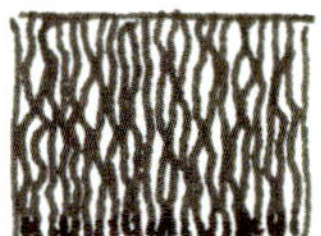
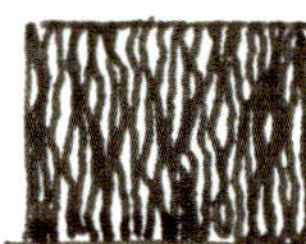

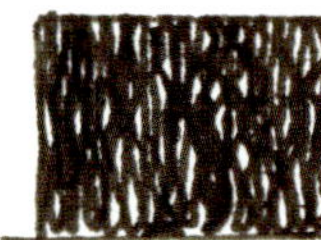
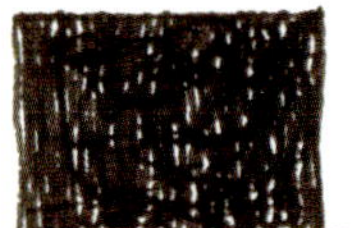

Verticals are useful for shadows on walls and the shaded sides of tree trunks.

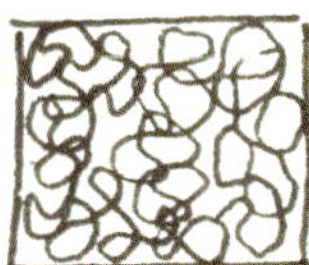
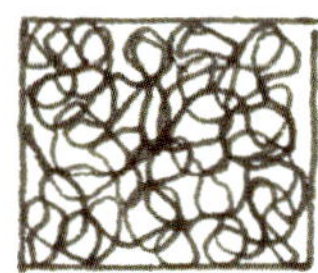
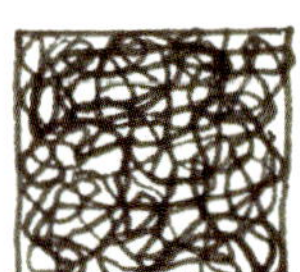
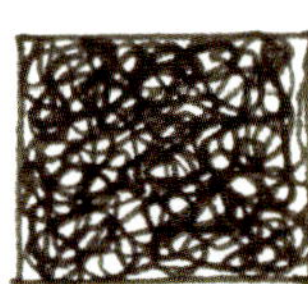
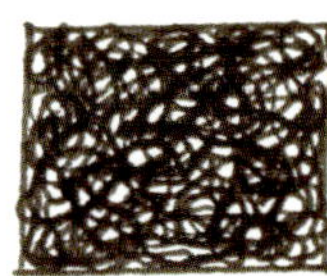
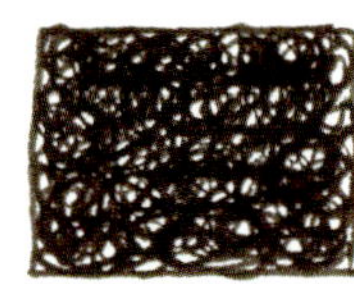
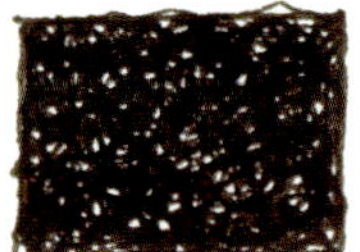

Irregular squiggles and scribbles can be used for foliage, shadows on trees or shrubs.

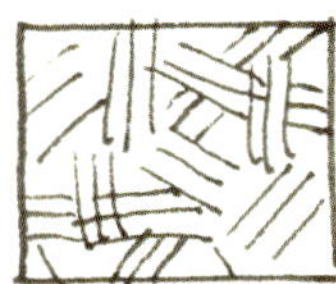
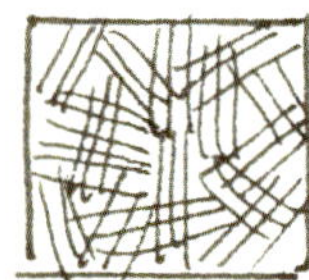
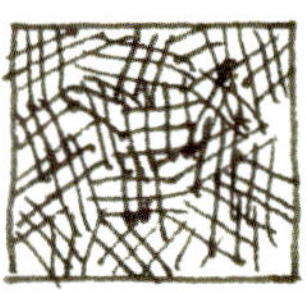
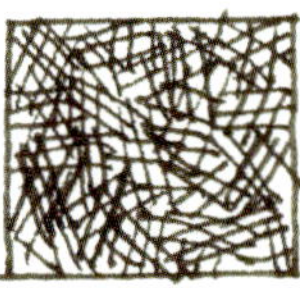
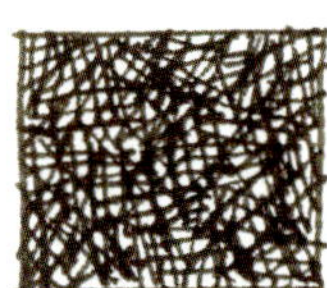
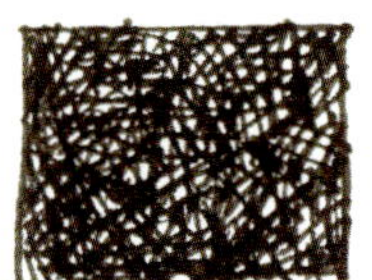
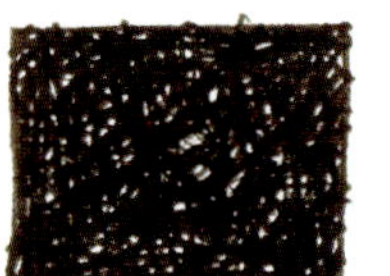

Short crossed lines can impart a stony look to boulders or stone walls.

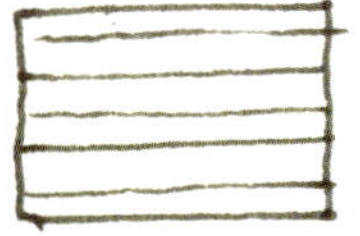
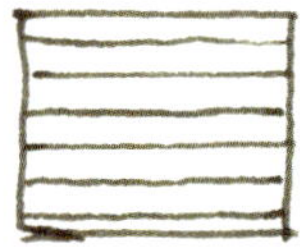
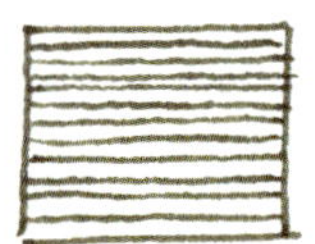
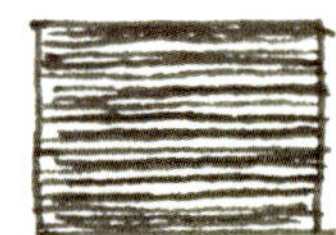

Horizontal lines can impart the look of flat surfaces and ripples or shadows on water.

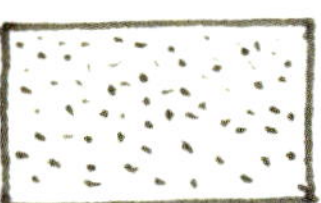
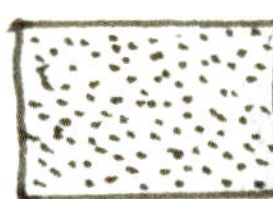
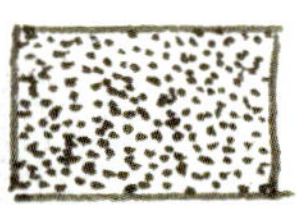

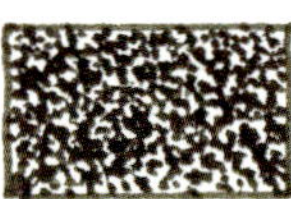
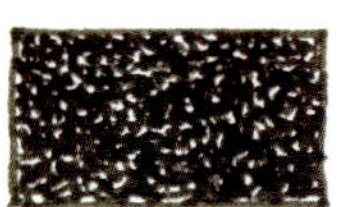

Dots can be used to look like sand, small stones and leaves. They are also useful for rendering textures such as leather.

QUICK & CLEVER EFFECTS!

Cross-hatching simply means drawing lines that cross. The more lines there are, the darker the effect.

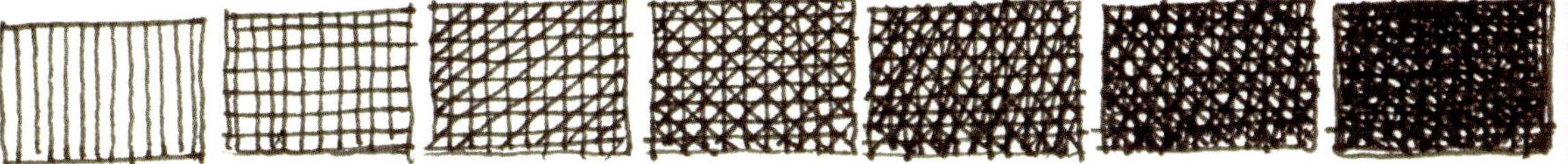

The denser the lines of the cross-hatching, the darker and deeper the shadows that the effect implies.

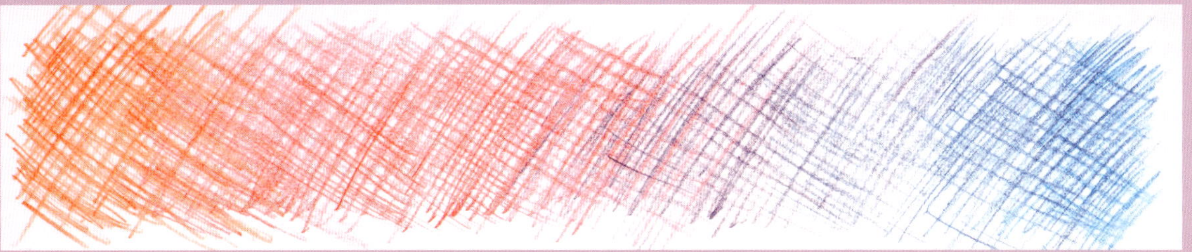

Cross-hatching is also effective with coloured pencils, watercolour pencils or hard pastels. Blend one colour into another using overlapping lines. This shades gradually from one colour to another, each area slightly overlapping the next one.

There are many illusions we can create when drawing with line. As well as tone, we can give an impression of still water with dark horizontal lines, foliage with tight scribbled lines, stones with random short lines, among many other effects.

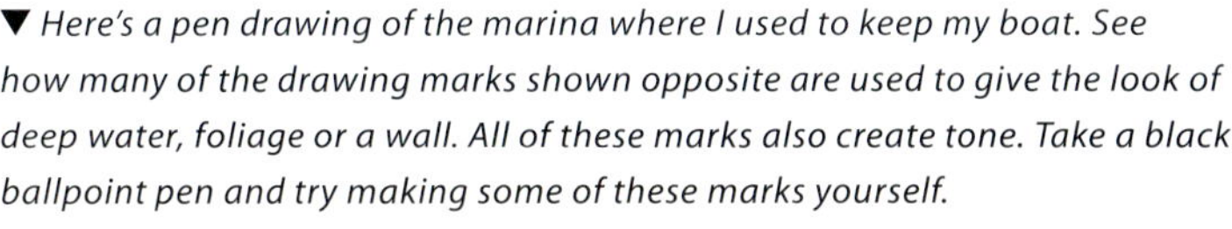

▼ Here's a pen drawing of the marina where I used to keep my boat. See how many of the drawing marks shown opposite are used to give the look of deep water, foliage or a wall. All of these marks also create tone. Take a black ballpoint pen and try making some of these marks yourself.

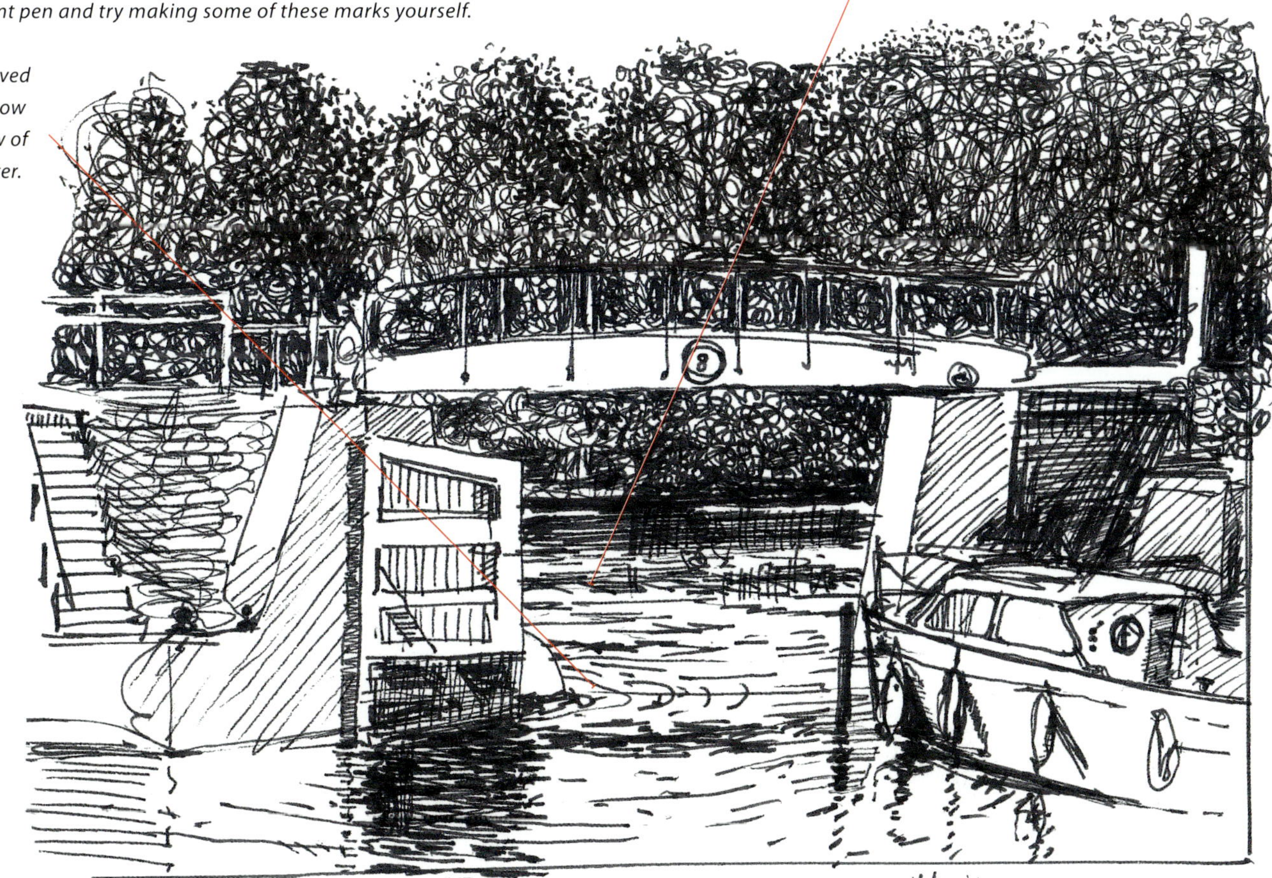

The darker lines show the change from light to shadow.

The curved lines show the flow of the water.

SCRIBBLING AND SMUDGING

Scribbling and smudging are useful ways to impart texture to a drawing.

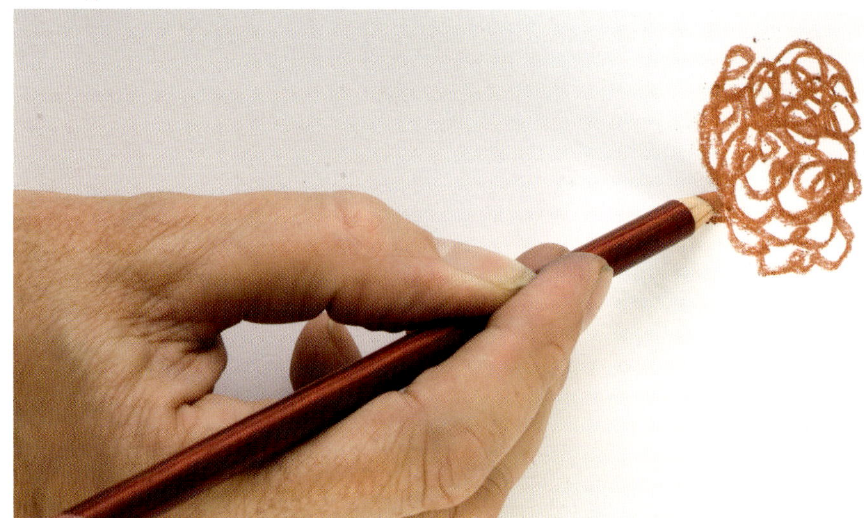

SCRIBBLING

If you are using pencils or pastel pencils, this effect is good for rendering bushes, trees and other greenery, especially if combined with dots to imply the shapes of leaves.

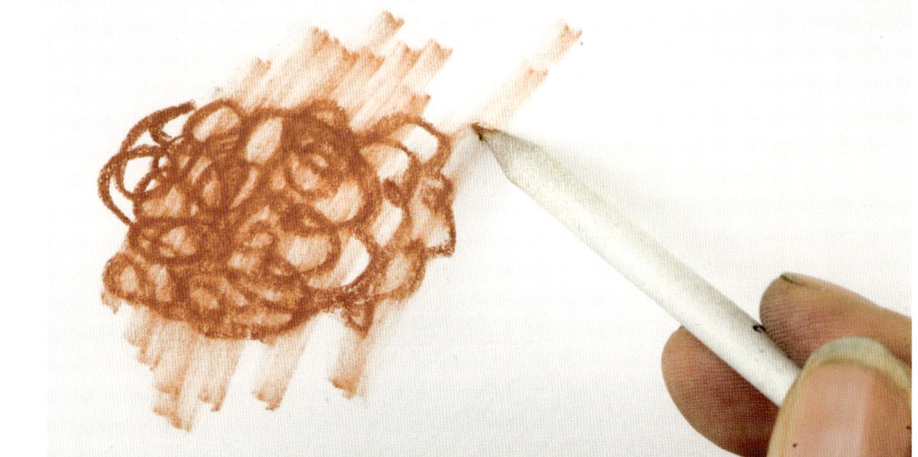

SMUDGING WITH A TORCHON

This will give a gentle, slightly blurry, effect. This scribbled effect can be built up gradually using different colours.

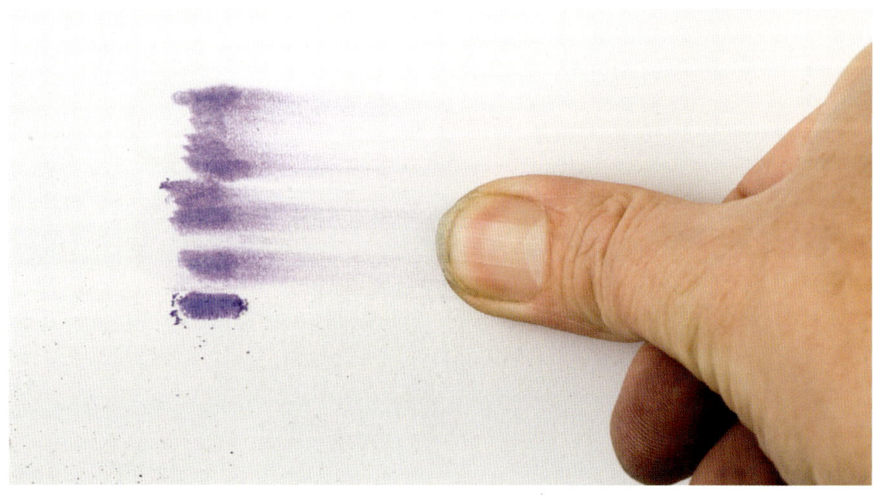

SMUDGING WITH YOUR FINGER

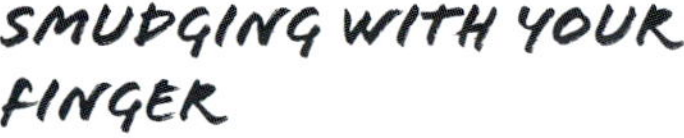

Marks made with soft pencils or pastel pencils can easily be smudged. This isn't a bad thing, as it can be used to show shadows, or to make reflections on water.

BLENDING

Hatching or scribbling with a pen or pencil develops an interesting texture. If either tool is a water-soluble type, there is a further option: adding a wash of water with a brush.

BLENDING WITH WATER-SOLUBLE PEN

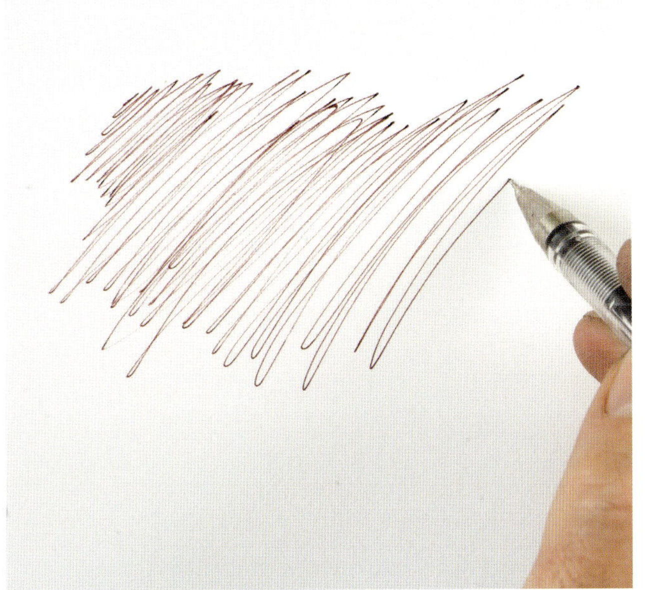

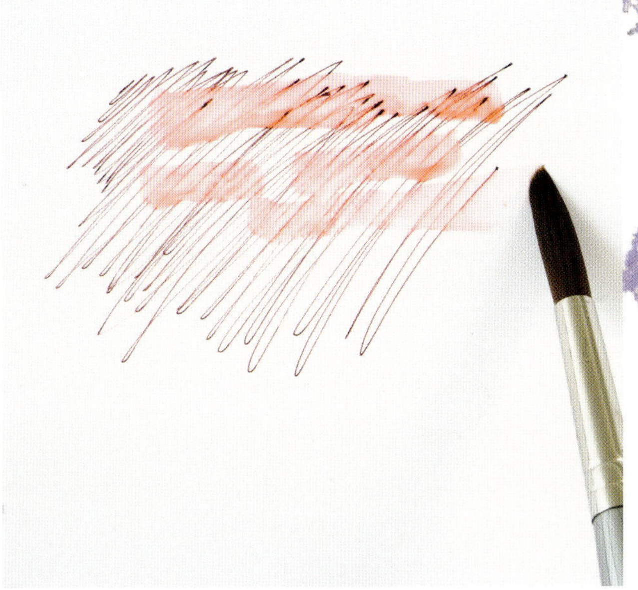

Washing water across the lines with a watercolour brush produces an entirely new colour! Some inks will still leave visible lines after water is brushed on, whereas others will dissolve into a watercolour effect. Experiment and see what your pens do.

BLENDING WITH WATERCOLOUR PENCILS

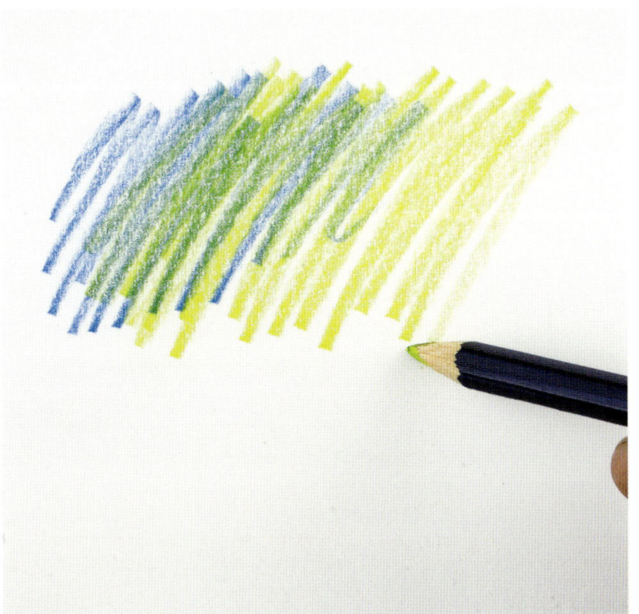

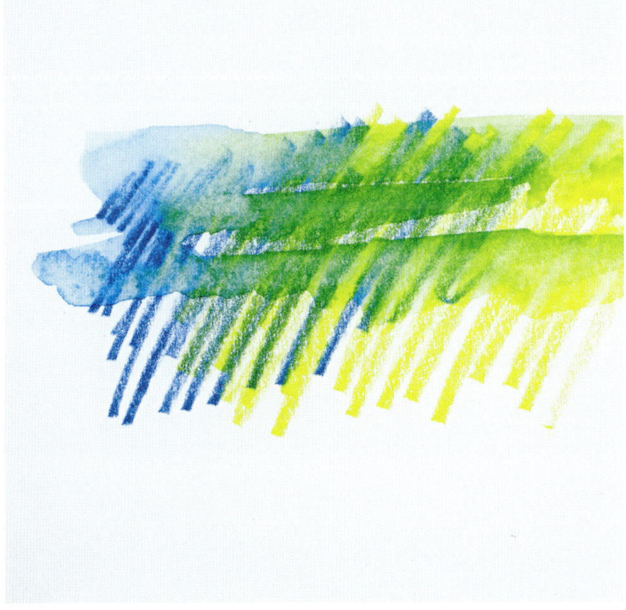

Hatching two watercolour pencils side by side gives a third colour if they overlap. Note how the blue and yellow produce a green between them when washed across with a brush.

ERASING AND MASKING

These are really useful techniques to make drawing easier, which is what this book is all about. These methods, or variants of them, are often used by illustrators and professional artists to save time when sketching ideas. I learned these techniques at art college way back in the 1960s, and I still find them useful. To create a simple yet striking scene of a building contrasting with a dark background, you will need a piece of paper (other than your drawing paper), a pair of scissors, a soft pencil and an eraser. I love watching people's faces when they see how this works!

1 BLOCKING IN
Hold the corner of the piece of paper firmly on the drawing pad. This is the mask. Take the pencil and sketch in some strong vertical lines, working upwards, over and away from the paper mask.

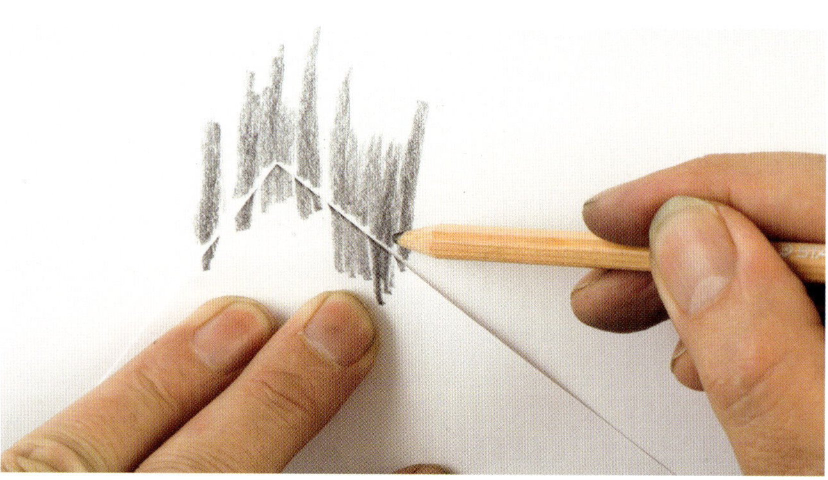

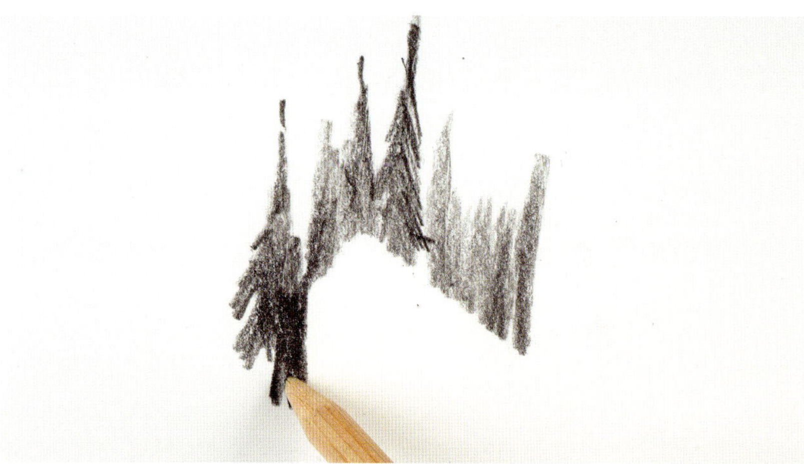

2 CREATING FIR TREES
Remove the paper and draw some diagonal lines out from the verticals to look like fir trees. Be careful; don't draw over the masked shape.

3 SMUDGING
Smudge across the base of the trees with a finger, add some short vertical lines for windows, and there's your house in the woods!

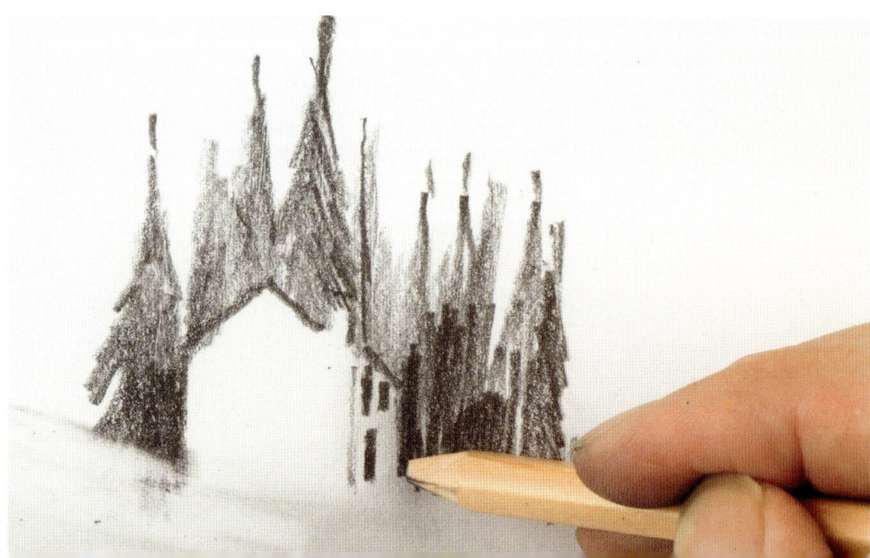

Another way of using a mask is to cut out the shape of the required subject, leaving a gap in the paper that is used to shape the erased area. Quick and clever!

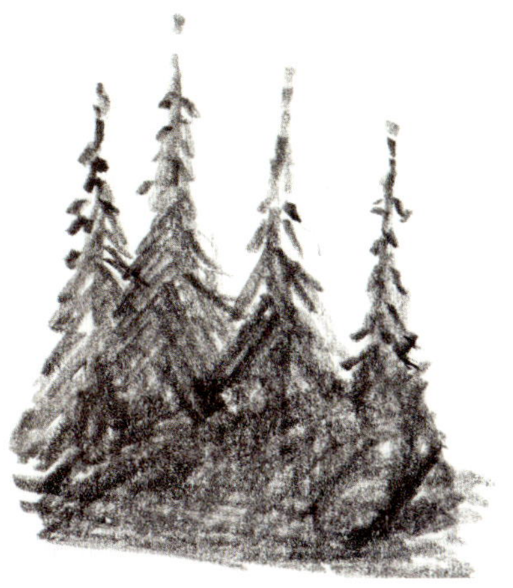

1 USING DARK TONES

Draw a simple shape of some trees, using a soft pencil. Make sure the tones are dark enough.

2 ERASING THROUGH THE MASK

To create the mask, you will need to cut out the required shape of the house on a piece of paper and hold it at the base of the trees where you want to position your house. Take the eraser and, rubbing inwards from the mask, carefully remove the pencil marks from the shape.

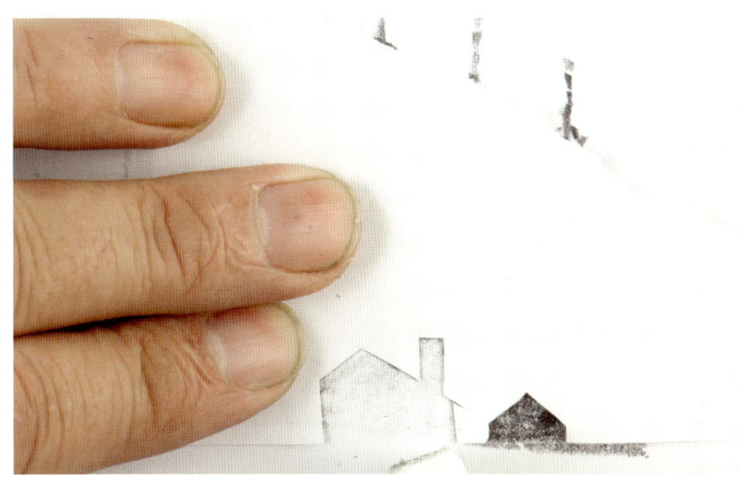

3 ADDING FINAL DETAILS

Add a few details; a couple of windows, a smudge across to look like a distant mountain, another smudge below the house. There you are. Practise a few times, then go and show your friends!

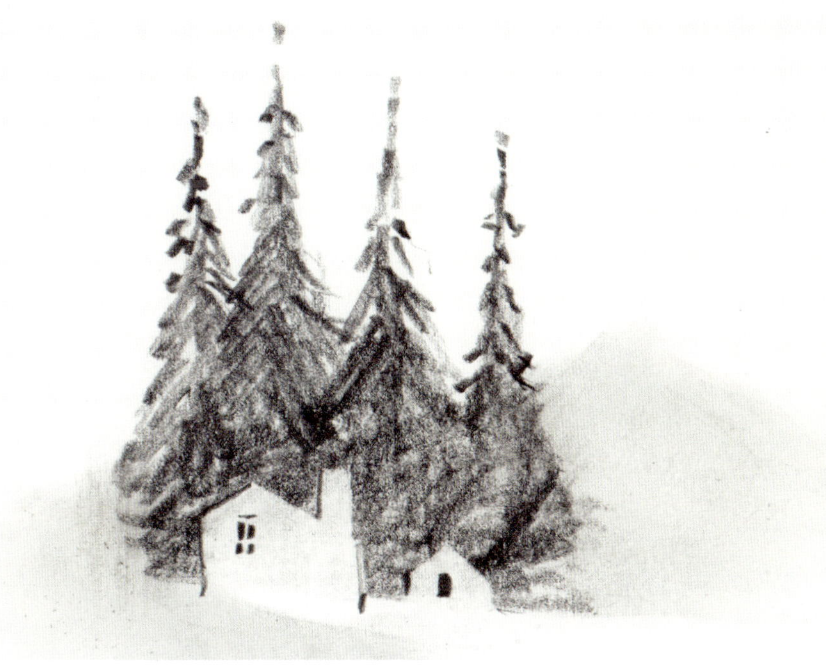

QUICK & CLEVER!

Sometimes erasers can get dirty with graphite, and don't work. If this happens, get a piece of rough paper such as watercolour paper and rub the eraser across it a few times to clean it. Or do what I do; I use the leg of my jeans!

INDENTING

This is another great quick and clever technique! When we draw with pencil, the only real difficulty is portraying thin, light shapes against a darker background, such as white fence posts in front of dark trees, light branches or brickwork. This simple technique makes the process easy, as you will see. To draw this architectural detail, you will need a cocktail stick or clean matchstick, and a piece of card.

1 INDENT THE WINDOW LINES

The shapes of the window and brickwork are drawn in and then indented with a cocktail stick.

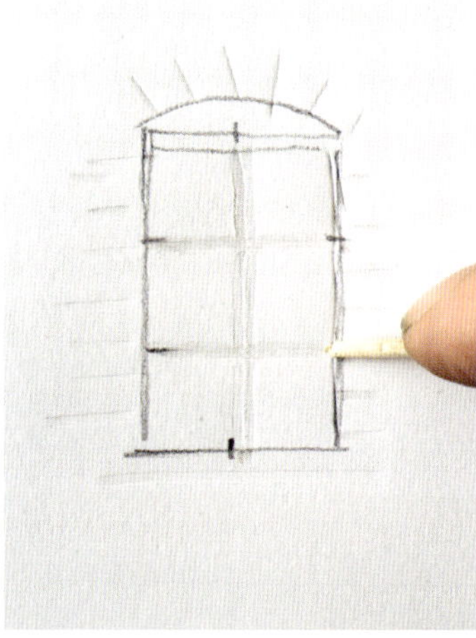

QUICK & CLEVER!

If you like using this method, collect objects that could be used for indenting. Combs, knitting needles and small pieces of wood can all be used to press onto paper to indent lines. Make sure they aren't too sharp or you'll rip the paper. Wooden objects are better for this purpose than metal ones.

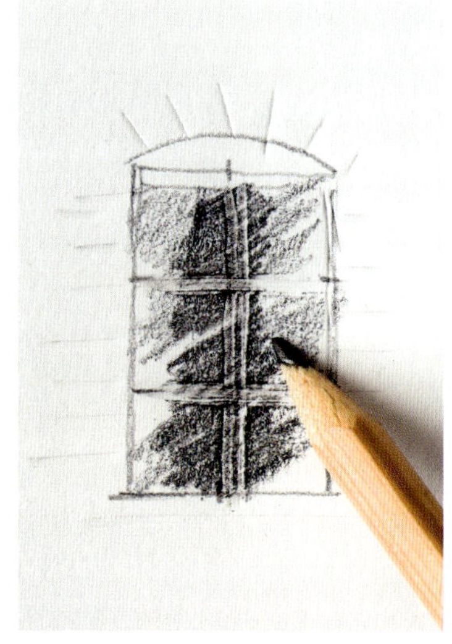

2 DEVELOP THE TONES

The window is shaded over and further darker detail is added.

3 REVEAL TEXTURE

The indents are then shaded over to reveal the brick texture around the window.

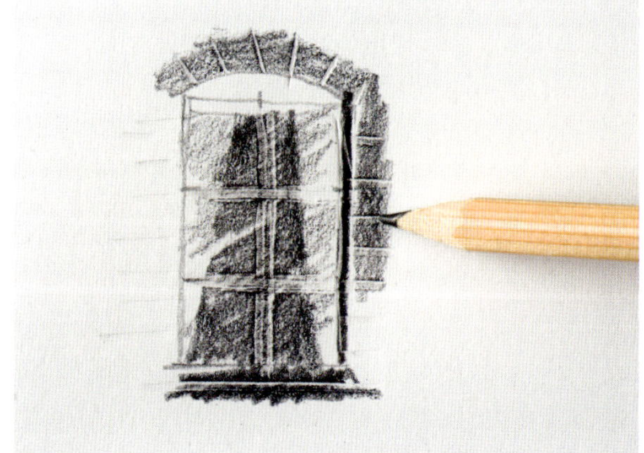

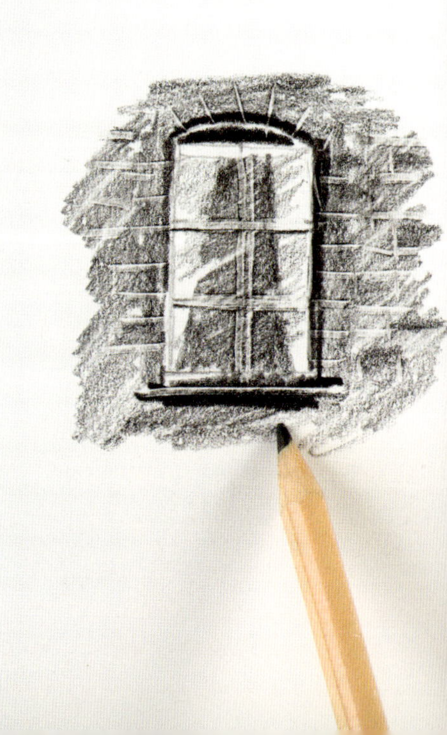

4 ADD DETAILS

Architectural details such as windows or brickwork are easily created with indenting.

INDENTING

SCRAPING AND RESISTING

Using oil pastels can be great fun. They are strong, vibrant and can be built up in layers. You can then scrape the layers back to show the colour underneath. Also, because they're oily, nothing with a water content will stick to them. This means they can be used as a resist, where the drawing is done with a few oil pastels, and then washed over with a watercolour.

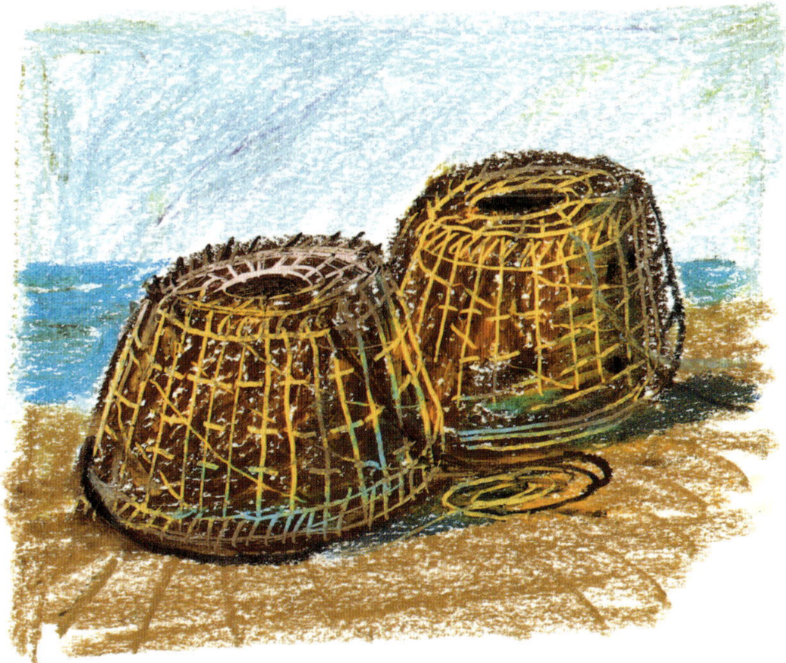

◀ *An exciting technique that works well is scraping back to show the colour of the underlayer. Fine lines are impossible to make by drawing with oil pastel because they are too thick, so this is the best method to use. To draw these crab pots I first scribbled a layer of orange oil pastel, and went over it with a darker colour. Using a cocktail stick to scrape the fine lines was easy!*

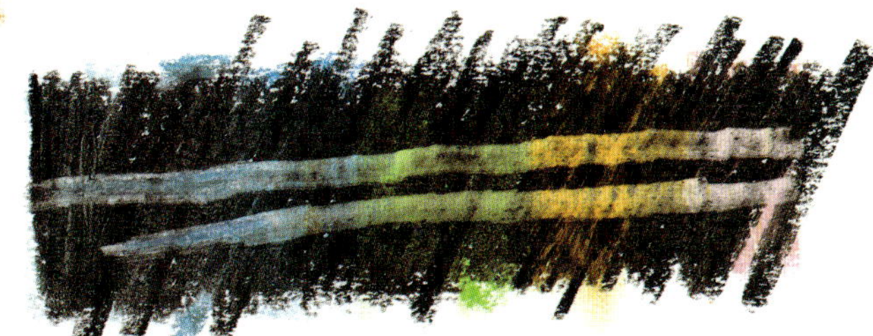

▲ *This technique involves scratching the surface colour to reveal the colours underneath.*

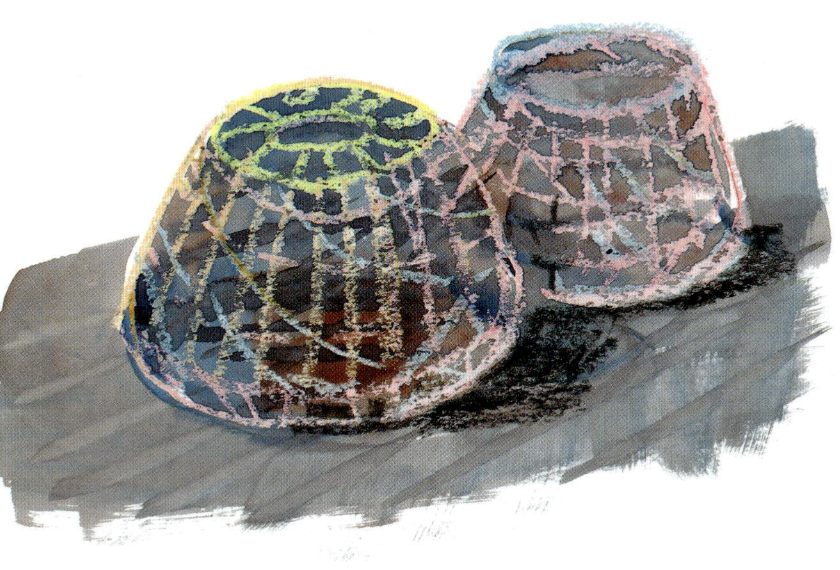

◀ *The same pots, this time drawn in various colours of oil pastel, and then washed over with a dark watercolour. For this to work well, the oil pastel must be in light colours and the watercolour very dark.*

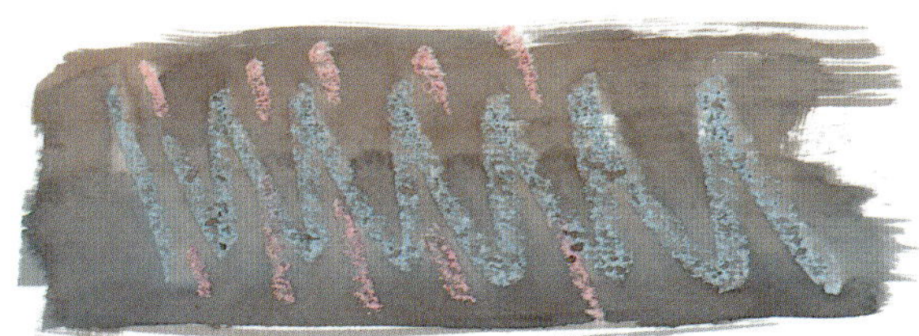

▲ *Use a water-resistant medium to establish your subject, then wash over it in a dark colour to really bring it to life.*

BRUSH DRAWING

Everyone is familiar with brushes; they're what you paint with. If used like a pencil, however, they can make very loose, expressive drawings. Many years ago, when I was a signwriter, traditional brush manufacturers still referred to small pointed brushes as 'pencils'. The best way to draw with a brush is to hold it well back along the handle, away from the metal part (the ferrule). This gives a more flowing movement.

QUICK & CLEVER BRUSH TECHNIQUES!

Use your brush in a variety of ways to achieve different effects.

INCREASING THE PRESSURE

One of the things that brushes can do that other drawing implements can't is spread the width of the line. This is achieved by increasing pressure on the brush as you draw the stroke.

FLICKING AND SPATTERING

Flicking and spattering are also interesting techniques to practise, but be careful who you sit beside when you do this!

THIN LINES

Thin lines can be very expressive, and strong flowing curves are equally easy to make with a bit of practice.

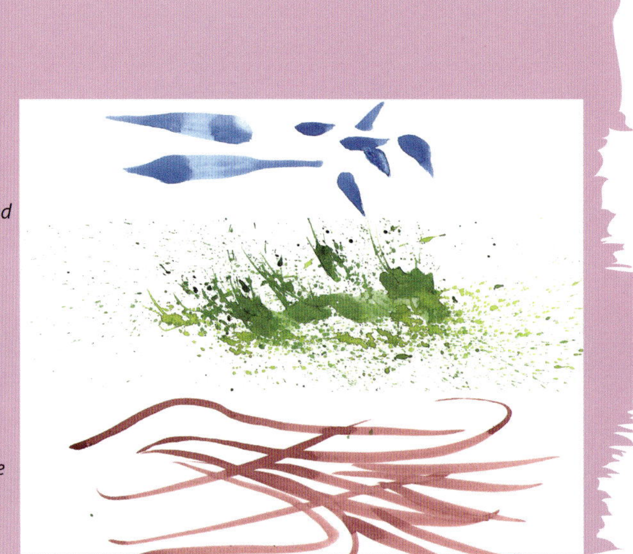

▼ *The ability to vary the brush line by pressing harder is used here to good effect. See how the line on the edge of the path becomes thicker as it moves down the page. This loose and spontaneous technique can be very useful.*

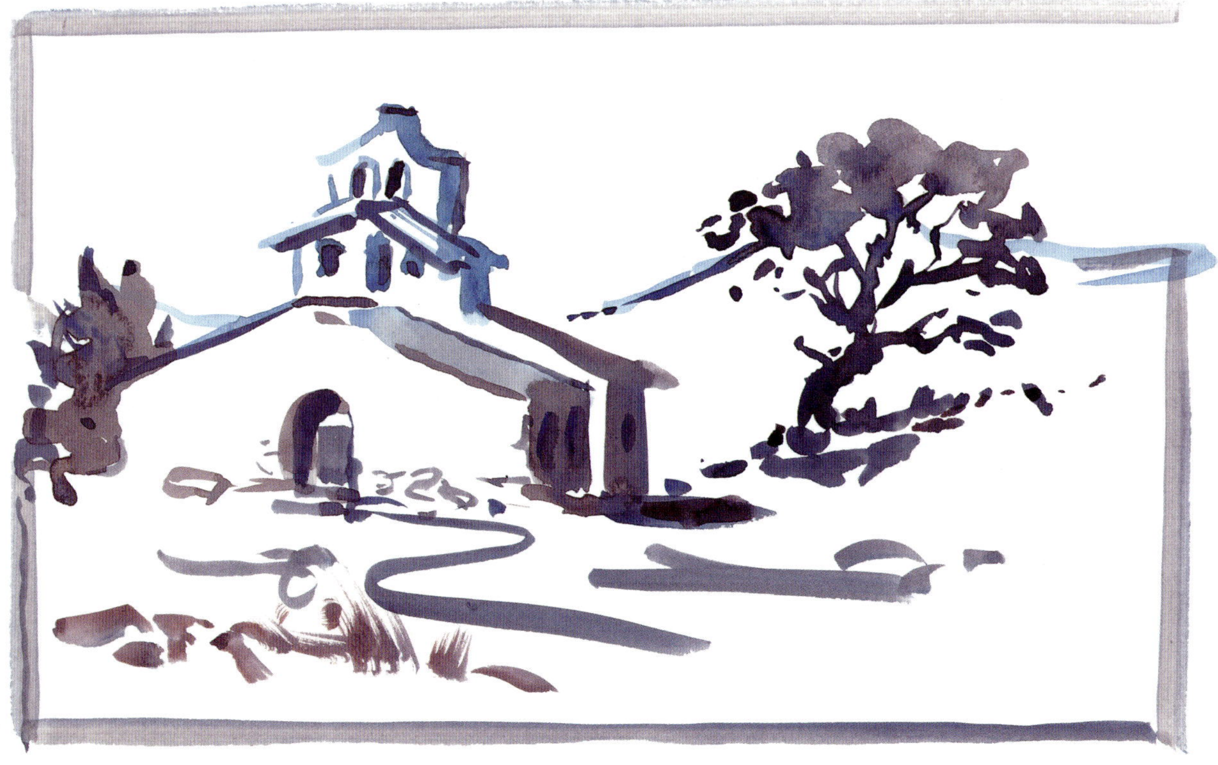

DOTS AND STIPPLES

Many years ago, when I was an art student, drawings made of dots were very fashionable. The method is very effective, especially if putting several tones together. Very subtle tonal gradations can be built up by adding carefully into the gaps between the dots. Technology has caught up with this technique; this is basically how pixels show colour in computer-generated images. The effect is particularly good for features such as leaves on trees or stonework. If you enjoy working slowly and carefully, this technique may be the one for you!

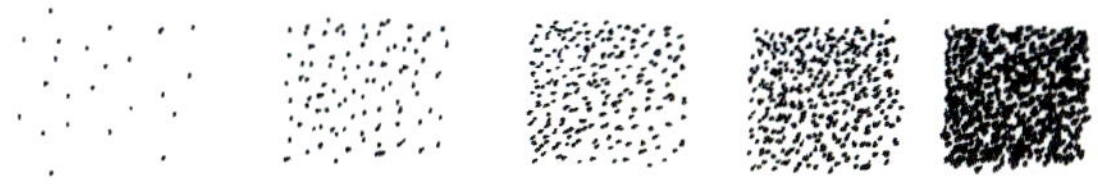

This is a simple tonal study, where more dots have been carefully added in areas where the tones need to be dark. It needs concentration, but the end result is an attractive image. It's important if using this method to have a simple drawing or photo to work from; complicated subjects can work, but will take a long time.

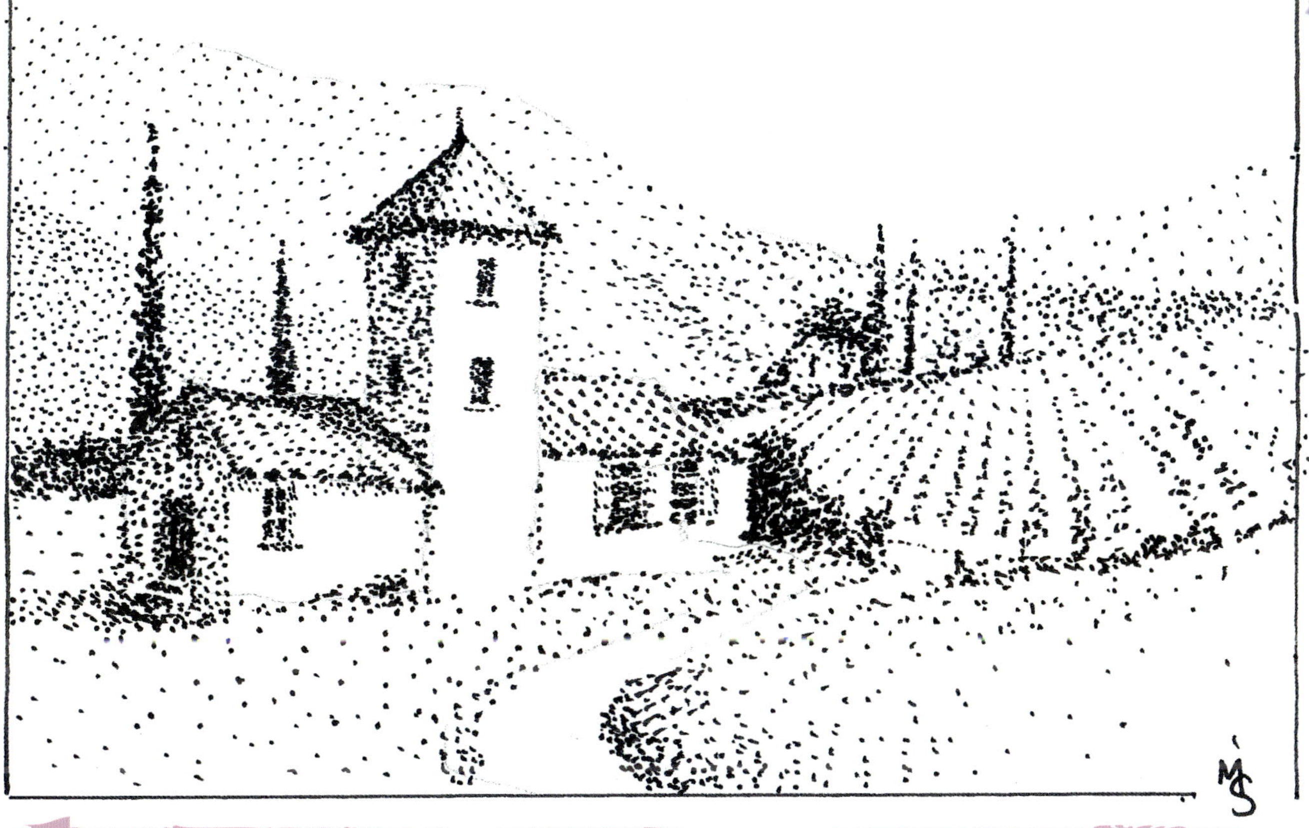

QUICK & CLEVER EFFECTS!

Coloured pencils can be used in the same way, to produce a shimmering effect.

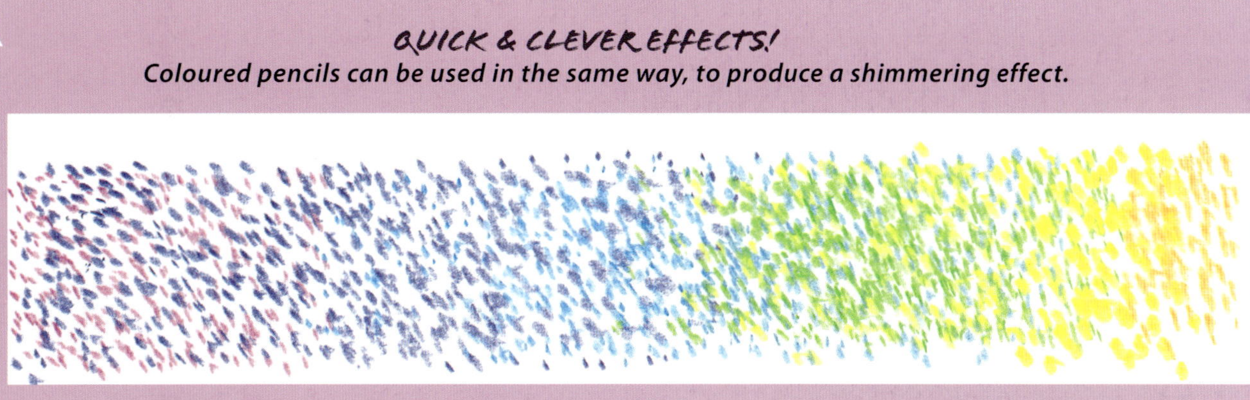

SOFT STREAKS AND STROKES

When working with coloured pencils, the effect can sometimes become too linear, with the lines predominating. This is a quick and clever way of softening the coloured pencil. You will need some medium-grade sandpaper and something to collect the dust in; a plate will do.

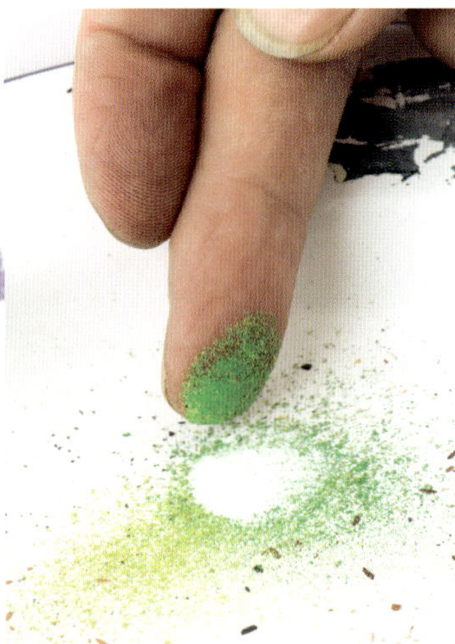

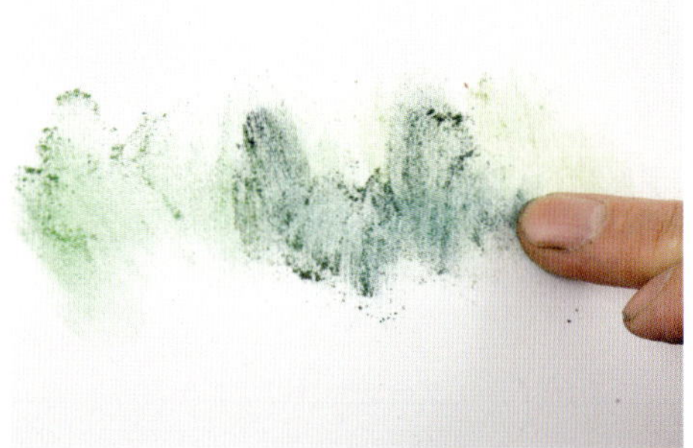

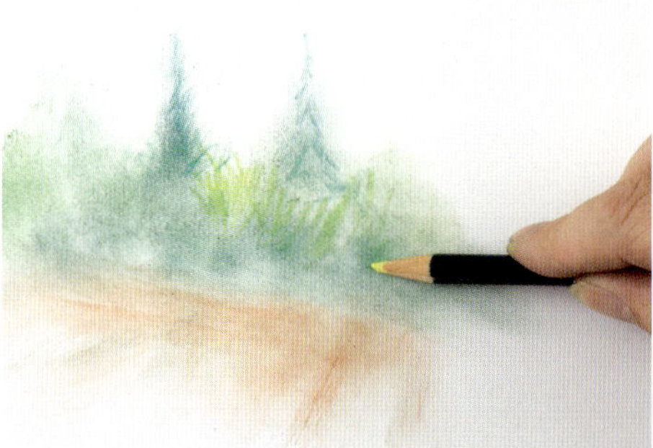

1 PICKING UP DUST Scribble some coloured pencils of the desired colour onto sandpaper and catch the dust on a plate.

2 SMUDGING Dip a finger into the dust. By using gentle or firm pressure, darker or lighter streaks can be applied to the paper. Add more colours as required.

3 ADDING DETAIL On this soft underdrawing, you can add more detail with coloured pencils, drawing fine lines where needed and blending on top of the previous colours.

4 SOFT EFFECT The final effect is much softer than using coloured pencils in the usual linear way.

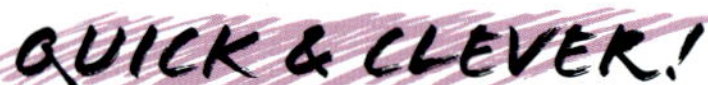

QUICK & CLEVER!

When using your fingers in this way, clean them between colours with a wet wipe or soap-impregnated tissue. Otherwise you'll get muddy colours.

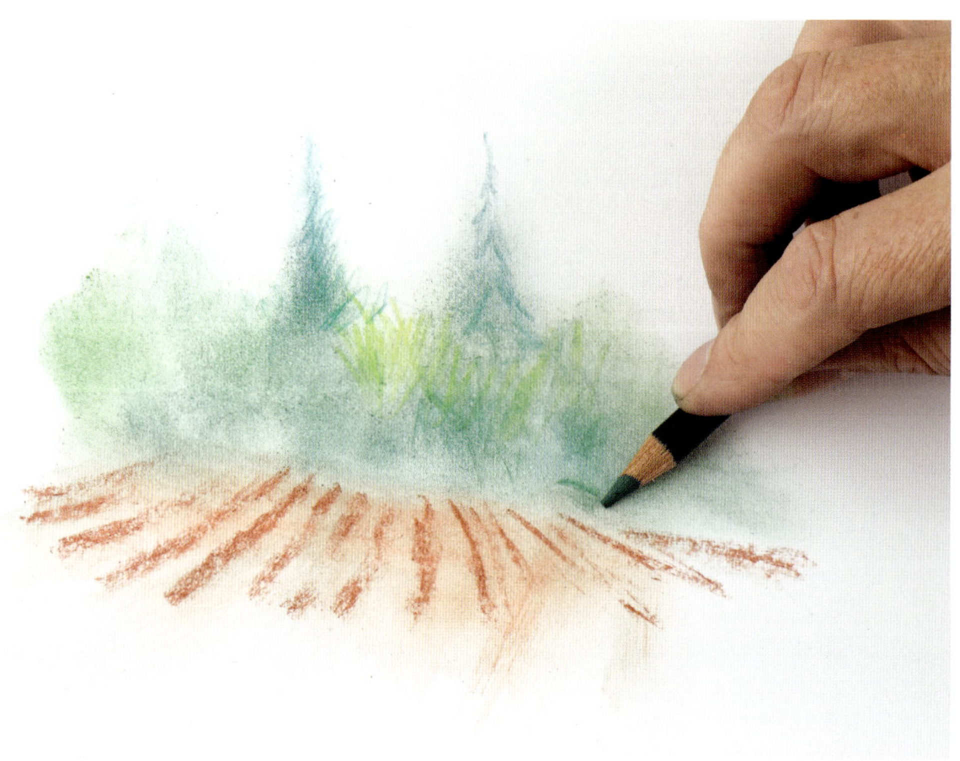

FROTTAGE

No, this is not a kind of French cheese! This drawing method consists of applying soft pencil or pastel on paper that is resting on a heavily textured surface. For this demonstration I used the photographer's metal camera case to rest on; the surface consisted of ripples and bumps. The effects are fascinating, as different textures impart different results. Try wood, plastic, concrete – anything with an interesting texture.

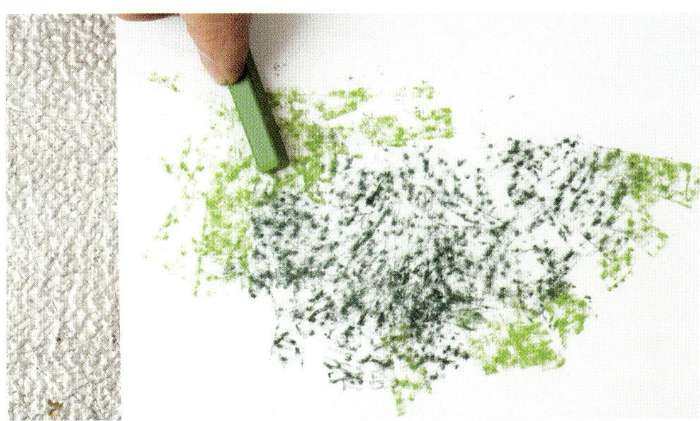

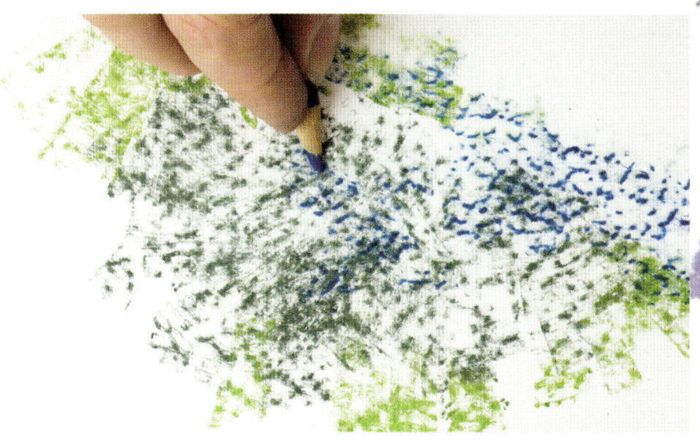

1 SCRIBBLING OVER SURFACE
Thin cartridge paper is placed on a rough surface, and scribbled over so that the imprint of this roughness shows through. Pressure can be varied to obtain differing densities of colour. Here I used two colours of hard pastel.

2 CREATING TEXTURE WITH COLOURED PENCIL
Colours can be built up as required, taking care that the rough effect isn't obliterated; too much pigment and the effect is diminished. After removing the paper from the textured surface and resting on a board, smooth lines or areas can be added.

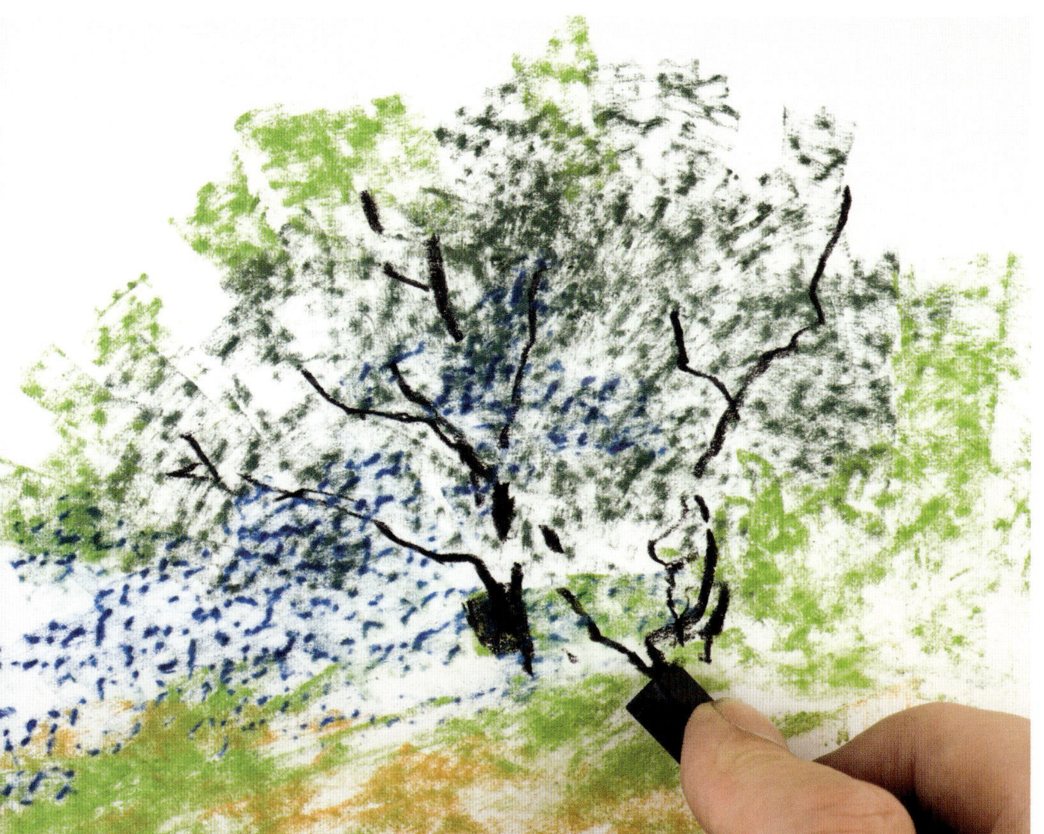

3 ADDING DETAIL
The texture used can take many forms, and each will impart a particular look that can be used to imply different features. The dotted look produced by the camera case reminded me of leaves, and so this image of a tree appeared. Try some different textures and see what you come up with.

QUICK & CLEVER!

Frottage works best if you use thin paper. Try combining several kinds of texture in the same image for an exciting effect.

LINE AND WASH

This is a very traditional method of working. A light pen drawing is done, without too much detail, and then colour is added to enhance the image. If you use a waterproof pen, colour can be added and the ink lines stay put. If you use a water-soluble pen, the lines run slightly and produce a different effect. Line and wash is particularly useful when working out of doors; you don't have much to carry, and you can give an idea of colour as well as shape. When surrounded by a wide card mount, in a nice frame, line and wash drawings look good and are very popular.

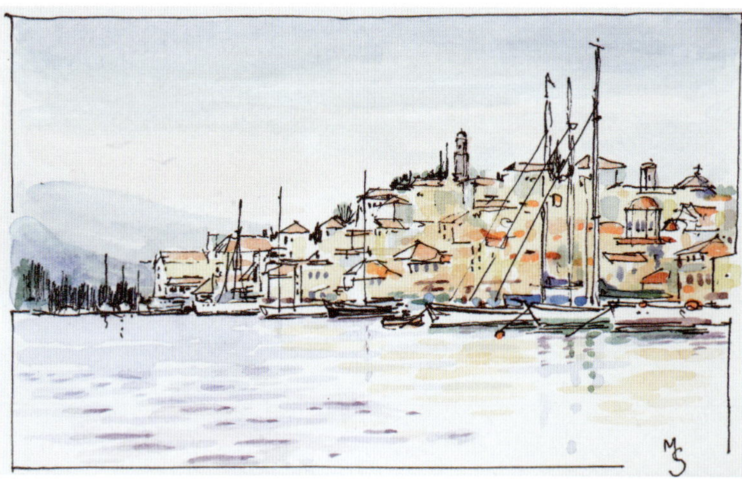

◀ *This sketch of Poros, Greece, was done quickly, and small touches of colour were added to enhance the warm feel of the place. A warm Raw Sienna and dilute Cadmium Red were used to enhance the buildings, with some orange, mixed from those two colours, in the terracotta roofs. Little touches of blue balanced the orange.*

QUICK & CLEVER!

Line doesn't have to be made with a pen; try using coloured pencil to make a drawing and add light washes of watercolour afterwards for a unique effect.

▶ *When I lived on a boat, I had to take her out of the water occasionally for maintenance. This little drawing shows the interior of the boat shed. I used a water-soluble pen and dilute washes of colour. I wanted to show the structure of the old shed, and line was effective for drawing the planking.*

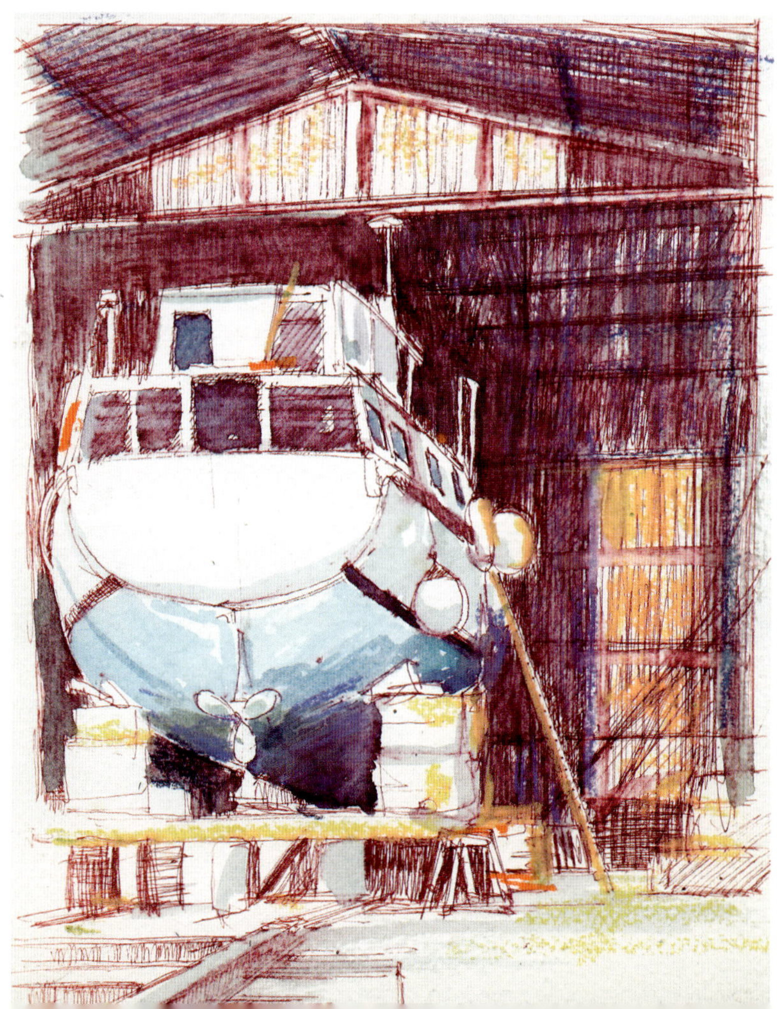

QUICK & CLEVER EFFECTS!

Water-soluble pens can be very effective in line and wash. When the drawing is finished, brushing on water will soften the lines.

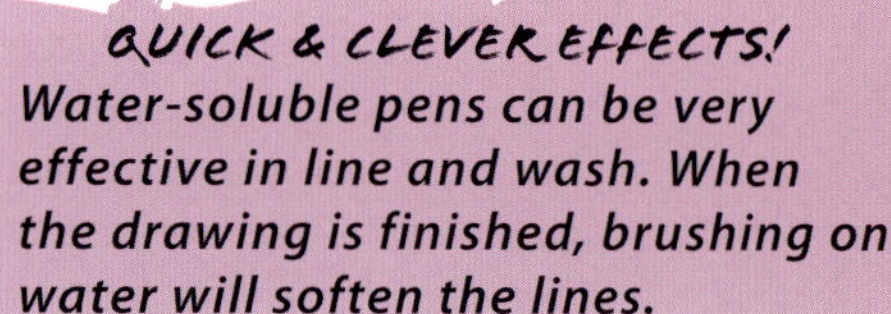

Washing water across the lines with a watercolour brush produces an entirely new colour!

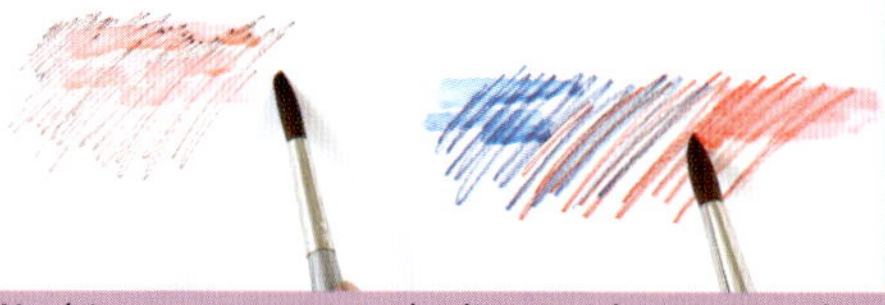

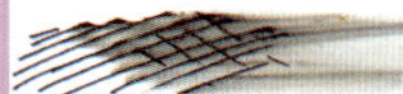

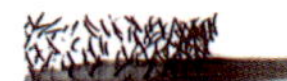

Some inks will still leave visible lines after water is brushed on, whereas others will dissolve into a watercolour effect. Experiment and see what your pens do.

PERSPECTIVE MADE EASY

Perspective is a subject that often seems to make beginners nervous. If you are worried about this, use my nice simple method, practise a few lines, then you can start to relax! The main thing to remember about perspective is that it is an illusion. It must be; if railway lines really did get closer together as they went away, the trains would fall off! But they don't. So, why worry about an optical illusion? For this lesson in perspective you don't need to learn anything new, or remember any complicated theory. All you need to learn is what to look for. Observation is everything with perspective.

HORIZONTAL LINES

▶ *Everyone can see whether something is level (horizontal) or not. Hold a pencil, horizontally, in front of your eyes, at arm's length. Is it level? Now look beyond it, and compare it to the line you want to draw. Ask yourself; 'does the line slope down to the left, or down to the right?' In this case, it slopes to the right.*

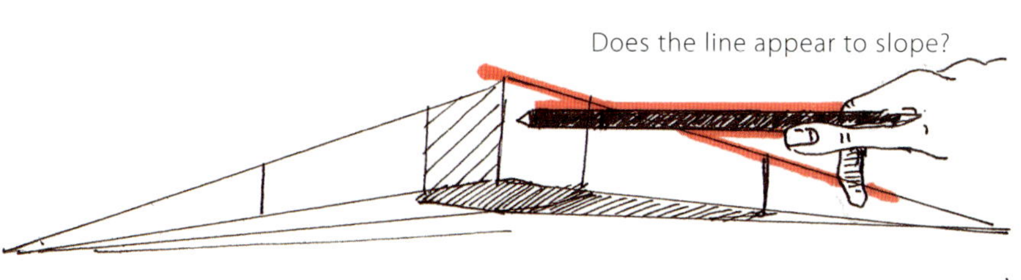

PROJECTING DISTANCE

▶ *When you've learned to look beyond the horizontal pencil in this way, you can ask yourself, 'does the line slope a little, or a lot?' All you need to do then is remember how much it sloped, and draw the same slope on your sketchpad. These lines have different angles; try and draw them now, freehand.*

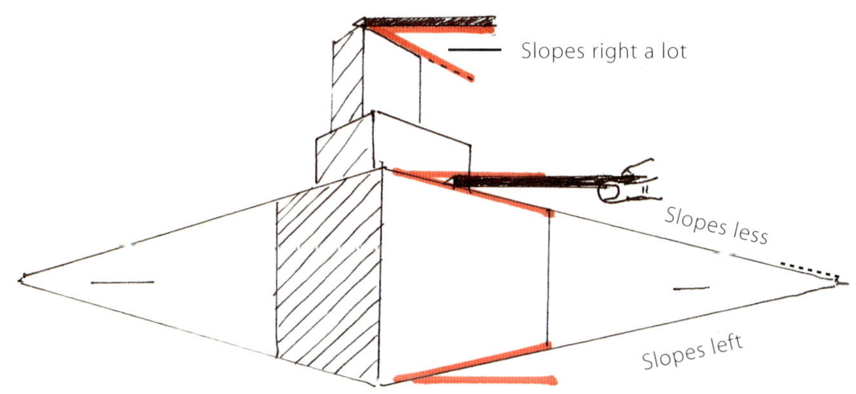

LOOKING DOWN

▶ *Here is a drawing of the top of an ornamental gatepost. Can you see which lines slope down to the left, and which slope down to the right? I drew this by holding a pencil horizontally, at arm's length, and looking beyond it. If you look closely, you will see that none of the lines are parallel. They all converge slightly. If you can see that, then you have learned the basics of perspective. Well done!*

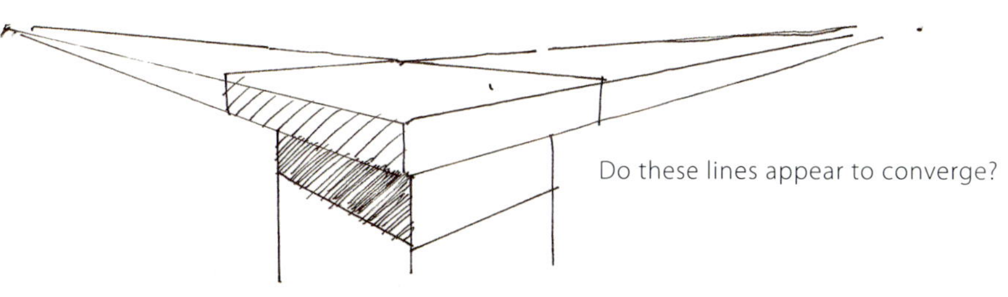

WORKING WITH COLOUR

THERE IS A MASSIVE RANGE OF COLOURED DRAWING MEDIA AVAILABLE, FROM WATERCOLOUR PENCILS TO SOFT PASTEL PENCILS. LEARNING TO DRAW WITH THESE MATERIALS WILL WIDEN YOUR RANGE OF TECHNIQUES AND MAKE YOUR IMAGES COME ALIVE. TO START WITH, IT'S A GOOD IDEA TO PRACTISE BLENDING ONE COLOUR INTO ANOTHER, IN A COLOUR WHEEL OR TRIANGLE.

COLOUR WHEEL

Colour wheels have been around for centuries, in one form or another. Ready-made ones can be found in most art shops, but making one is a very good exercise. It will teach you how to mix many colours from a few, and also how one colour relates to its neighbours on the wheel.

If you buy sets of coloured or pastel pencils or watercolour pencils, then the larger the set, the more variety of each colour you will have. With careful practice, it's not too difficult to blend or hatch one colour onto another to achieve a third one.

It's best to start with yellow, as that is the palest colour and is most easily overpowered by others. Then move round, gradually adding touches of the next colour. The best sequence is:

1. Lemon yellow, mid-yellow, orange-yellow
2. Orange, orange-red
3. Bright red, mid-red and deep red
4. Red-violet, violet, blue-violet
5. Warm blue, mid-blue, green-blue
6. Turquoise, dark blue-green, green
7. Mid-green, yellow-green, lime

5
4
6
3
7
1
2

QUICK & CLEVER!

When experimenting with colour, it's a good idea to make notes of the colours you used on the back of the paper, so you don't forget which ones worked successfully.

◀ *This colour wheel is coloured pencil on the outside, watercolour pencil (washed with water) in the middle, and pastel pencil on the inside.*

COMPLEMENTARY COLOURS

There are some combinations of colour that work well together; they just seem to 'go' with one another. Sometimes clashing colours are exciting, but harmonious combinations are easier on the eye. For centuries artists have understood that certain colours 'complement' one another when used in a composition.

Complementary colours work like this: there are three primaries; red, blue and yellow. When two primaries are mixed together, they produce another colour, the 'secondary' colour.

The complementary of blue is a mix of the other two: yellow and red, which gives orange.

You can work this the other way. Take a secondary colour; green. It's made from yellow and blue. The primary colour that's left – red – is the complementary of green.

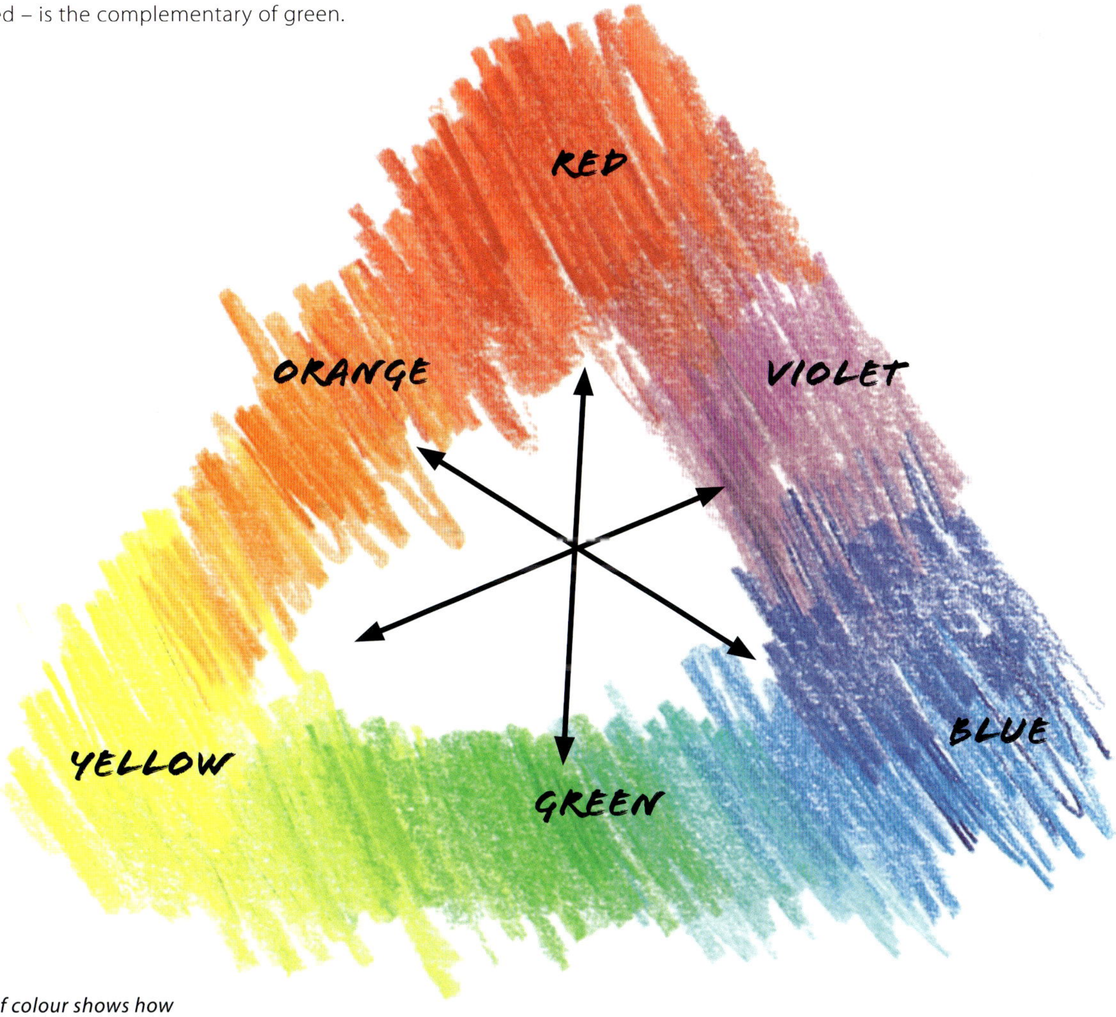

RED
ORANGE
VIOLET
YELLOW
GREEN
BLUE

▲ *A triangle of colour shows how complementary colours work. You can start with a primary at each corner and work out what the complementary colour is. It is the one produced by mixing the other two primaries.*

COLOUR TEMPERATURE AND AERIAL PERSPECTIVE

One of the most important effects to learn to create is a sense of distance in a drawing. As with colour theory, this can become second nature with practice. Every colour has a 'temperature', which simply means whether there is blue or red in it. Any colour that has a hint of red is called a warm colour; if it contains blue it's termed cool. There are, of course, colours that don't contain either, and they can be thought of as neutral in temperature. So how does this all work?

What you need to remember is that warm colours appear nearer than cool ones. Warm colours advance; cool colours recede. So, if you draw a mountain with a red barn on it, the barn will look as if it's hovering in front of the mountain, not placed on it. Warm colours such as browns, oranges, reds and warm yellows should be near the 'front' of the drawing, i.e. near the bottom. The distance needs to recede, and so receding colours should have blue in them. Greens should be blue-green and pale, in the distance, gradually becoming warmer and darker as they get nearer.

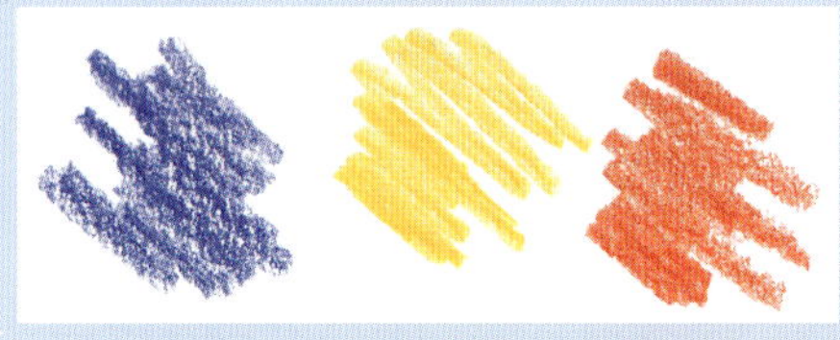

WARM COLOURS

Can you see the difference between the left-hand colours and those on the right? The ones on the left are 'warm' colours; those on the right are 'cool'.

COOL COLOURS

▶ This little image of Tuscany works on the principle that warm colours such as browns and reds need to be at the bottom (front) of an image, whereas cool colours such as pale green and blue need to be in the distance. Although the house has an orange tinge, it is very pale, so doesn't look out of place.

COOL

WARM

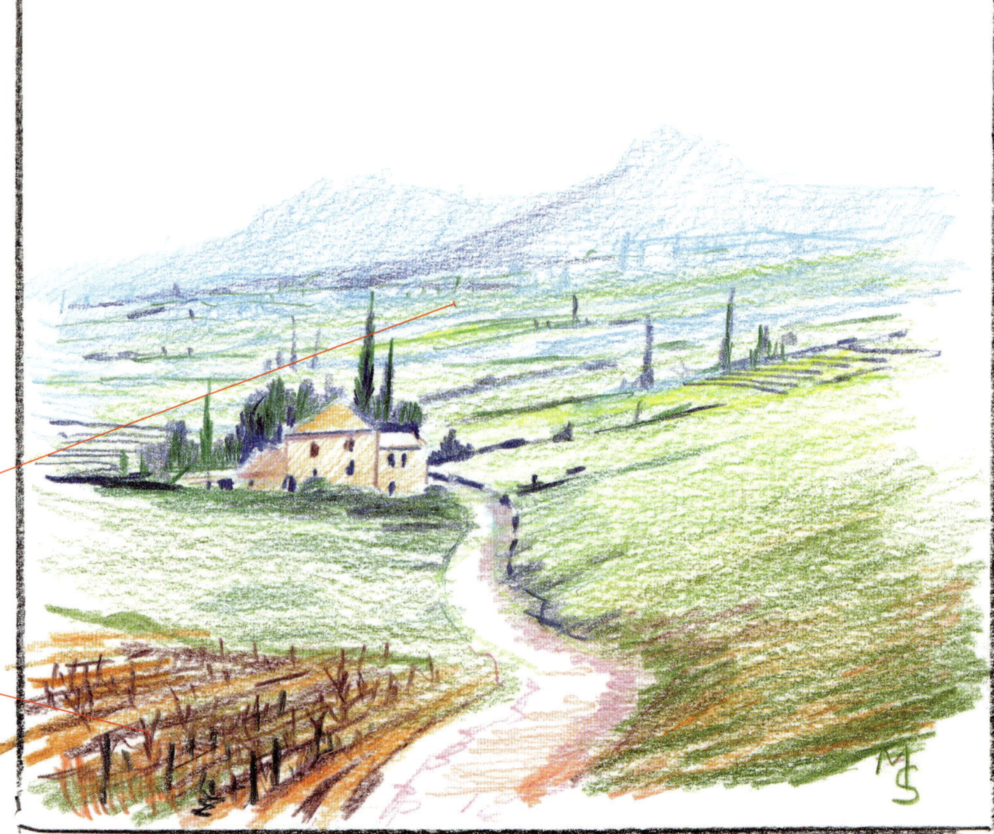

COLOUR COMPOSITION

Now you understand the principles of warm and cool colours, choosing colours should be much easier. Using complementaries in a composition is also an advantage. All of this can be planned with confidence, as long as you remember that distant objects look pale and cool, while closer elements look brighter and warmer. It's a good idea to make little thumbnail sketches before tackling bigger drawings, especially if you're going to be using colour later. Working out which colours are going where is easier if you have done a bit of planning. These little sketches can be quite simple.

▼ Here is one of my preparatory sketches for a bigger drawing. You see, they don't have to be neat and tidy!

QUICK & CLEVER!

Always have a sketchbook handy. You may get an idea for a drawing, or see something that you could record quickly. Maybe your train is delayed or you face a long wait in traffic. In those circumstances, a sketchbook and pencil or pen is an ideal way to spend the time.

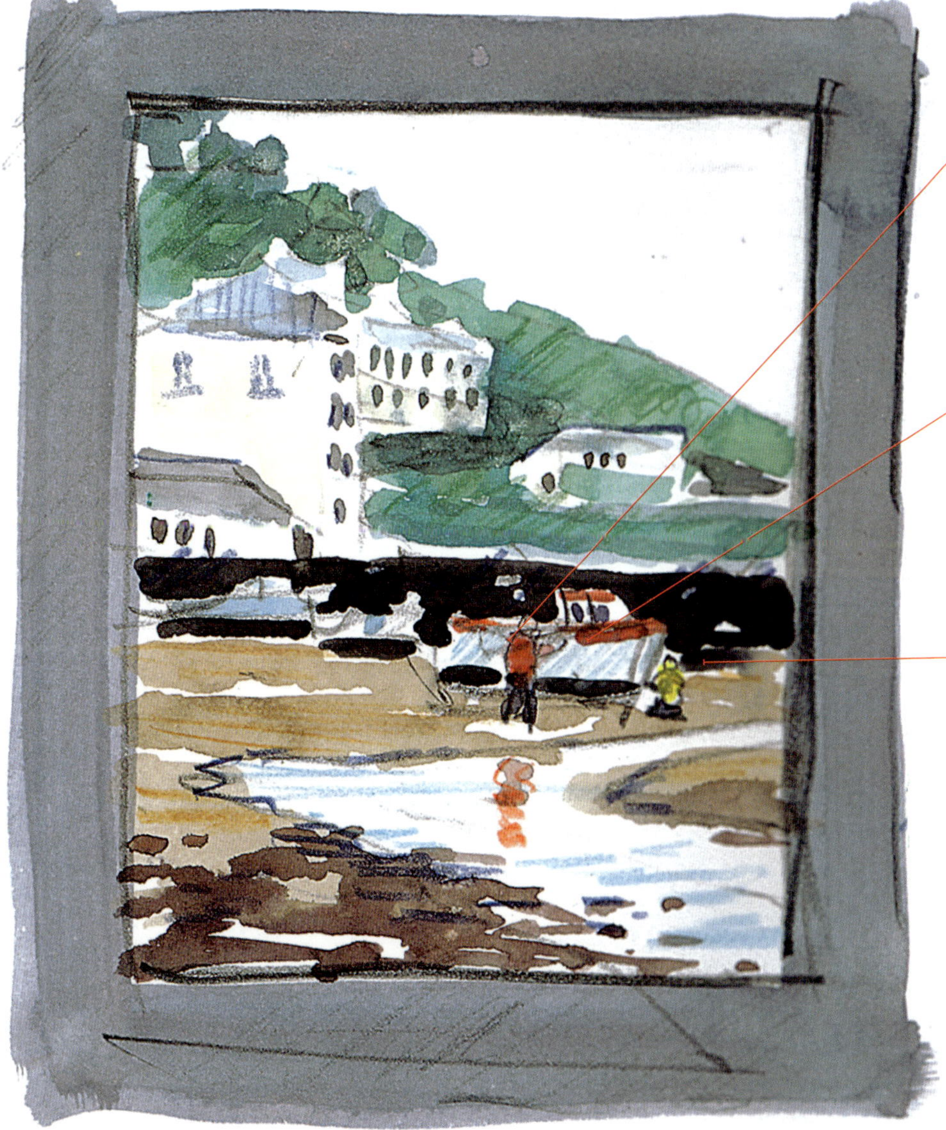

I chose red for the figure because there is a lot of green in the background. Red is a complementary colour of green, remember?

I don't want the red figure right in the centre, and, if the boat is blue, the bright paintwork on it should be orange (complementaries again).

The little yellow figure on the right of the boat should have some violet-grey behind it.

CROSS-HATCHING, BLENDING AND TONAL STRIPS

Coloured pencils are a most expressive medium. Light and easy to carry, they are very adaptable. As well as being used for lines, they can be used to stroke colour onto the paper, building graduated colour variations of a subtle nature. They can be bold and expressive or quiet and subdued.

QUICK AND CLEVER EFFECTS!

Hatching in two or more shades builds up colour using the linear quality of the pencils.

One of the easiest ways to begin combining colours is to use cross-hatching. This is where one colour is drawn using lines, and another set of lines is superimposed on it in a different direction. Several layers can be built up in this way.

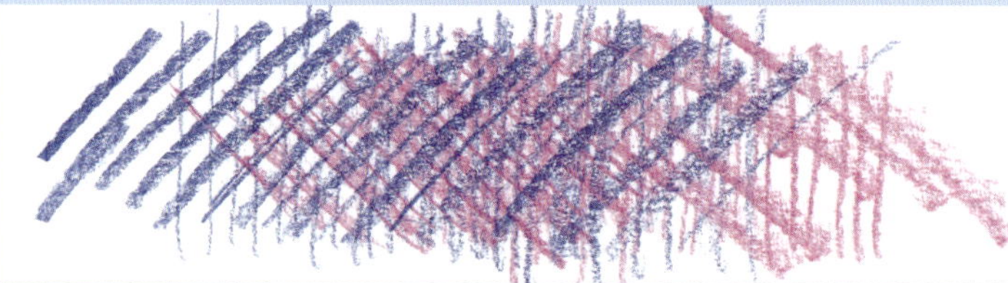

CROSS-HATCHING

Another method is what I call the soft scribble. This is where the pencil is stroked over the surface of the paper without much pressure until the desired density of colour is produced.

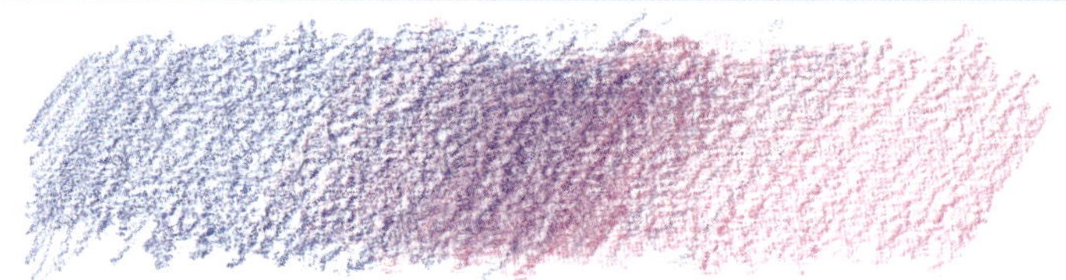

SOFT SCRIBBLE

Blending is a technique that produces strong effects, and entails working on top of one layer with another layer using a softer pressure so the top colour gradually affects the base – changing a yellow into a green by gentle application of blue, for instance. Blended colour mixes can be more exciting than having just one colour alone.

BLEND

HARD PRESSURE

LIGHT PRESSURE

◀ *Any pigment possesses tone, as well as its main attribute, which is colour. So you can produce a range of tonal values from any colour. Try this tonal strip with as many colours as you have. Try to produce four tones from each colour. In these examples, I think the blue is darker than the others, at full strength. What do you think?*

LAYERS

Layering is a method of building up dense colours that is most useful with coloured pencils. Because coloured pencils are mainly transparent, colours applied over others allow the bottom colour to show through. This can be used to build rich, vibrant effects. Colours can be made very dense in this way. The effect depends on the quality of the coloured pencils and the strength and quality of the paper.

QUICK AND CLEVER EFFECTS!

Experiment by building up layers of primary colours. you can vary the amount of layers and colours to produce different effects.

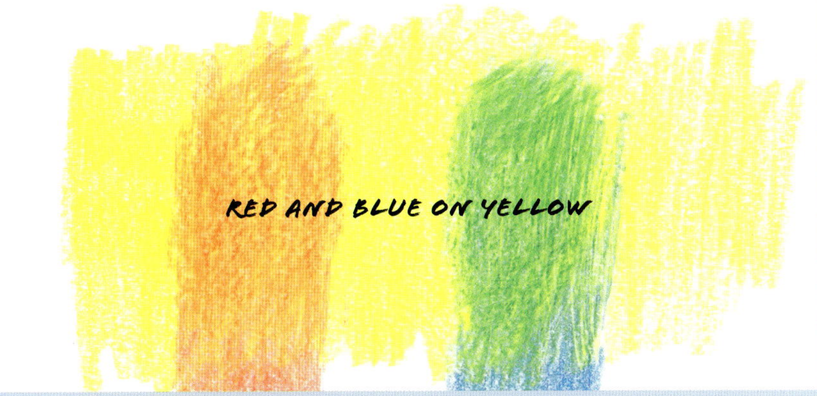

▲ *Red and blue coloured pencil applied over yellow produces orange and green.*

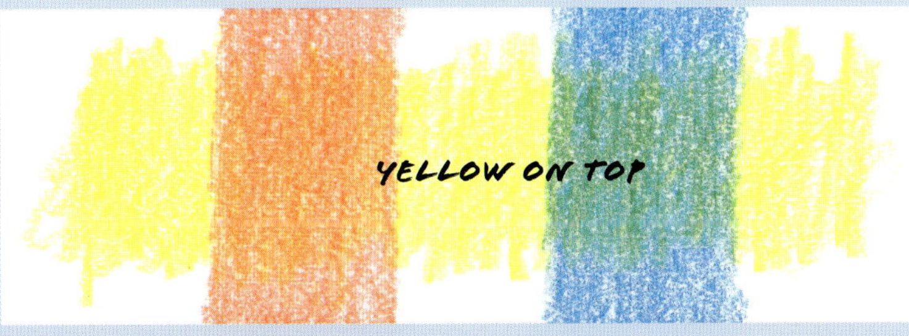

▲ *Yellow applied over red and blue has a more subtle effect, because yellow pigment is less opaque.*

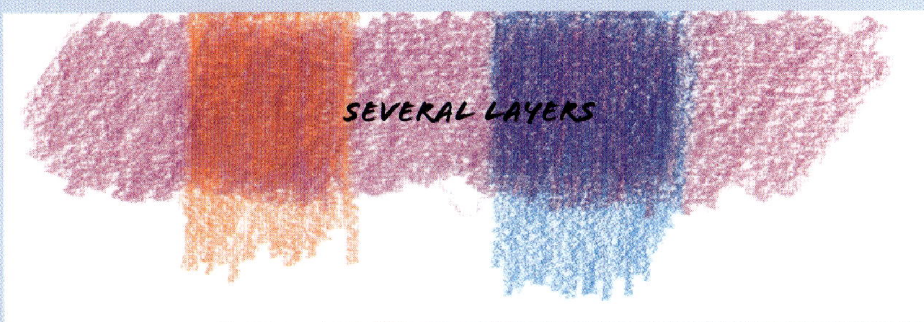

▲ *Working coloured pencils with heavy pressure can build really dense layers of colour.*

QUICK & CLEVER!

The larger the range of coloured pencils you get, the more choice of colours you have. Some colours, especially bright oranges and reds, cannot be made by blending or layering. If the colours you have aren't bright enough, adding others by mixing won't improve things. Buy the largest set of quality coloured pencils you can afford – they'll last for years!

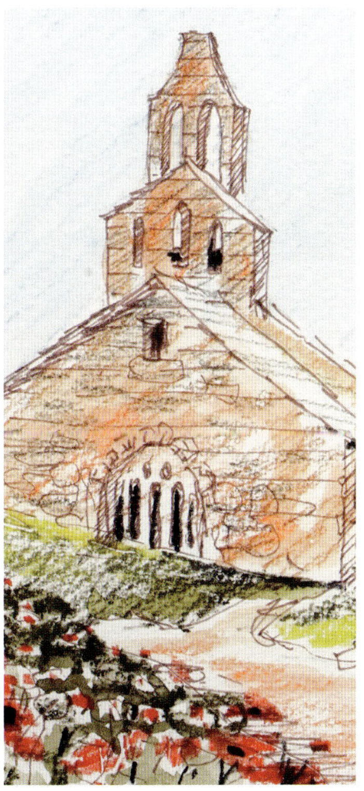

▲ *Layering means that you can adapt and change as you work. In order to make the orange colour on the building less strident, a grey was gently layered on top. This is known as 'subduing' a colour; it makes it more subtle.*

WATERCOLOUR WASHES

When using watercolour pencils, it's possible to lift colour straight from the tip of the pencil. If you use them in this way, you can produce traditional watercolours, especially if you work on good-quality watercolour paper. This method is a unique cross-over between drawing and painting and has the advantage of being easy to use.

QUICK AND CLEVER EFFECTS!

Colour lifted off watercolour pencils.

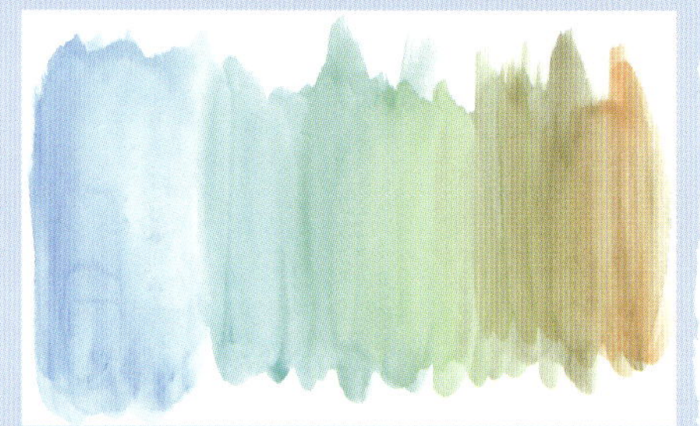

These colours were lifted from the watercolour pencils and applied onto damp paper. Use only watercolour or heavy cartridge paper for this; light cartridge paper isn't robust enough, and will buckle.

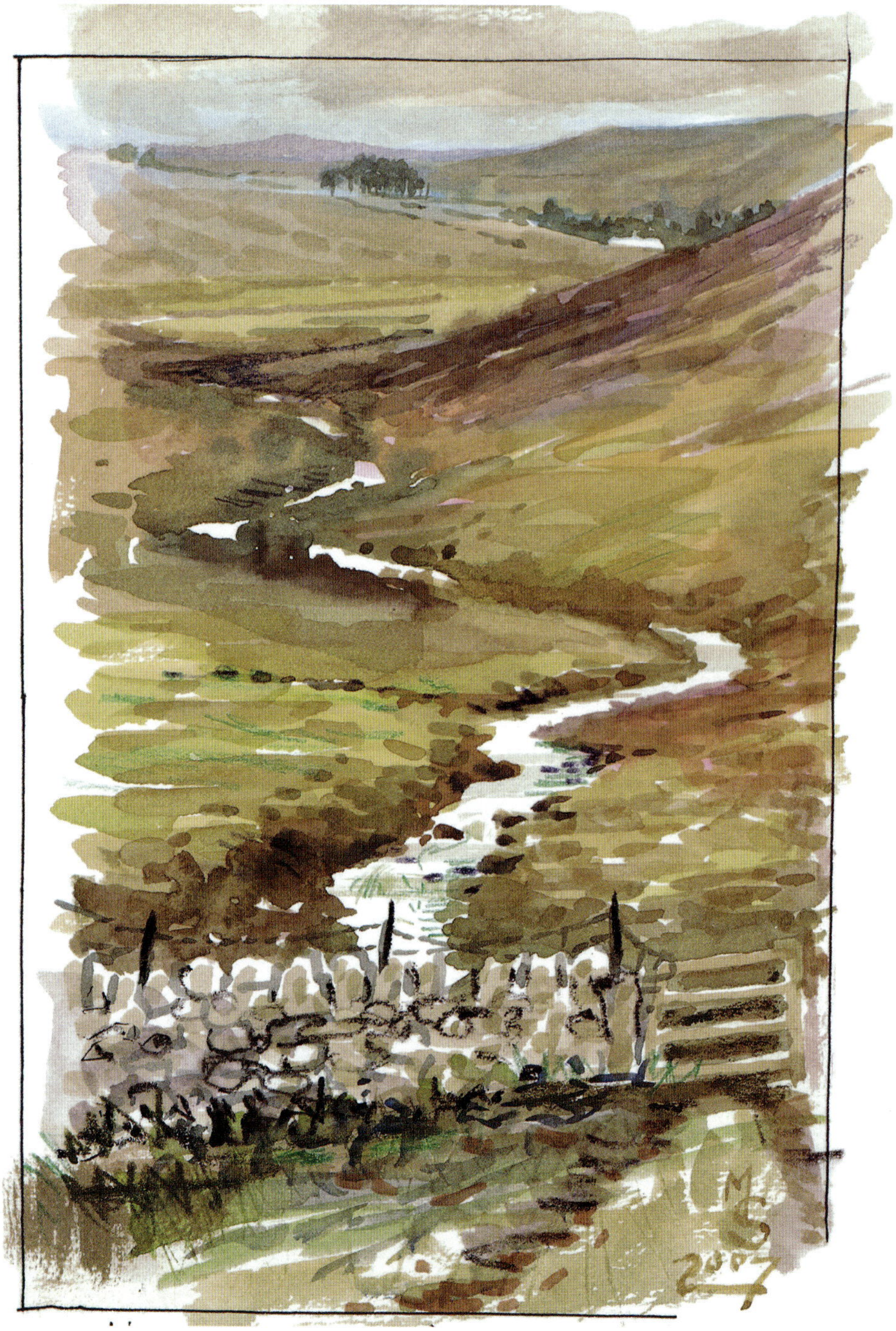

▶ *This little painting was made by lifting pigment from watercolour pencils and transferring it to a piece of heavy cartridge paper. Each colour was chosen and applied individually, then mixed on the surface of the paper where needed. The only places where the pencils were used directly on the paper were the shadows at the base of the wall and between the stones.*

QUICK & CLEVER!

Watercolour pencil pigment works well on damp paper. Brush clean water on to watercolour paper. To check when paper has changed from wet to damp, look carefully. When the shine has gone it's damp. Sometimes you will need to re-wet paper as you work, especially in hot weather.

TONAL VALUES

This is a term that, put simply, means contrast. Using tonal values is probably the most important thing an artist can master. It means looking at the darkness or lightness of an element in the drawing and comparing it with other areas. Think about the two Cs: compare the contrast. If a drawing doesn't appear to have 'depth', then tone is the aspect that should be considered first. Drawing a tonal strip, also known as a grey scale, will help you practice this.

▶ *Here you can see how short marks and dots can be used to create tone and texture, such as the leather finish on the binoculars. The more these tonal marks run into each other, the darker they become. These tones imply the form of the object. If the drawing were in line only, there wouldn't be any illusion of depth. The careful hint of shadow on the flat surface helps fix the binoculars so they don't 'float' in space. Even the strap casts a pale shadow. Tones are important for applying shadows, and shadows are important for making drawings look 'real'.*

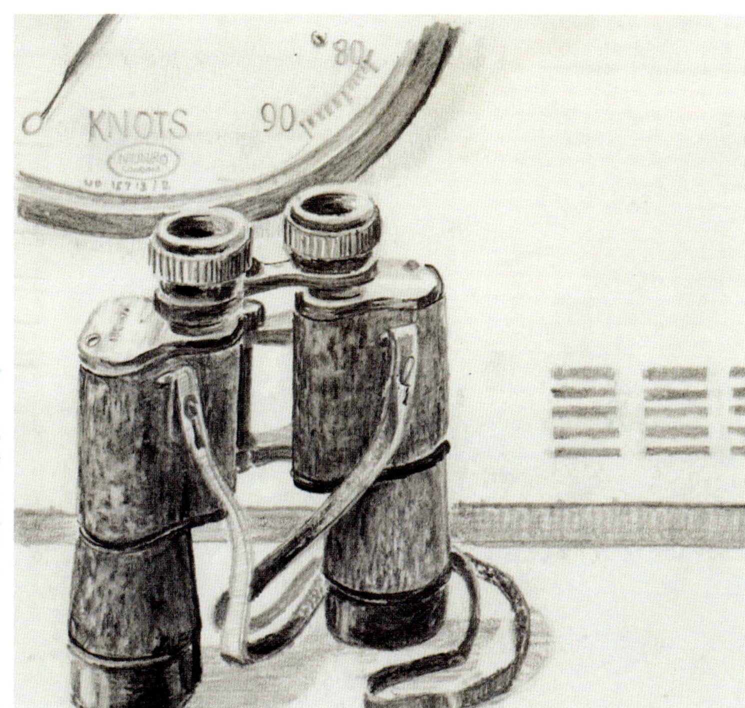

GREY SCALE

Being able to create several tones is what drawing is all about. Have a go at making a tonal strip or grey scale like this with your pencils, for practice.

The secret of making a grey scale is to start as dark as you can, and make the next rectangle quite a bit lighter, all the way through to the lightest tone, with the merest hint of grey.

QUICK & CLEVER!

When checking a photograph for tones, this device will help. Punch or cut several small holes in a piece of mid-grey paper, about 2.5 and 5cm (1 and 2in) apart. You can then position this on the photo, so different areas of tone show through the holes. Tonal differences are easier to see when separated like this.

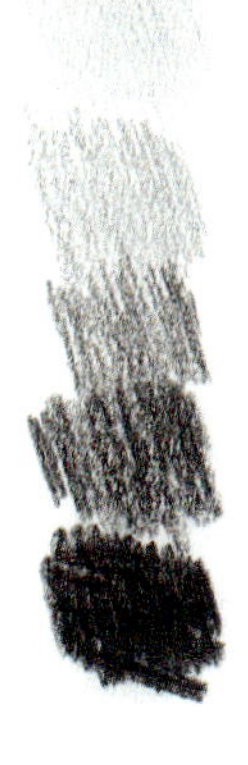

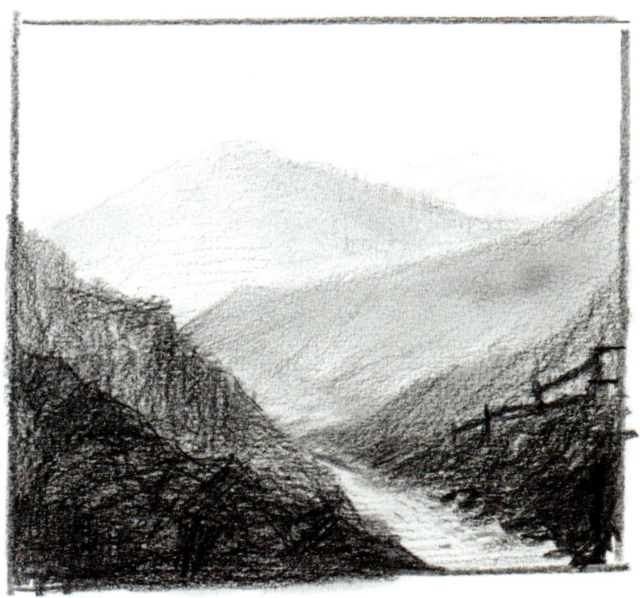

▶ *One of the main uses for tone in drawing is to create the illusion of space. The further away something is, the paler it appears. So, in order to make this image work, the distant hills must be very pale. The next hill is slightly darker, and so on. The darkest tones should be nearest. The term 'mid-tone', which you will sometimes hear, means the middle, between the lightest element and the darkest.*

WORKING FROM BLACK AND WHITE PHOTOGRAPHS

Sometimes a photograph looks difficult to interpret tonally. I find it helps to make a black and white photocopy from a colour photo, as this immediately defines everything as a grey-scale image. You can then draw onto the copy to plan the drawing.

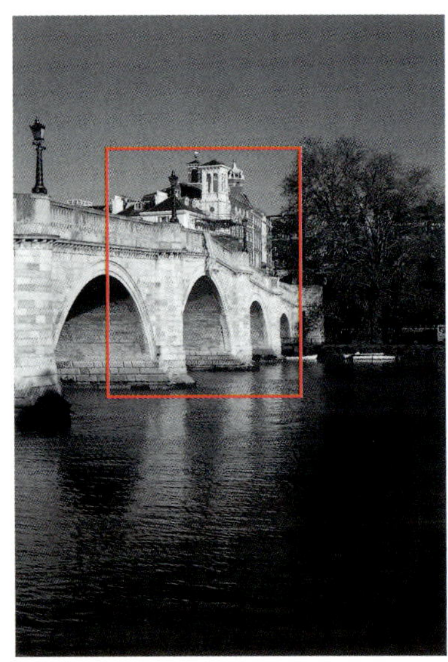

◀ *In this example, I took the black and white picture and drew a rectangle onto it, cropping the image to create an interesting composition. Sometimes it's best to omit large areas of a photo that don't offer much interest. I've excluded large amounts of dark water, which could create a boring image, and left out quite a bit of sky for the same reason. I thought the trees on the right didn't look too interesting, so they had to go as well, leaving the interesting buildings and unusual angle of the bridge.*

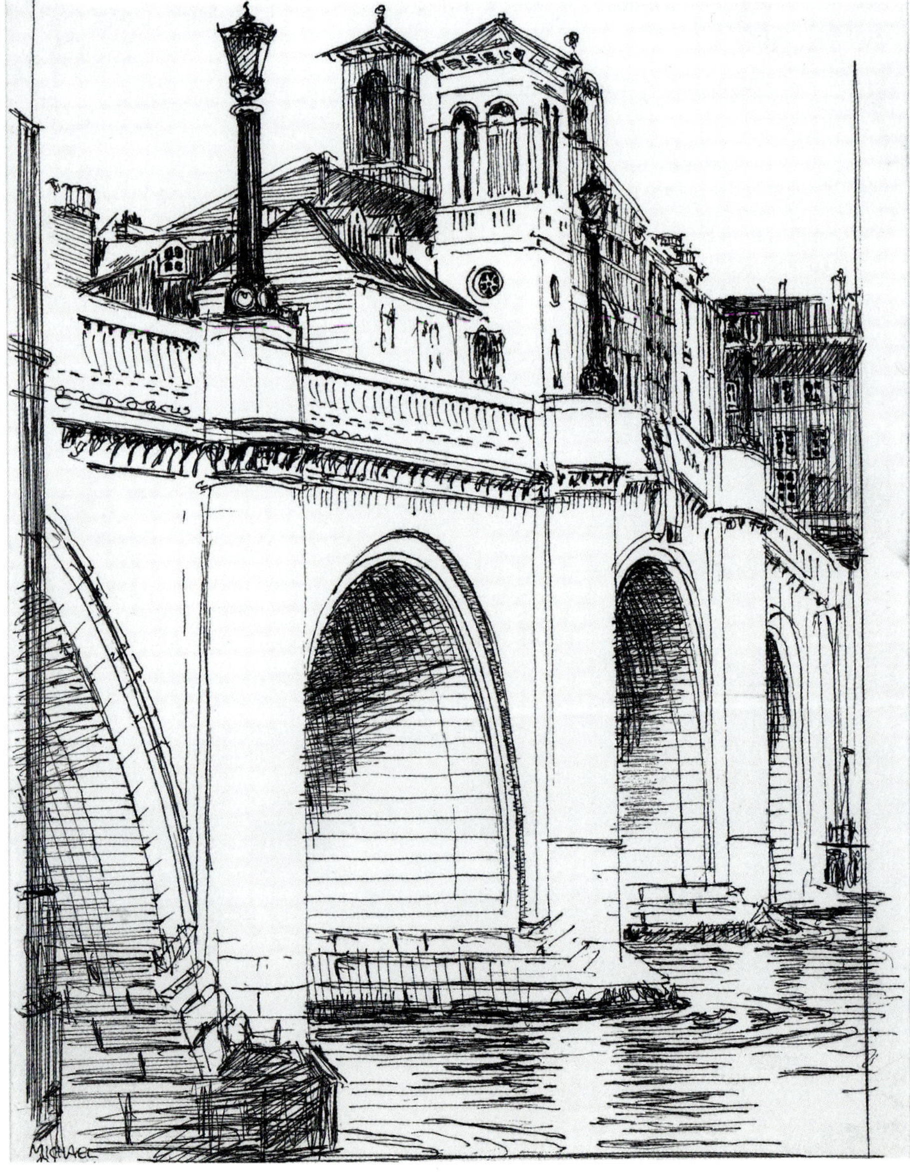

▶ *I used the assessment of tones and the cropped image to produce this pen drawing. There were some minor improvements in composition, such as inventing some ripples around the bridge piers, and I've simplified the buildings somewhat.*

AERIAL PERSPECTIVE WITH TONE

Tone enables artists to create the illusion of depth. The more tones you can produce with your pencil, the more chance you have of creating this effect successfully. The only way to obtain the required amount of tone is through practice. Have a go at the grey scale on page 41, then try this little drawing.

This pencil drawing uses very pale tones for the mountains, and becomes progressively darker and clearer as it gets nearer. Working in this way, it's important to get the distance pale and soft enough, while any dark areas in the foreground need to be sharp and dark.

Most beginners will make the distance here too dark, and then have problems making the nearer parts of the image dark enough, when compared to the background. This means you lose the illusion of distance. The thing to remember when working with tone is that it's quite easy to add more, and darken an area, later, but it's very difficult to make things lighter once they've been put in.

If you have difficulty drawing this image, practise the grey scale again, then start on the distant mountains, using very gentle pressure on the pencil. Stop shading before it becomes too dark! Then, for the nearer parts of the landscape, such as the trees on the right and the scrub on the left, use a softer grade of pencil. Remember, the higher the number on 'B' grade pencils, the darker the effect.

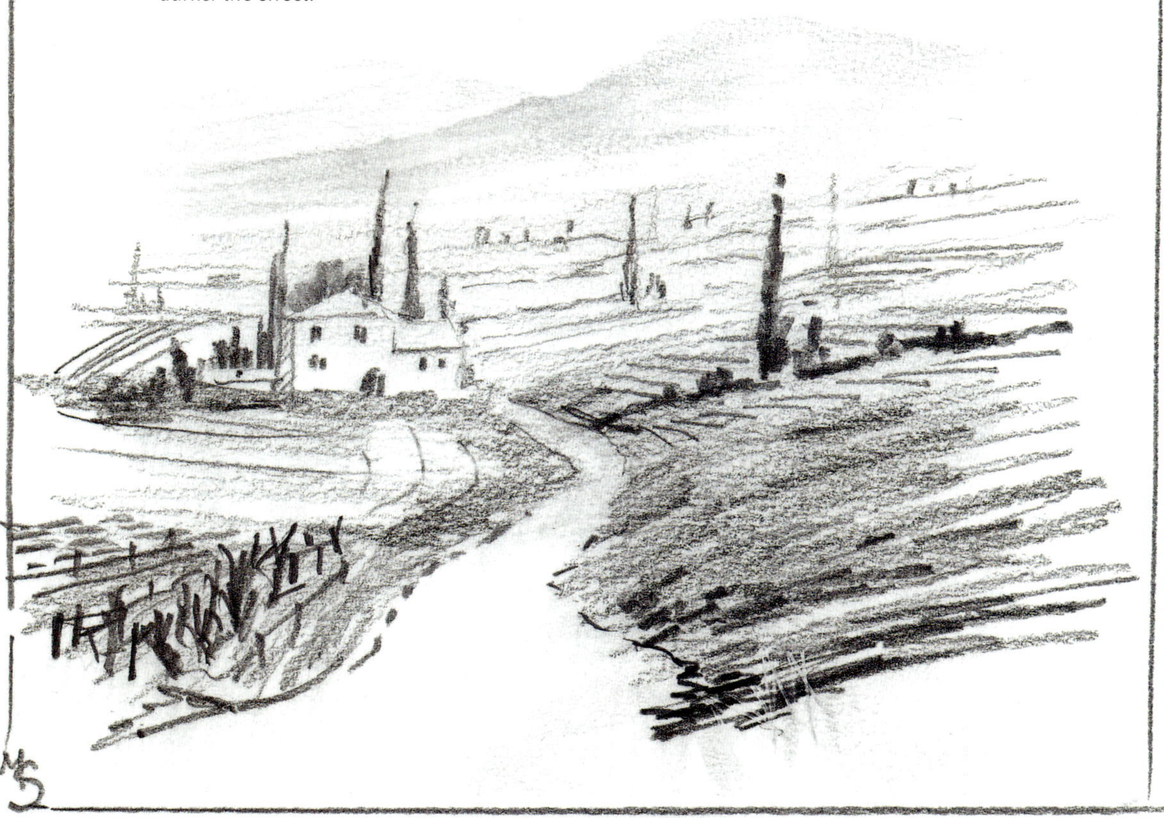

START DRAWING!

Now let us get started on some real drawings!

The projects that follow will guide you through the processes involved in producing some lively and dynamic drawings in a variety of materials, including pastels, regular pencils, coloured pencils, watercolour pencils, inks and tinted charcoal. At the start of each project I demonstrate a few of the techniques that are used to complete the main drawing featured, or that will be useful to you when drawing a similar subject. You should give yourself plenty of time to practise these before attempting the real thing.

Once you have got your skills up to scratch and are feeling confident and raring to go, try doing the complete drawing as I have, step by step. I have described each stage for you. The close-up shots show you how each material is handled and applied.

In these projects we tackle a variety of subjects to whet your appetite for drawing. All of these are pretty straightforward to do and will give you the confidence and enthusiasm to go out and find your own subjects, using the techniques you have learned. To start with, we've shown you how to create a seascape with islands and a yacht; then we move on to capturing buildings and trees in a landscape. Next we tackle vibrant Venetian and Spanish scenes, before building up to the final project: drawing a self-portrait.

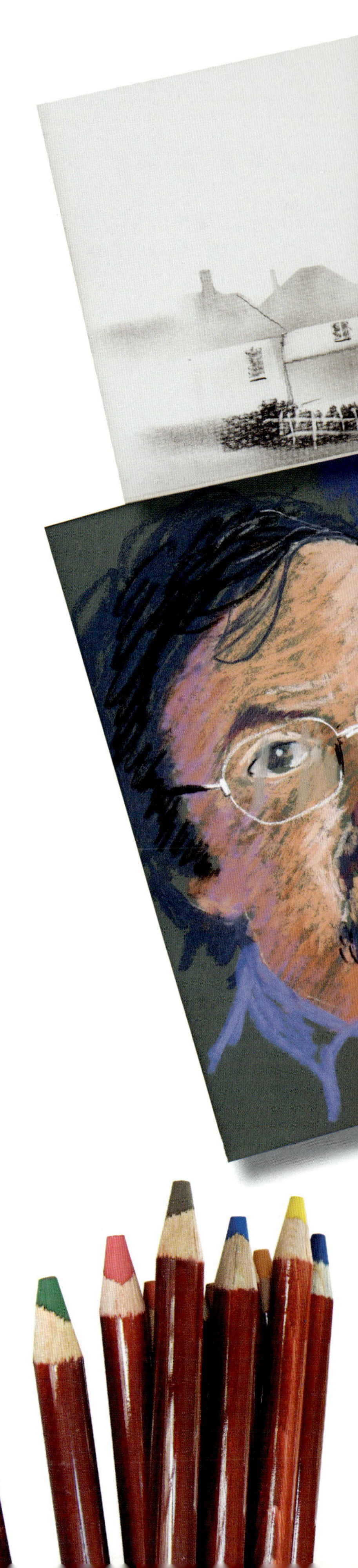

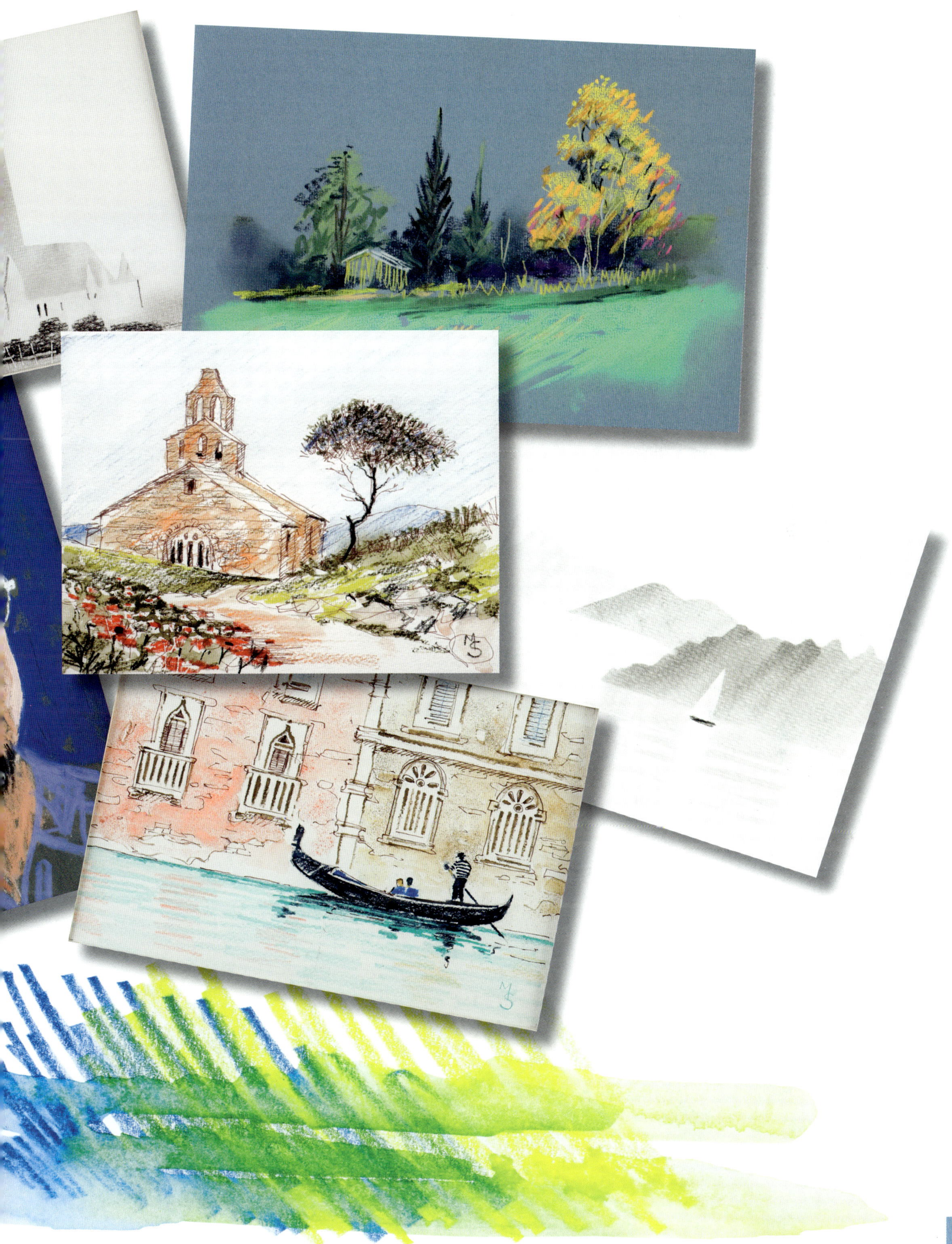

PROJECT 1

QUICK & CLEVER

LAND AND SEA

The aim of the first two projects is to get you to loosen up. Most people who haven't done much drawing get quite tense when confronted by a pencil and paper, but all I'm going to ask you to do is scribble, tear and smudge – all the things you were told off for doing when you were a child at school! At the start of each of the projects in this book I've included some practice techniques that will enable you to feel more confident when you start on the main drawing. They will be almost like 'playing', so you can relax and enjoy yourself. Please practise these exercises, but don't take the techniques too seriously; art is meant to be fun! If you make a mistake and things go wrong, just take a break and try again. Eventually you will be able to create your own versions of these drawings.

PROJECT 1

YOU WILL NEED:

- Reasonable quality sketchbook
- A couple of pastels in dark colours, or pastel pencils: blue, green, violet and grey would do
- Rectangular eraser
- 4B and 6B pencils
- Sharp scissors
- Card mount, such as that used for photographs, or 2 L-shaped pieces of coloured card

ISLANDS WITH A YACHT

(SEE PAGE 55)

This is a simple drawing just to get you started, but it looks very effective when mounted in a nice cardboard mount. To start with, don't make the image too big; something about the size shown here will do, or even a little smaller.

PENCILS:

4B

6B

PASTELS:

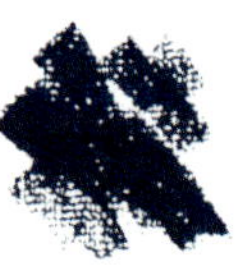

Indigo

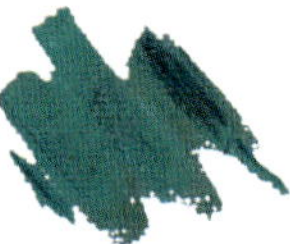

Sap Green

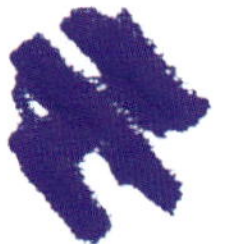

Violet

Grey

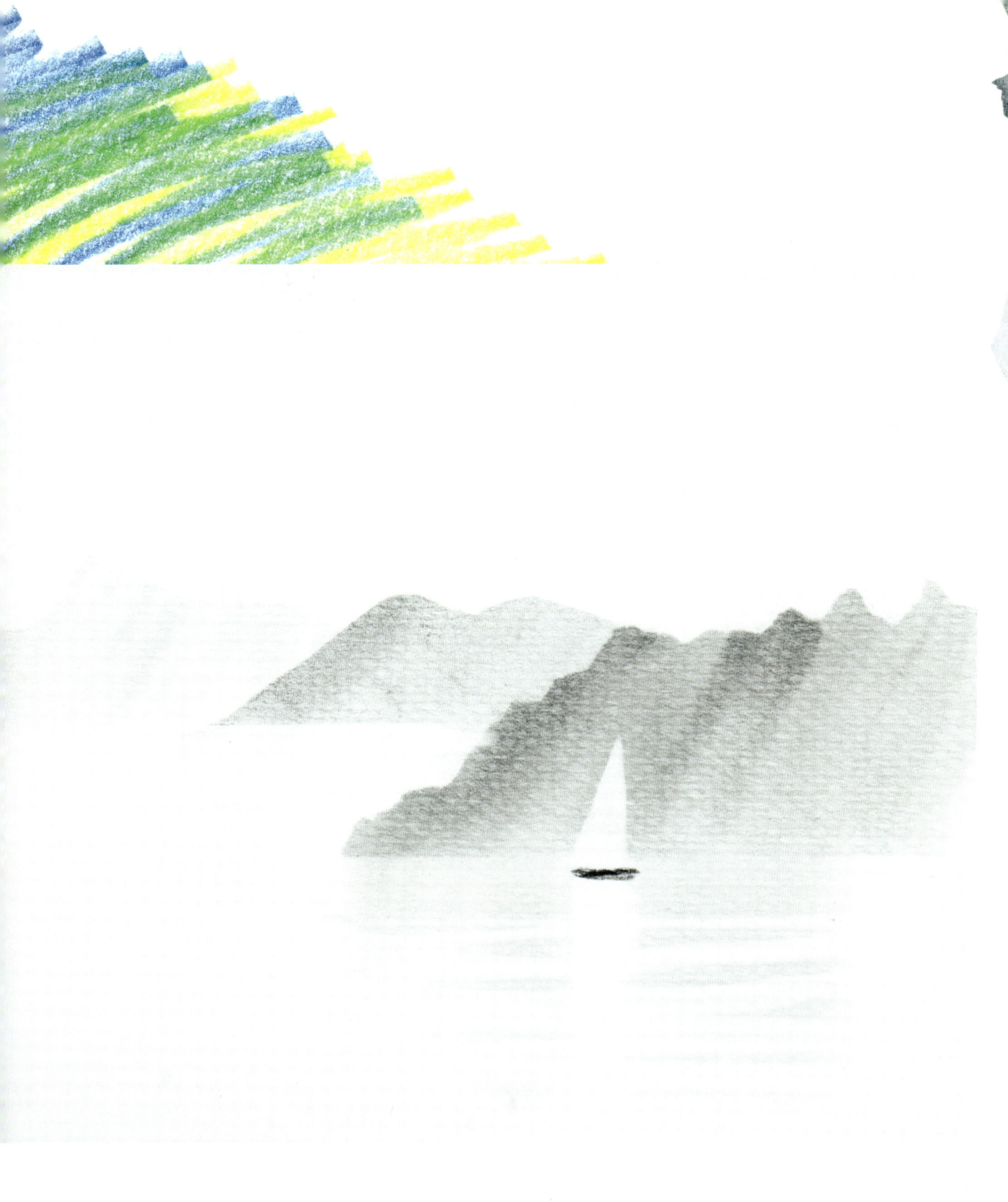

TECHNIQUE – SMUDGING EXERCISE

Drawing is not necessarily about making lines; some very effective techniques use little or no line-making at all. Often when I run a beginners' class, someone will say 'I can't draw'. When this happens, I get them to scribble on a piece of paper, then tear the paper, and then I simply talk them through this little smudging project. Afterwards, the most rewarding thing is the expression on their face when they realize that they have made a drawing, just with cutting, scribbling and smudging! Everyone needs to overcome the tiny voice that says 'I can't draw'. Before you start on the first project, try these easy techniques. You will be able to build them into a nice, achievable drawing on your first attempt. Honest!

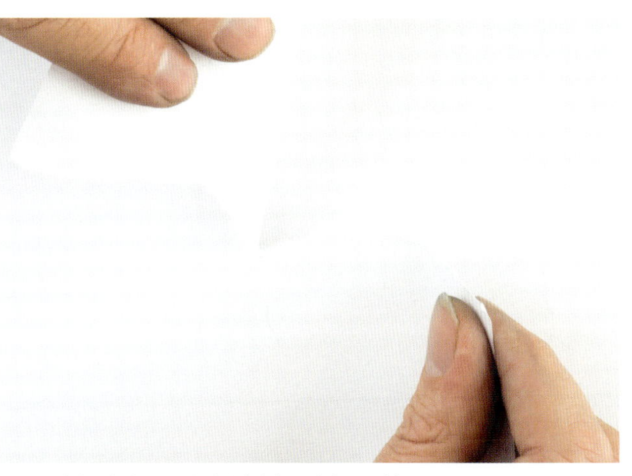

1 TEARING A PAPER STENCIL
This is easy! Imagine the shape of a range of hills. Then tear out their shapes. Work quite small; 15cm (6in) or so will be fine. Any bit of paper from your sketchbook will do, as long as it's not too thick. Don't worry about how they look – hills can be almost any shape. Now, discard your hill shapes and keep the other piece of paper.

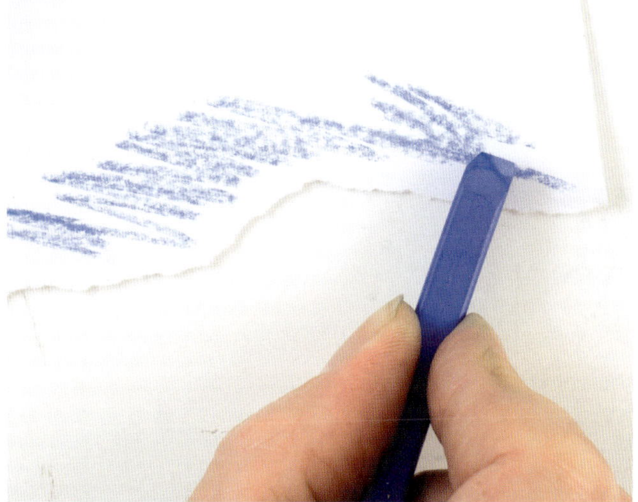

2 SCRIBBLING ON THE STENCIL
Take a stick of pastel or pastel pencil. Scribble on your piece of paper (remember, not the hills, the other piece). Blue or green colours would be good (I used Indigo hard pastel). Make sure that you scribble close to the torn edge and put plenty of colour on.

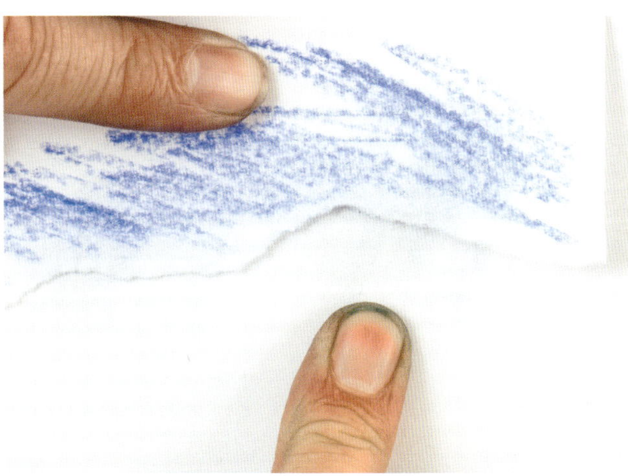

3 SMUDGING TO MAKE CLEAR SHAPES
Take a clean page of your sketchbook, and put your scribbled-on piece somewhere just above the centre, on the left. Holding firmly, smudge downwards with your finger, using a steady movement and light pressure, until some of the pigment has rubbed off onto the page all the way along.

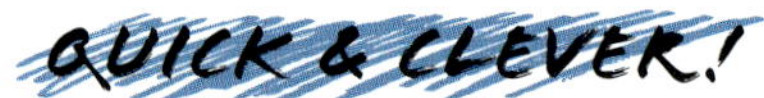

If you have long fingernails, rubbing pigment may not be easy because you will scratch the paper. Try using a piece of scrunched-up kitchen paper instead.

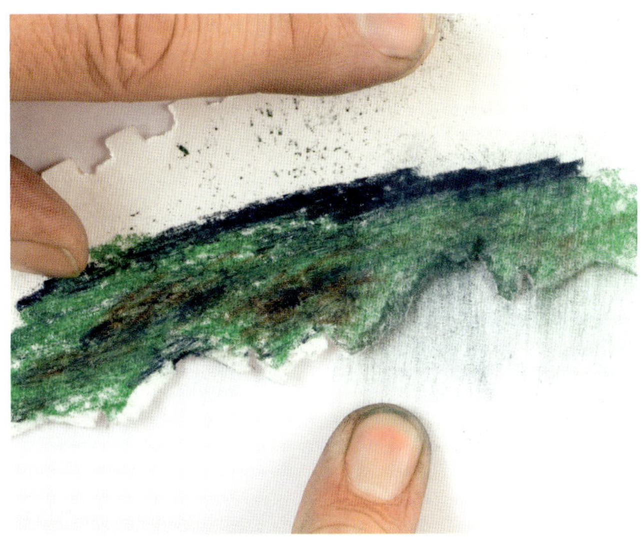

4 ADDING TONAL CHANGES

Tear another range of hills; you should be getting good by now! Scribble more colour on with a darker pastel, such as Sap Green. This is effective, as nearer hills look darker than distant ones. Put these on the right, and drag the colour down with firmer pressure than previously.

5 QUICK AND CLEVER RANGE OF HILLS

When you remove the paper, your image should look a bit like this. If it is too indistinct, you haven't put enough pigment on, or maybe didn't use enough pressure when rubbing. If so, simply try again. For best results, the smudged pigment should come down quite a way, as shown.

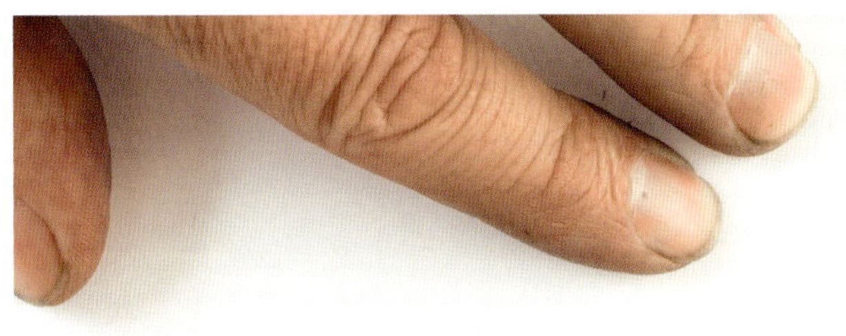

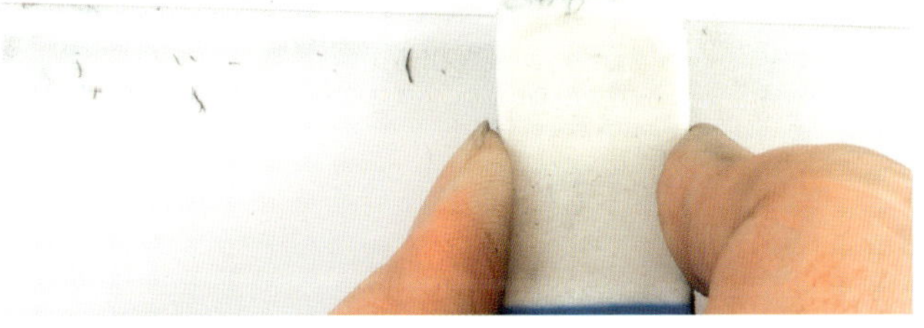

6 DRAWING WITH THE ERASER

Now we're going to turn the hills into islands. Take a piece of paper with a straight edge, and place it so it almost covers the distant range of hills, with the straight edge horizontal and bits of colour showing at the bottom. Then use the edge as a stencil, and rub carefully along the edge with the eraser to remove all of the colour showing. Repeat this, slightly lower, for the nearer island.

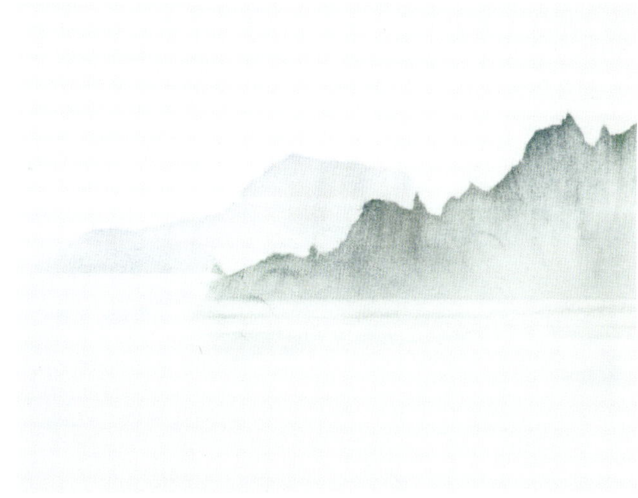

7 A SIMPLE ISLAND IMAGE

If you have rubbed out along the straight edges carefully, and removed the pigment, your image should look a bit like this. If your line is wobbly, maybe you moved the paper stencil as you used the eraser. Or perhaps the eraser went up under the stencil. If yours looks something like this, well done!

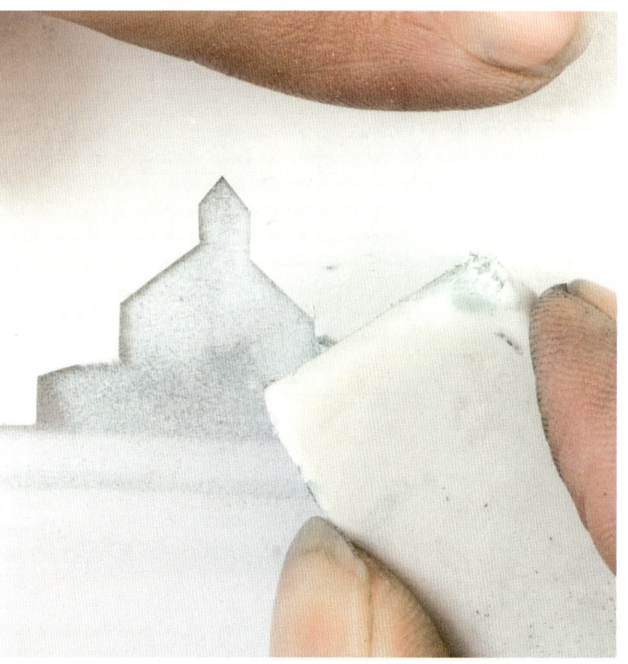

8 ERASING THROUGH A CUT STENCIL

With sharp scissors, cut a simple little building shape out of a piece of paper, like this. Then, holding this stencil firmly in place over the toned area, use an eraser to carefully remove pigment, rubbing from the edges in. If the eraser becomes coloured with pigment, rub it on a piece of scrap paper to remove the colour.

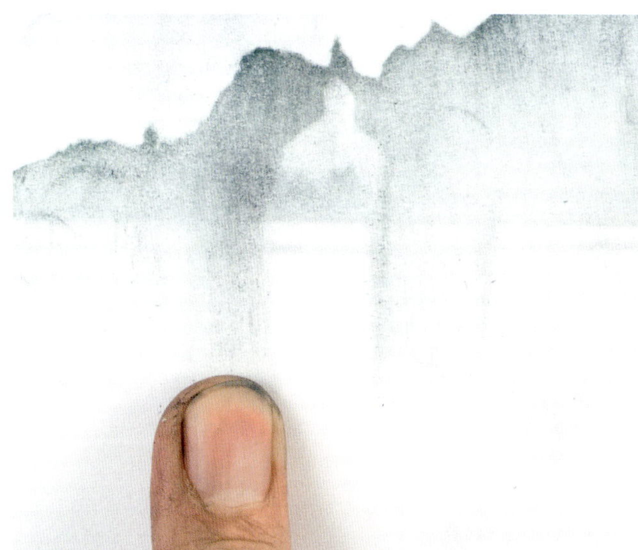

9 SMUDGING TO MAKE REFLECTIONS

Remove the template and use your (clean!) finger to make some vertical smudges. These should be made carefully, avoiding the area underneath the building. This will have the effect of a reflection, and begin to create the look of water.

10 ERASING RIPPLES

Use the edge of the eraser to make thin horizontal lines in the water. These add movement and create a watery look. Don't add too many, or the effect will be lost.

QUICK & CLEVER!

Coloured pencils are often waxy, so don't smudge very well. To get the best results from the technique, use pastels, pastel pencils or soft graphite pencils (4B or 5B).

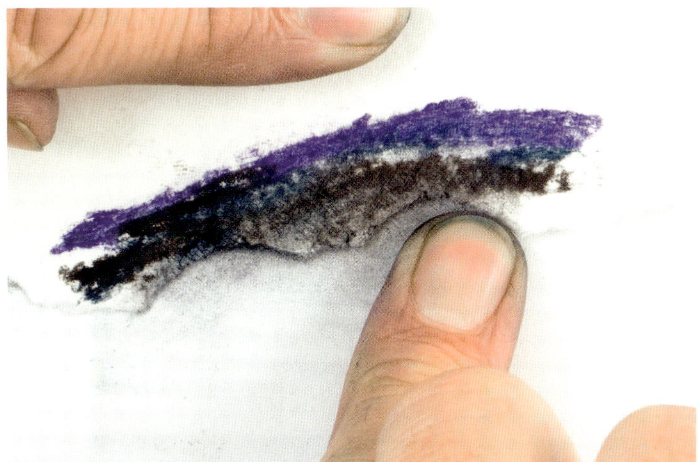

11 INCREASING THE TONAL RANGE

Add depth to your image by using a darker colour to create an island. Dark grey or violet would be good; to achieve this colour, scribble plenty of pigment on to a piece of torn paper and place it so that it overlaps the hills on the far right. Rub the pigment down vigorously, and use the eraser to lift the horizontal edge to create the water effect.

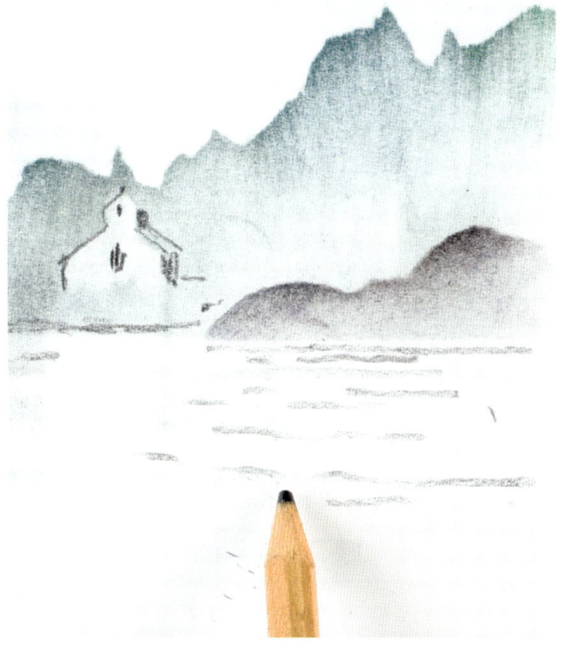

QUICK & CLEVER!

When practising drawing techniques such as smudging, don't work too big. A large expanse of paper can be quite intimidating and time-consuming to work on. Draw to a size that you are comfortable with.

12 DRAWING A FEW LINES

Add some short lines around the edge of the chapel or your chosen shape with a graphite or pastel pencil. Then add a few horizontal ripples on the water. Lines like this will sharpen the image and create a 'drawn' effect.

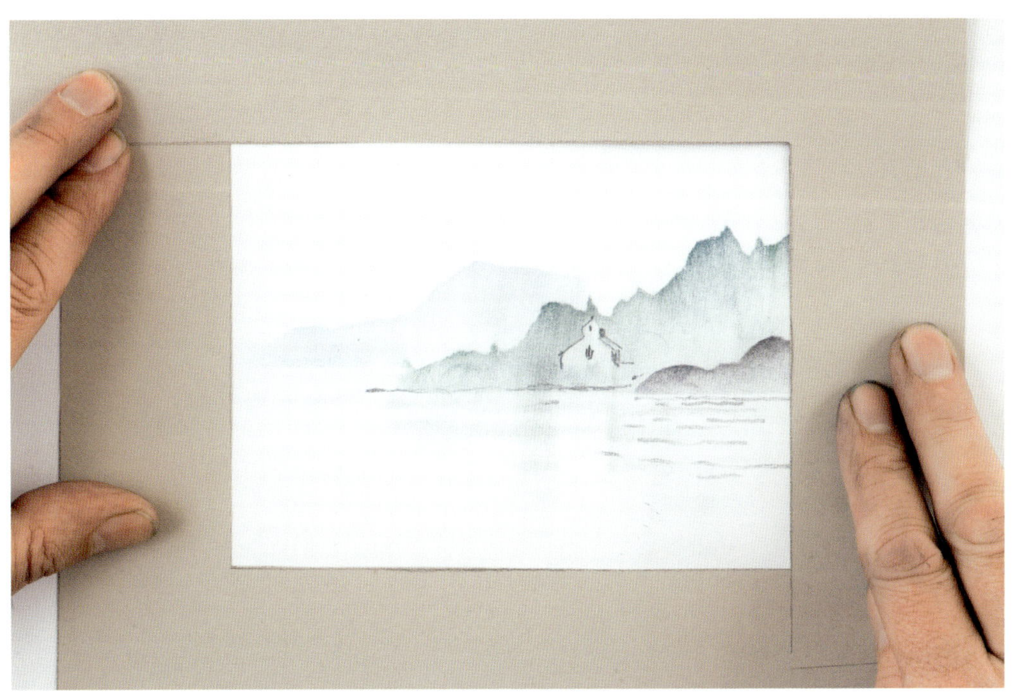

13 ADDING A MOUNT

Use a couple of L-shaped pieces of coloured paper or card to make a simple frame or cropping mask. By moving this around you will be able to crop parts and alter the image. In this instance, the chapel is the focal point and shouldn't be in the exact centre. Using the mask to crop the right-hand side moves the focal point away from the middle.

QUICK & CLEVER DRAWING

ISLANDS WITH A YACHT

This little drawing uses the smudging property of soft graphite pencils and introduces tonal values. Tones – the relative darkness or lightness of objects in an image – impart a logic to a picture. In general, objects further away are paler, while nearer objects are darker. These smudges are simple techniques, but most of us were told off at school for smudging and being messy, so we think they're bad things to do. Well, now I'm giving you permission to be untidy. Smudge away as much as you like – go on, be a rebel! Just keep an eye on the tones.

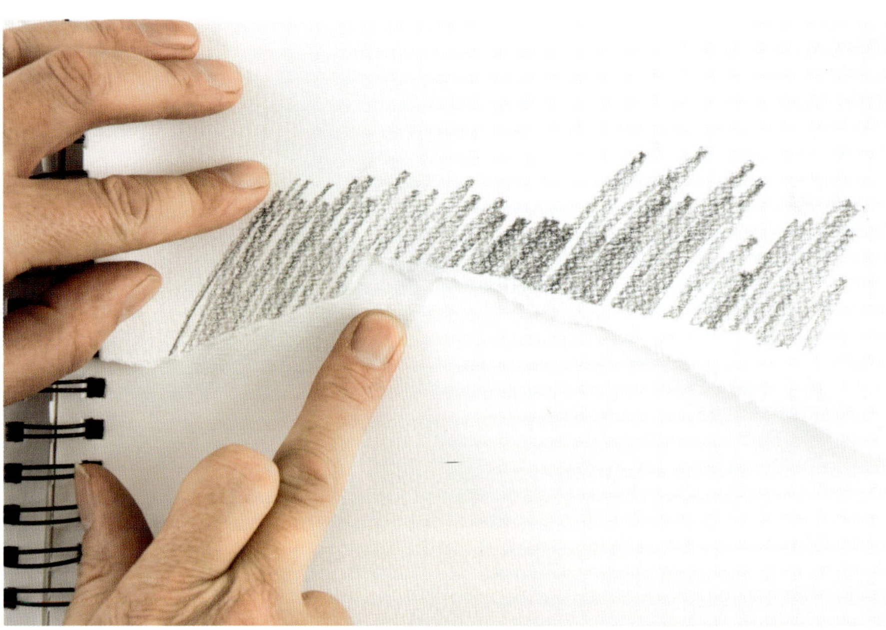

1 TEARING A MASK FROM SCRIBBLED PAPER

Use a 4B pencil to scribble on a scrap piece of thin paper. Cover an area roughly 10 x 15cm (4 x 6in). Make sure that the scribbles are fairly close together, and that you apply moderate pressure. Now tear the paper through the scribble, to create the shapes of hills. Place this torn paper left of centre on your sketchpad, and rub the graphite down onto the page, using light finger pressure.

2 CUTTING SHAPES FOR MOUNTAIN TOPS

Scribble on the scrap paper again, with a 4B pencil, making a darker and denser application. Near objects look sharper as well as darker; to make a sharper edge, use a pair of scissors to cut out another mountain shape. This will look nearer than the other one.

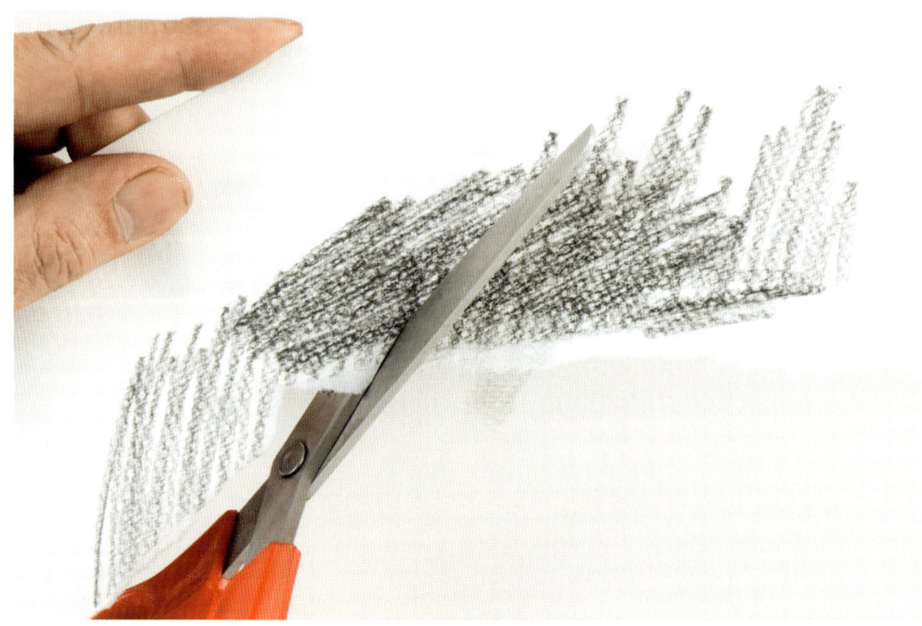

3 CREATING PALE AND MID-TONE SHAPES

Rub this down as in step 1, on the right of the first shape but overlapping it slightly, near the middle of the page. Use moderate finger pressure. You should have a pale shape, and now a mid-tone shape, which will look nearer.

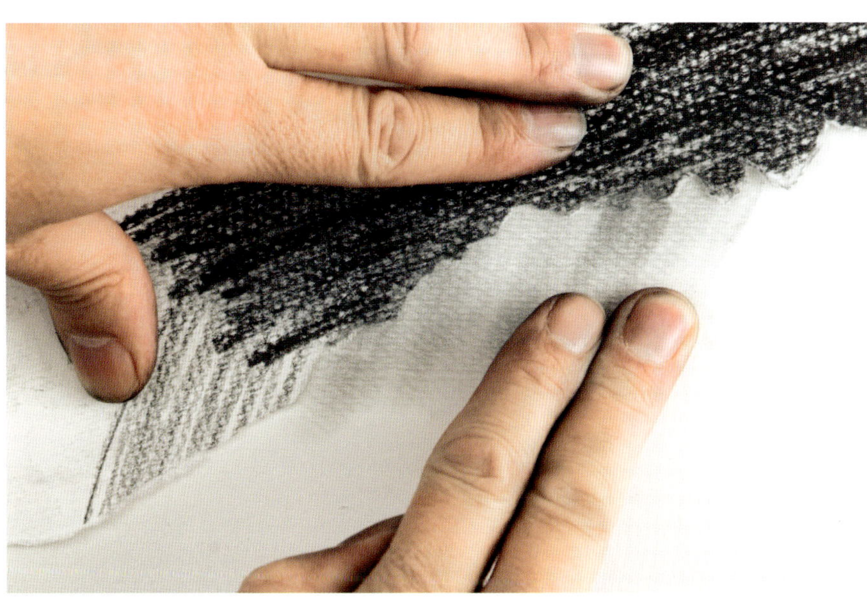

4 ADDING HEAVIER SHADING

Scribble on the scrap paper once again, with a 6B pencil for a darker application. Press firmly and make sure that the area is covered. Cut out a more jagged hill shape. Place this on the right-hand side of the page, overlapping slightly, and rub down it with strong finger pressure to create the nearest and darkest shape.

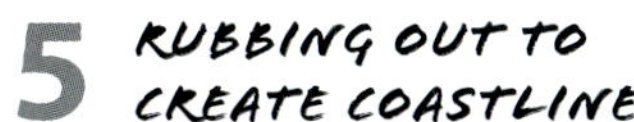

5 RUBBING OUT TO CREATE COASTLINE

Use a straight edge of a piece of scrap paper, held horizontally, and an eraser to create a shoreline, starting with the distant, palest shape (see p. 54). Rub carefully along the edge, not across it. Move the paper down, erasing each time, to achieve the same effect on the nearer shapes.

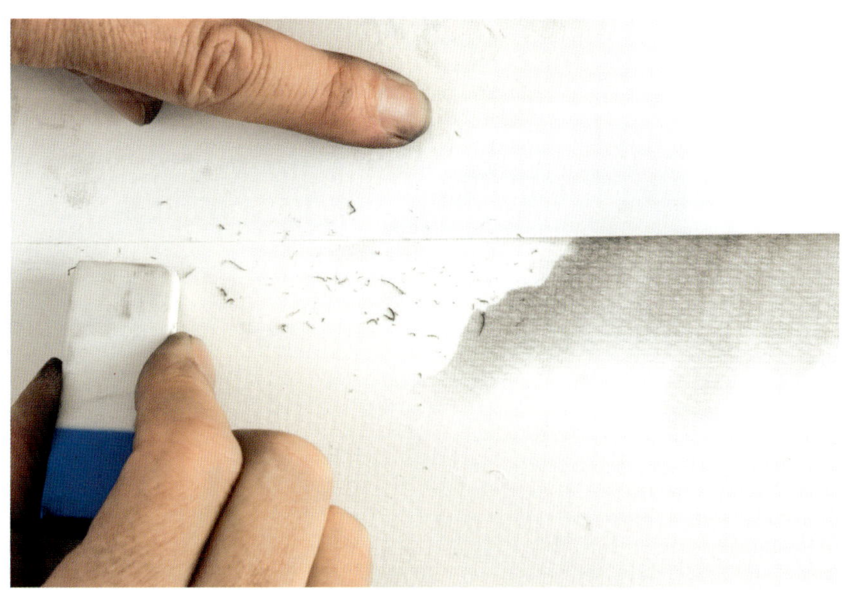

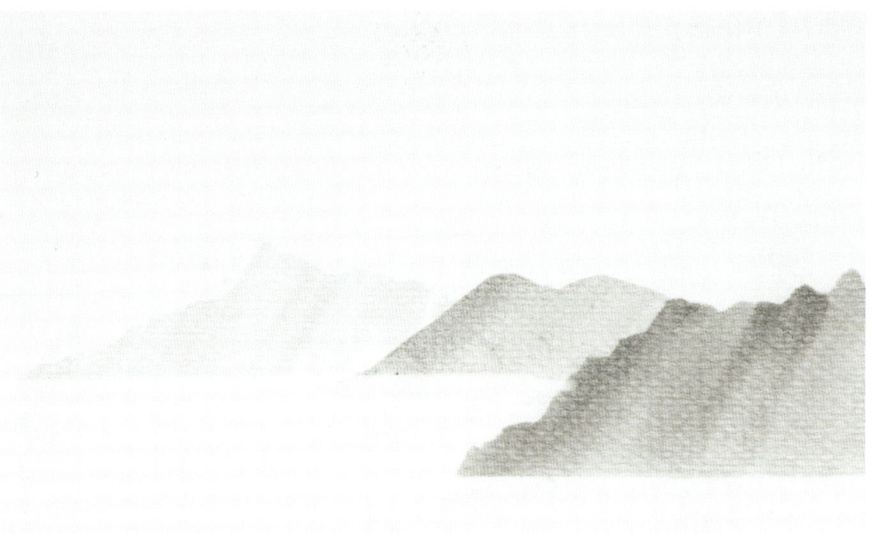

6 CREATING A RECEDING SHORELINE

The tonal values should give the appearance of a receding shoreline, with the palest and most indistinct tone away in the distance. This is one of the easiest ways to produce a receding effect. Now we'll add a simple detail.

7 CUTTING OUT THE YACHT STENCIL

Use scissors to cut a basic stencil of a tapering triangle out of the scrap paper. Don't make it too big. This will form the little sail of the yacht.

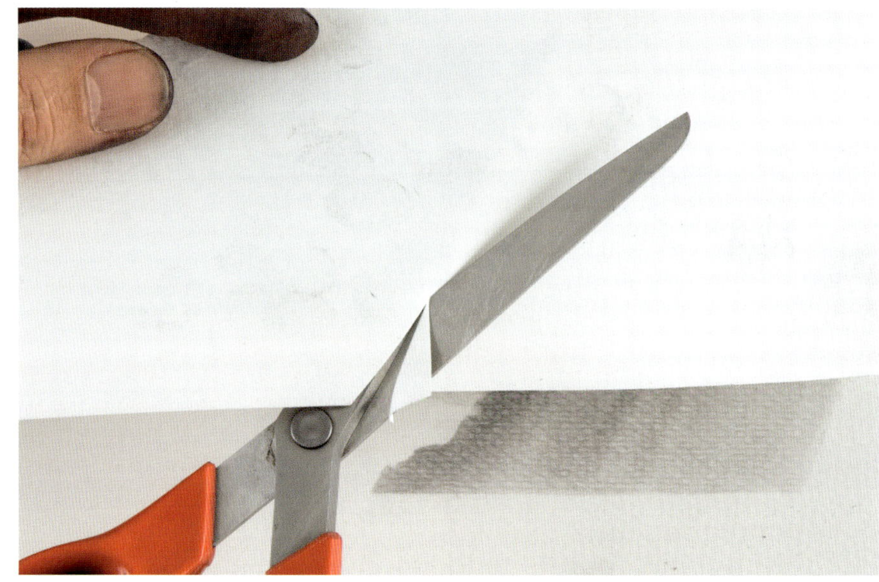

8 RUBBING OUT SAIL SHAPE

Decide where you want the sail to be. This will become the focal point for the image, so it's best if it doesn't go in the centre. For maximum contrast, it should be on the darkest area. Take an eraser and rub down the triangle shape, making sure the eraser is clean.

9 SMUDGING FOR REFLECTION

Use your pencil to draw in the hull of the boat (a simple horizontal line will work). Then smudge some vertical lines down from the darkest area to make reflections. Don't put too many in, or you'll spoil the effect. By avoiding smudging below the sail shape, you will create the look of a reflection of the white sail.

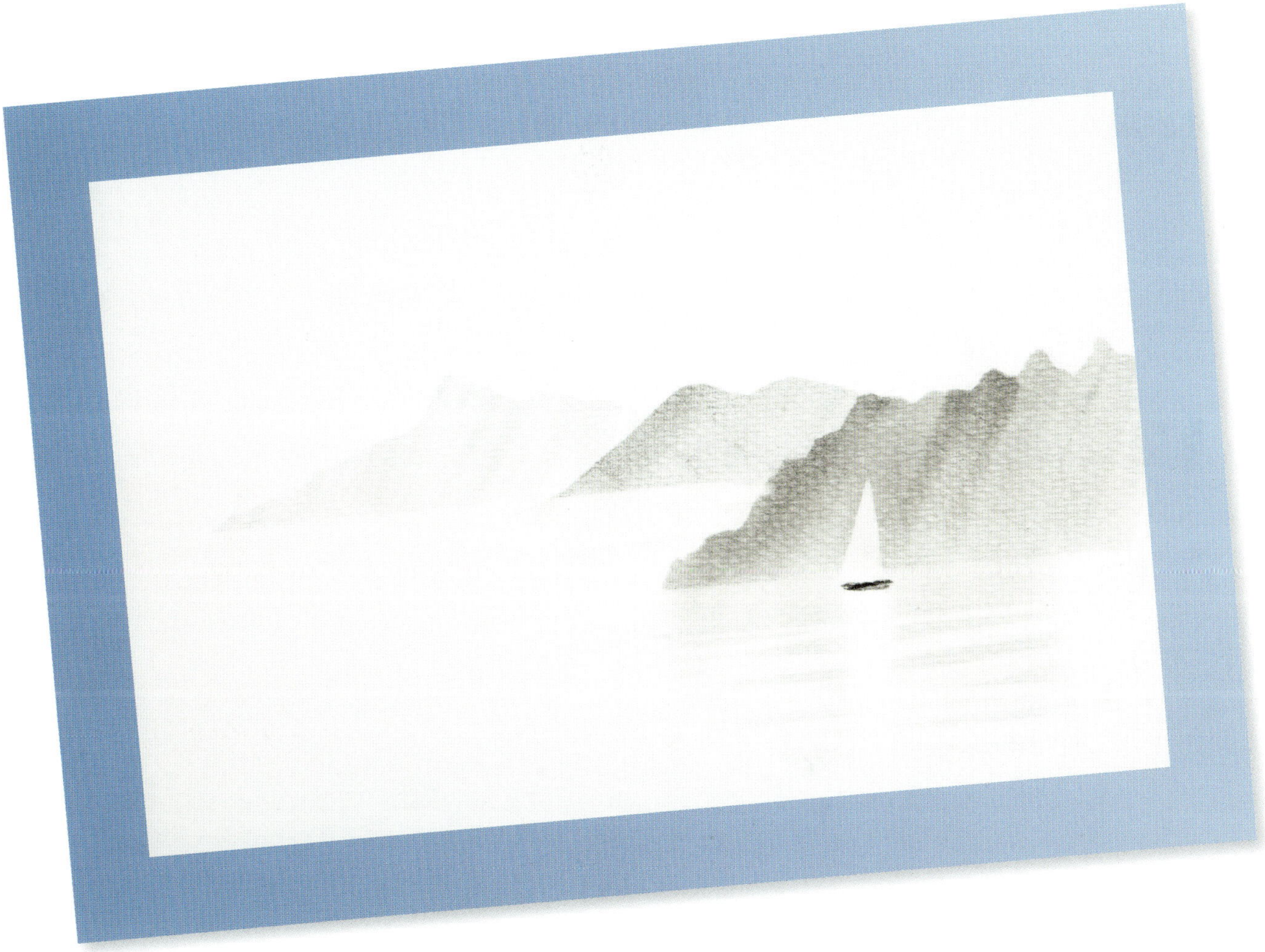

10 ERASING TO CREATE RIPPLES

With the edge of the eraser, rub out some ripples through the smudged reflections, making sure to keep them absolutely horizontal. Now sit back and have a break; you've earned it! What you have achieved with this little exercise is actually quite complex: the creation of tones to imply distance, the positioning of a focal point, and adding marks to imply movement of the water. And you told me you couldn't draw!

PROJECT 2

QUICK & CLEVER

BUILDINGS MADE EASY

Buildings can be intimidating for the beginner; all those lines and angles! What I'd like you to do is forget that you are going to make buildings, and just think of them as shapes. This simple exercise will give you the confidence to try to create your own images of houses, barns, churches and more. First, before starting the project, let's look at some techniques that you will find useful, including planning where the subject will go, simple ways of enlarging an image, and easy methods to make symmetrical shapes. Have a go at these, and then try the project.

PROJECT 2

YOU WILL NEED:

- A sketchpad
- 2B, 4B and 6B pencils
- A pencil sharpener
- An eraser
- Cocktail sticks or matchsticks
- A pair of scissors

PENCILS:

2B

4B

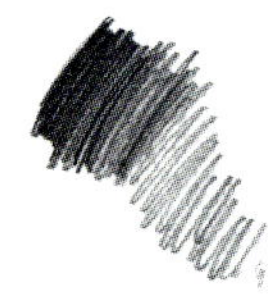

6B

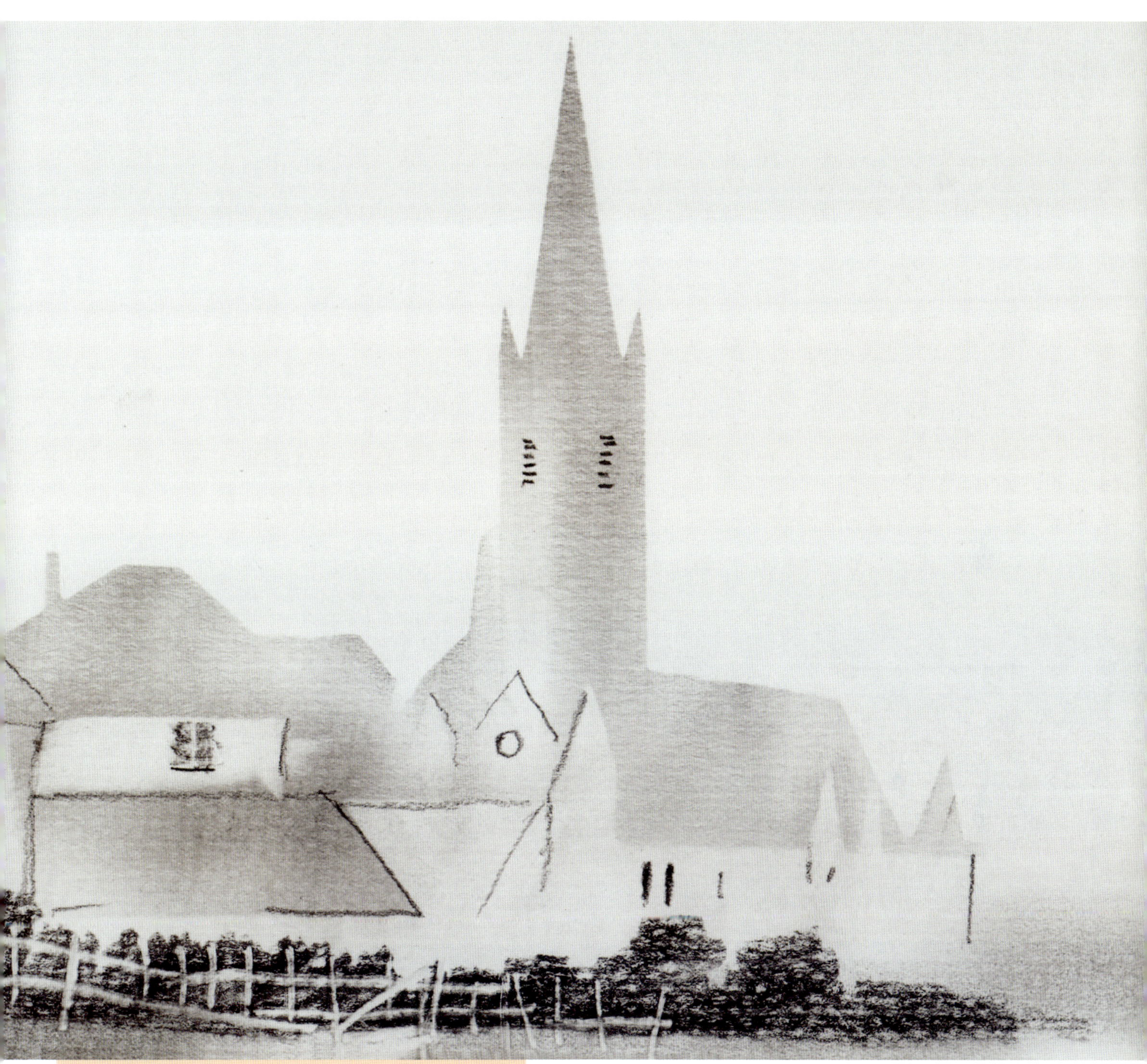

CHURCH SPIRE

(SEE PAGE 65)

Beginners are often put off drawing buildings because they seem complicated, but this little image is easy! If you are handy with a pair of scissors and can smudge, you'll enjoy doing this. Working with the simple techniques that follow will make everything straightforward, so take some time to practise them.

TECHNIQUE – PLANNING

Before starting to draw a 'proper' drawing, it's a good idea to do some planning so you know where features are going to be placed. One of the most common errors is to put the subject (the most important thing) in the middle. There is a good reason for not doing this; it's boring! You don't want to make boring pictures, do you? I thought not. So, what you need to do is make little drawings like these, no bigger than a matchbox, just to see how things will look.

Composition is made easy with thumbnail sketches. Making small drawings like these thumbnail sketches is quick, and gives you good practice. They don't need to be detailed or accurate. And you don't have to show them to anyone!

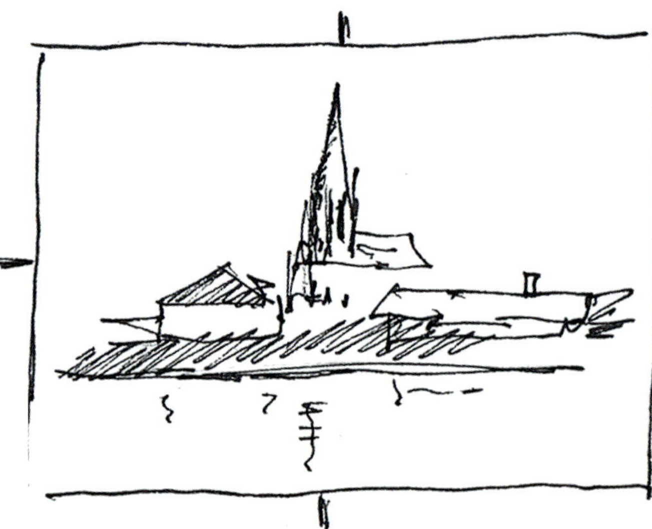

1 WHAT NOT TO DO This composition would result in an uninteresting drawing. The spire is the important part of the image – the 'focal point' – so it should be slightly to one side. Having the focal point in the centre looks boring.

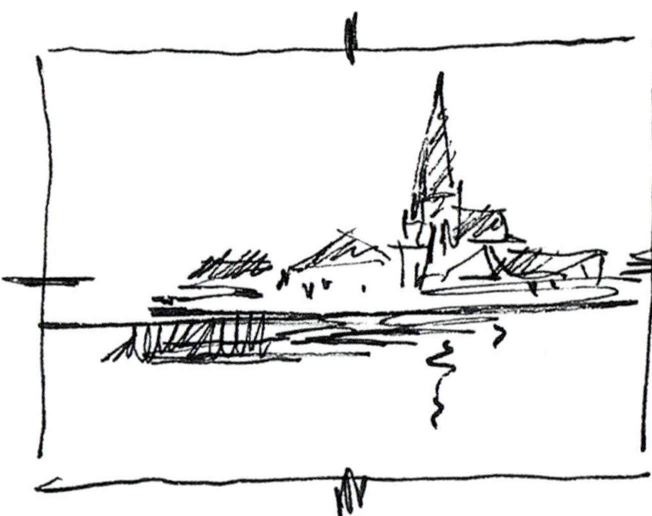

2 USE THE RULE OF THIRDS This is a better composition because the spire is not central. As a general rule, if the main subject (the focal point) is about a third of the way in from the side, it looks better. This image can still be improved on though, because the edge of the water cuts right across the centre.

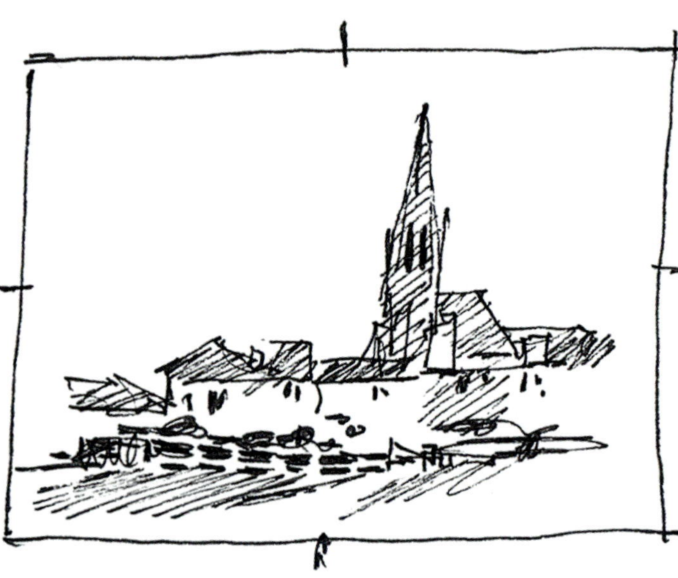

3 CROPPING THE IMAGE This one is better. I've changed the content of the drawing to concentrate on the buildings rather than the water. Also in this sketch I've invented a fence, and the hint of a pathway, to lead the eye into the image.

TECHNIQUE – ENLARGING

Every artist will need to enlarge their work at some time or other. With computers and photocopying available, it's possible to use these to do the enlarging for us, but there are limitations. Photocopies can't be made onto heavy-weight paper or textured surfaces, for instance. So it's a good thing to be able to enlarge by pencil and eye!

My favourite method is to divide the small image into four equal sections. Then divide the larger paper into four also. All you need to do then is look at each section in turn, and transfer the lines in their correct position. If one part of the image contains a lot of detail, simply divide that area again, into four more sections.

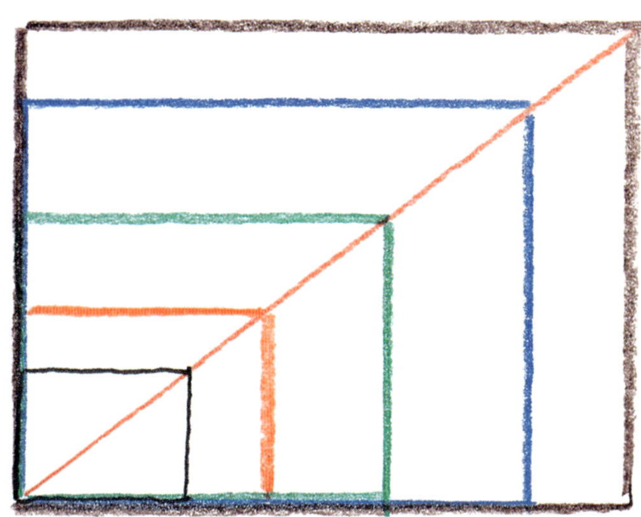

PROPORTION

To keep the same proportion of image shape, place your small image into the bottom left-hand corner of the larger piece of paper. Then very lightly use a ruler to draw a line across from one corner of the small image to the other, and extend this line out into the larger paper. Now, any horizontal and vertical lines that meet on this diagonal will enclose the same proportion as the small image.

1 DRAW THE GRID ON THE SMALL IMAGE

Use a ruler to measure the height and width of the image, and divide each side in half, putting marks on the half-way point. Draw lines between the points to divide the image into four quarters.

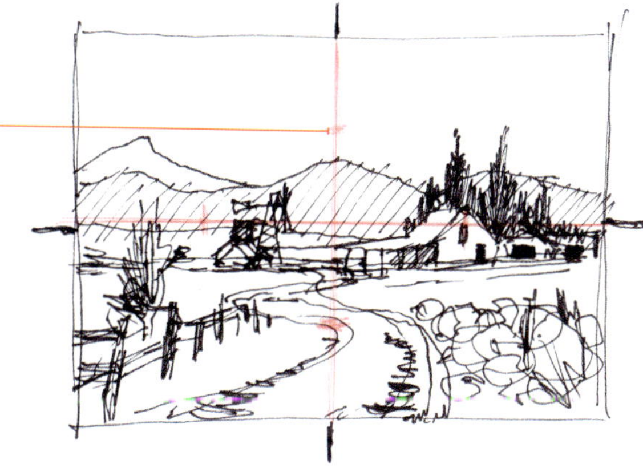

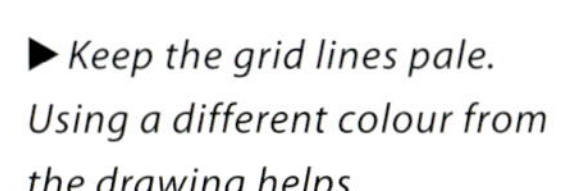

▶ *Keep the grid lines pale. Using a different colour from the drawing helps.*

2 CONCENTRATE ON ONE AREA AT A TIME

Decide on how much bigger you want the larger drawing to be. If the dimensions of your small image are 2 x 3in, your larger one could be 4 x 6in, or 6 x 9in. As long as you keep the proportion between the sides constant, it can be any size you want. Draw the lines lightly with a soft pencil, so they can be removed later. Look for the important parts of the image first, and make guide marks where they should be. Use a light pressure, and work on each section in turn, putting guidelines in to indicate where all the important parts of that section occur. Finally, start drawing lines to link the sections together.

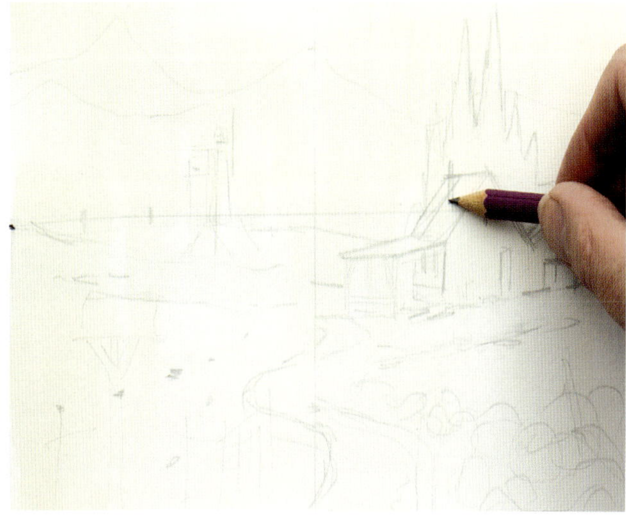

▶ *When transferring lines, work with a light pressure to start with so it's easier to make corrections.*

TECHNIQUE – EASY SYMMETRY

Symmetrical objects can be difficult to draw; it's very difficult to get both sides looking the same. Objects that can cause problems are bottles, glasses and goblets, flowerpots, church spires – in fact, anything that's the same shape on both sides can be difficult. Well, I don't like to do things the hard way, so here's the easy way to do it!

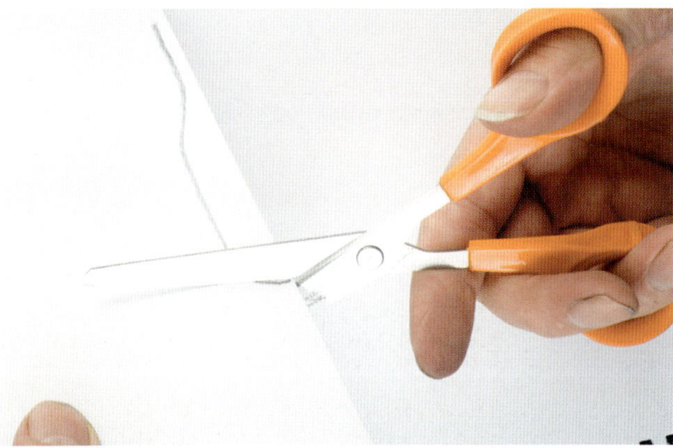

1 DRAWING SYMMETRICAL OBJECTS THE EASY WAY
You only draw one side! Take a single piece of thin paper. Fold it in half. Draw one side of the object. Make sure that the side you draw looks OK. Then take a pair of scissors and, holding the fold together, cut through both sides of the paper.

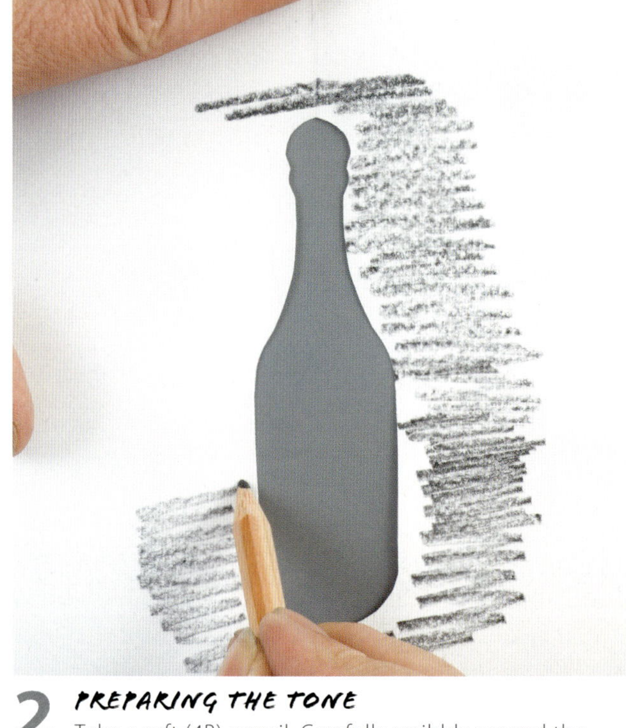

2 PREPARING THE TONE
Take a soft (4B) pencil. Carefully scribble around the edge of your shape. Make sure to press quite hard so you get plenty of graphite on the paper.

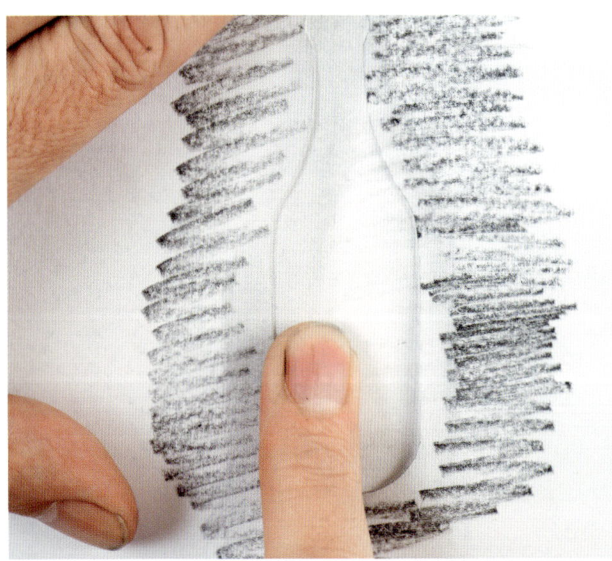

3 CREATING THE SYMMETRICAL IMAGE
Place your cut-out image over the paper you want to transfer it to. Holding it down firmly, wipe your fingers across from the outside in, all the way round. You can use a torchon for this if you wish.

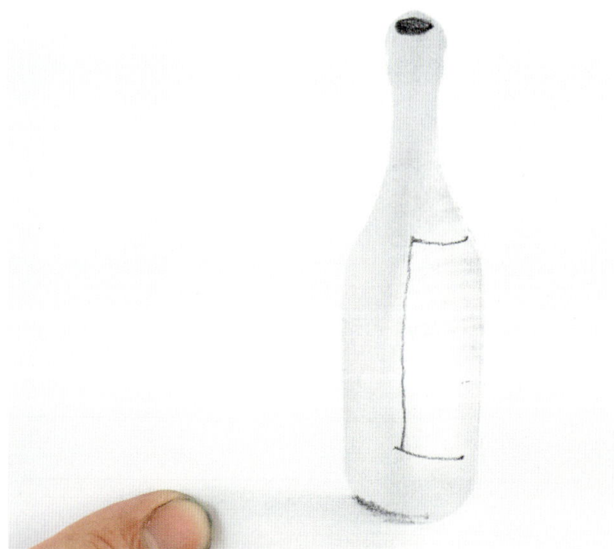

4 ADDING DETAIL AND FORM
To make something look solid, often all you have to do is imply that it's casting a shadow. Use a finger and drag some of the graphite across the paper from one side of the object. This makes a quick shadow.

TECHNIQUE – INDENTING

Sometimes, all a drawing needs is to suggest or imply a feature. Indenting works well with subjects that contain lots of detail and could be complicated if you tried to draw every element. Foliage, grasses and leaves could all be suggested, by indenting first and then working pencil on top. The end result looks more effective than a tight, complicated drawing, and is more fun to do!

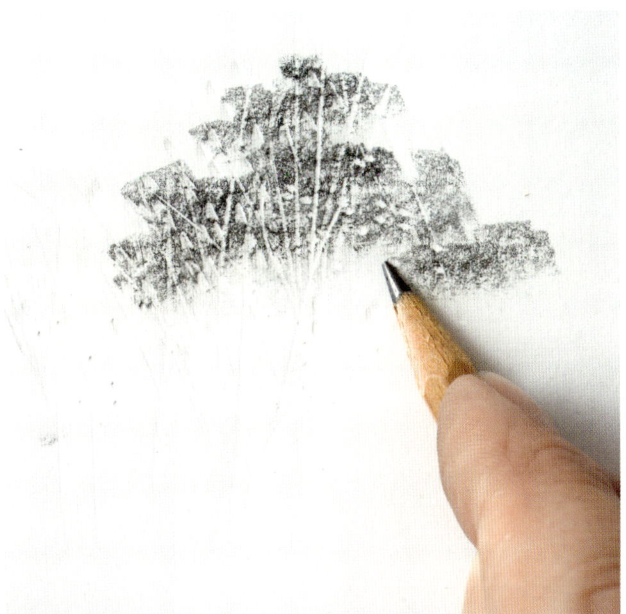

1 SCRIBBLING OVER INDENTS
Interesting textural marks can be produced by indenting with a cocktail stick and then working over gently with a soft pencil. This is ideal for grasses or branches.

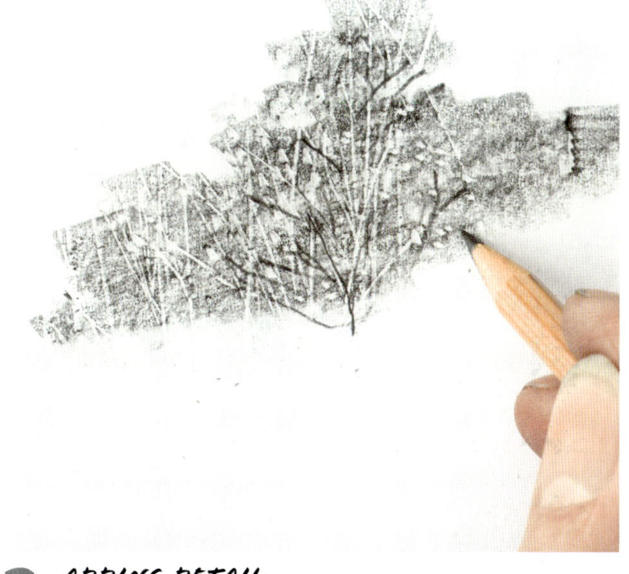

2 ADDING DETAIL
The pencil can be used to develop these shapes, without putting in too much detail. Following the shapes of the indented lines will add realism, as this will then look like light and shade on twigs and branches.

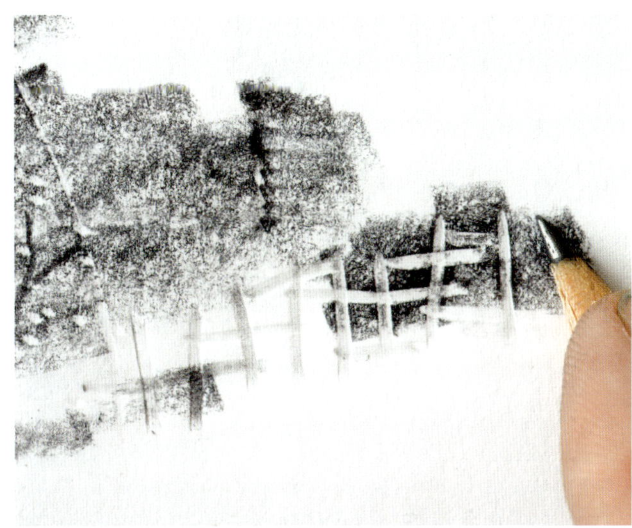

3 REVEALING THE FENCE POST
If you use a thicker implement to indent with, such as a knitting needle, elements that are useful in the foreground, such as fence posts or gates, can be added. These can then be carefully worked over with a soft pencil.

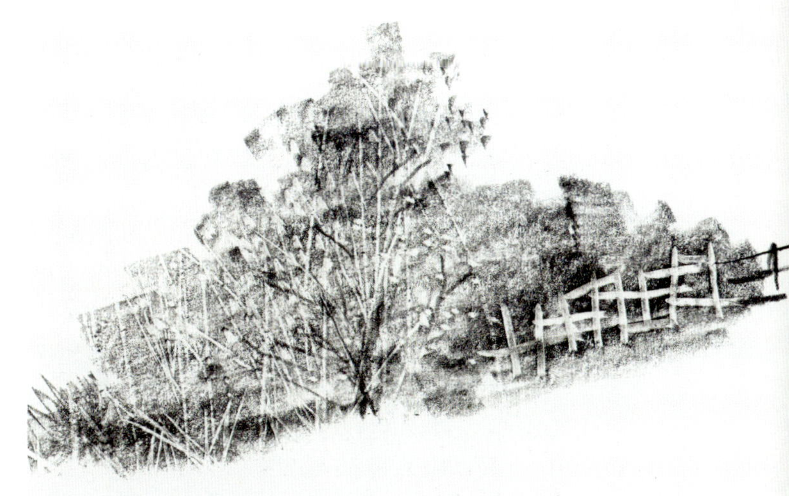

4 FINAL IMAGE
This would serve as a foreground for a landscape. There isn't much detail, but the textures imply grass, twigs and branches, and the fenceposts serve to lead the eye up into the drawing.

PROJECT 2

QUICK & CLEVER DRAWING

CHURCH SPIRE

I hope that you've now had a bit of practice at cutting out symmetrical shapes and indenting and are feeling ready to tackle the main project. This kind of image appears quite complex to draw, yet can easily be simplified. When working from a photograph like this, the tendency is to try to copy every element. It is better to make changes and simplifications so that the image appears pleasing and uncomplicated. That's what we're going to do.

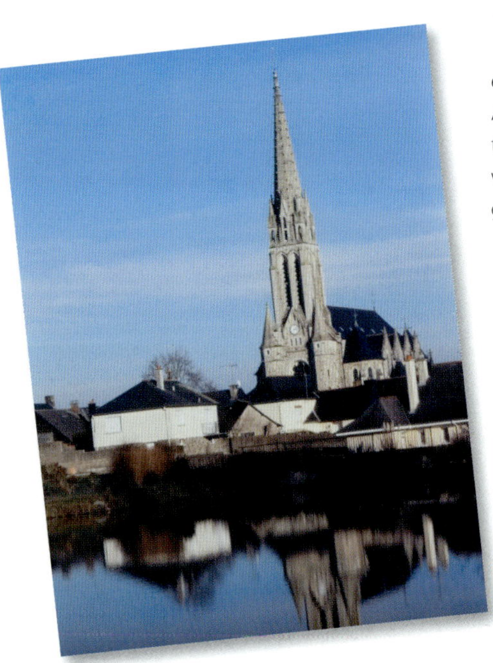

1 REFERENCE SHOT

The spire is the focal point, so remember to place it to one side, not exactly in the centre. You could try a small thumbnail sketch to see how it looks. Although the water is nice to look at, I've decided to ignore it and concentrate on the buildings. After you've practised doing this sketch you may like to do another with the water included. You've done reflections in project 1, so I bet you'll do a good job!

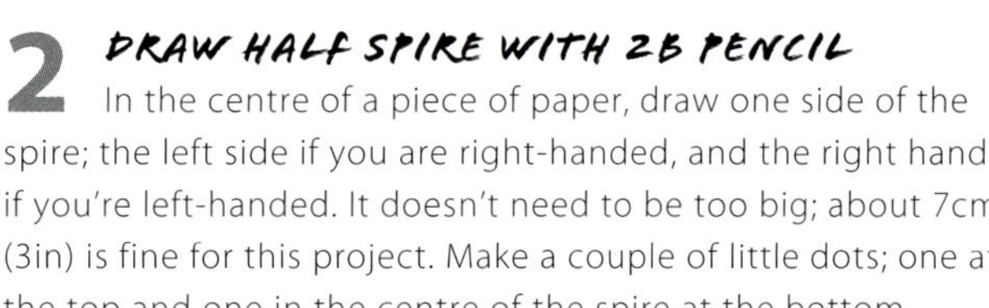

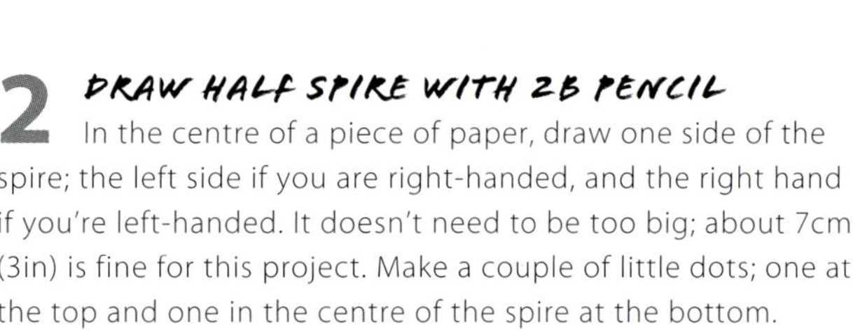

2 DRAW HALF SPIRE WITH 2B PENCIL

In the centre of a piece of paper, draw one side of the spire; the left side if you are right-handed, and the right hand if you're left-handed. It doesn't need to be too big; about 7cm (3in) is fine for this project. Make a couple of little dots; one at the top and one in the centre of the spire at the bottom.

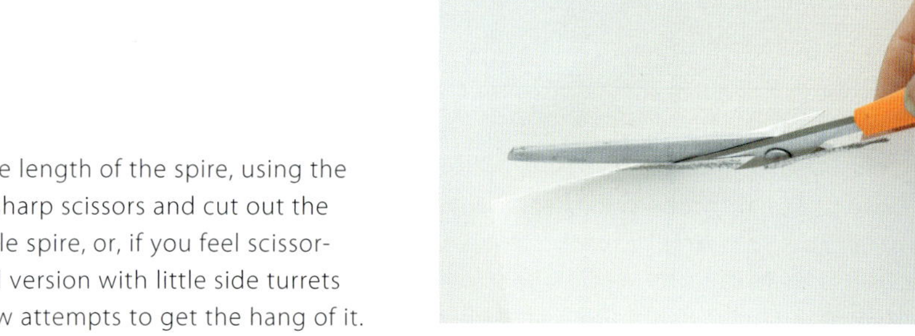

3 CUT SPIRE SHAPE

Fold the paper along the length of the spire, using the dots as guides. Take a pair of sharp scissors and cut out the shape. You can choose a simple spire, or, if you feel scissor-happy, go for the complicated version with little side turrets like I have. You may need a few attempts to get the hang of it.

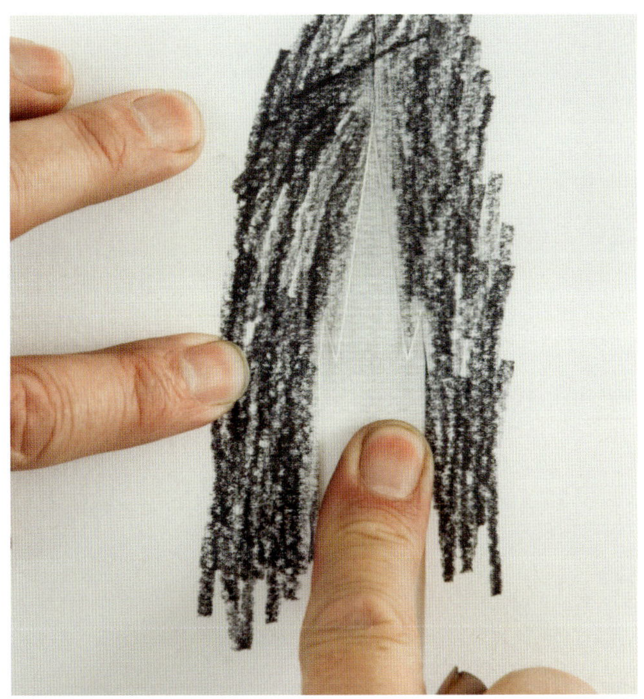

4 DRAG IN GRAPHITE TO CREATE SPIRE
Use a 4B pencil to scribble around the shape using firm pressure. Place the stencil on the sketching paper; be careful to avoid putting it dead centre! Also, make sure it doesn't slope. Then, while holding the stencil firmly, carefully pull the graphite from the scribble into the spire shape, working from the outside in.

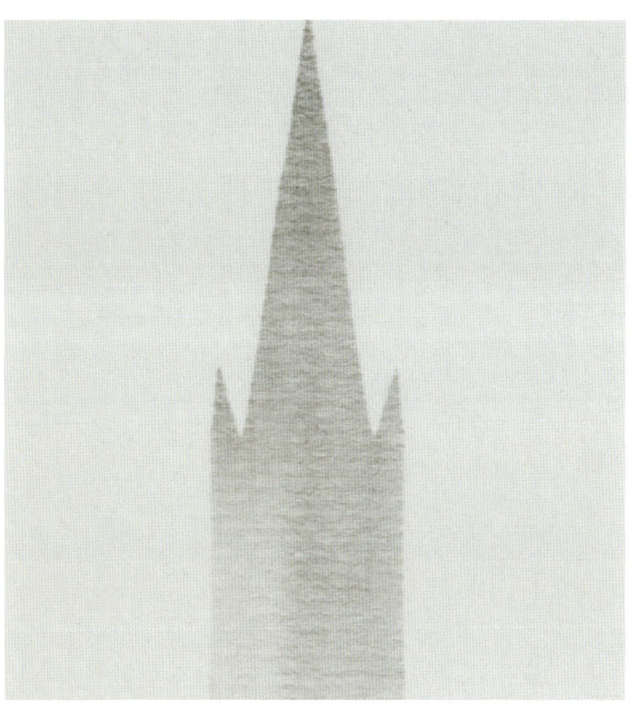

5 ASSESS SPIRE
When you've rubbed through the stencil it should look something like this. If it doesn't, don't worry; it could be too wide or too narrow, or perhaps it tapers. Whatever is wrong will be easy to fix. Simply fold another piece of paper and try again with a slightly different shape.

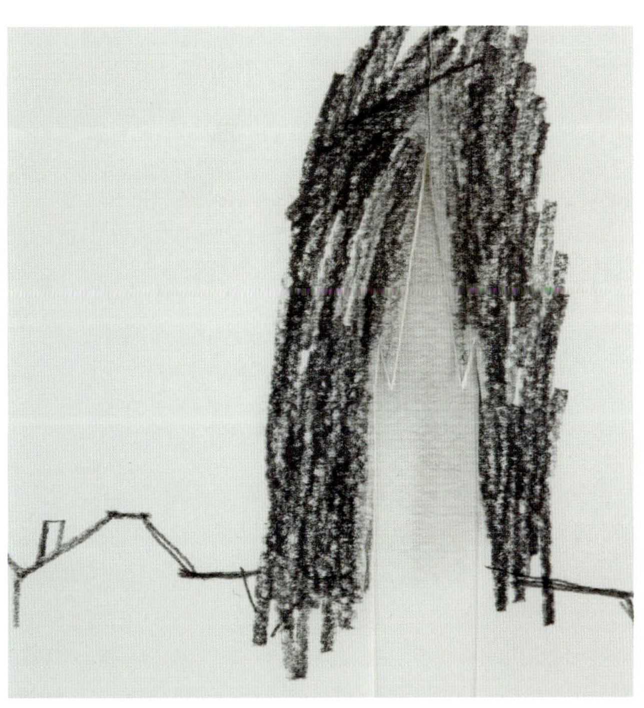

6 DRAW IN ROOFLINE ON MASK
Draw some simple roof shapes below the spire, keeping it very simple. Just a few lines will do. If you look at what I've drawn you will notice that I haven't copied the photo exactly, but interpreted it.

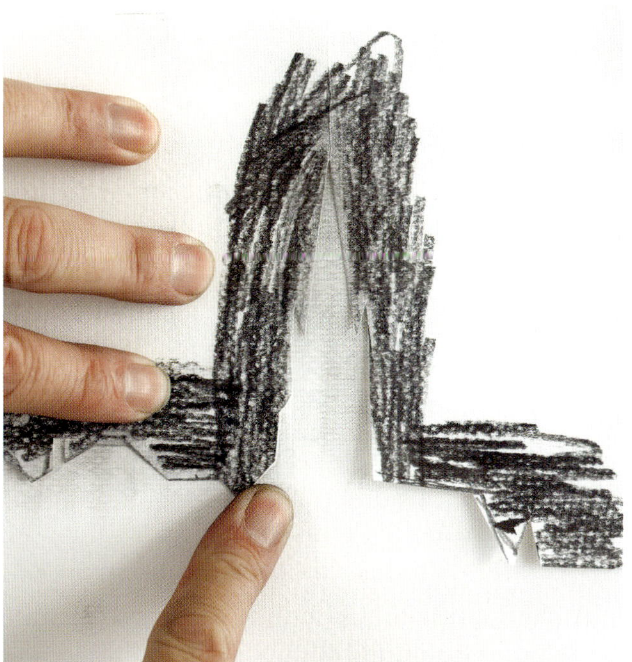

7 DRAG DOWN GRAPHITE TO CREATE ROOFLINE
Cut out the roofline carefully with sharp scissors, and scribble around it with a 4B pencil. Hold down firmly, making sure that it is in the correct position beneath the spire. Then smudge the graphite in as before.

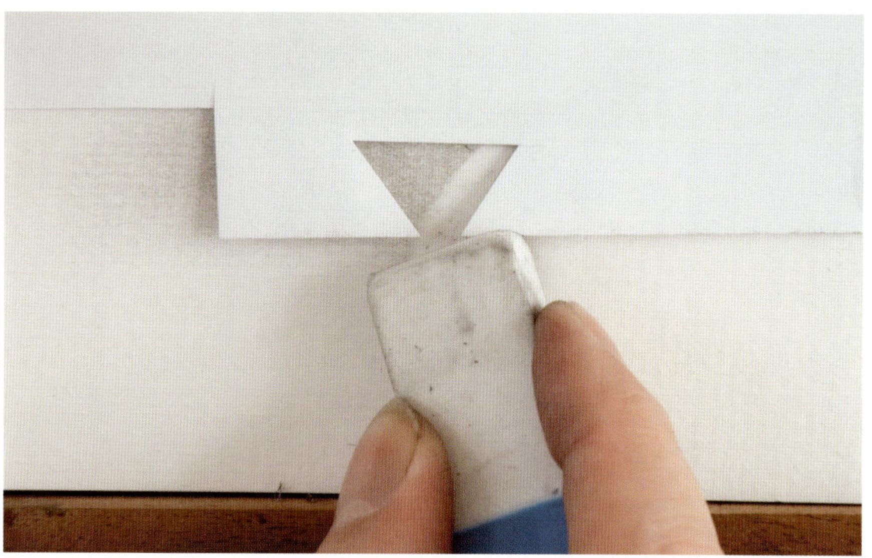

8 CREATING A GUTTERING MASK

Cut a couple of small triangular and rectangular shapes. These will be the mask for erasing the guttering and side of two of the roofs. Position the mask and hold firmly. Use the eraser to rub out some of the graphite. Work carefully with a gentle pressure along the edges of the mask.

9 DEFINING ROOFLINE

Your image should now be looking a bit like this. If the roof edges are a little indistinct, use a 2B pencil to draw some defining lines. The point of this method is not to draw too many lines, so don't overdo it! If you have fuzzy edges you're probably moving the stencil as you work.

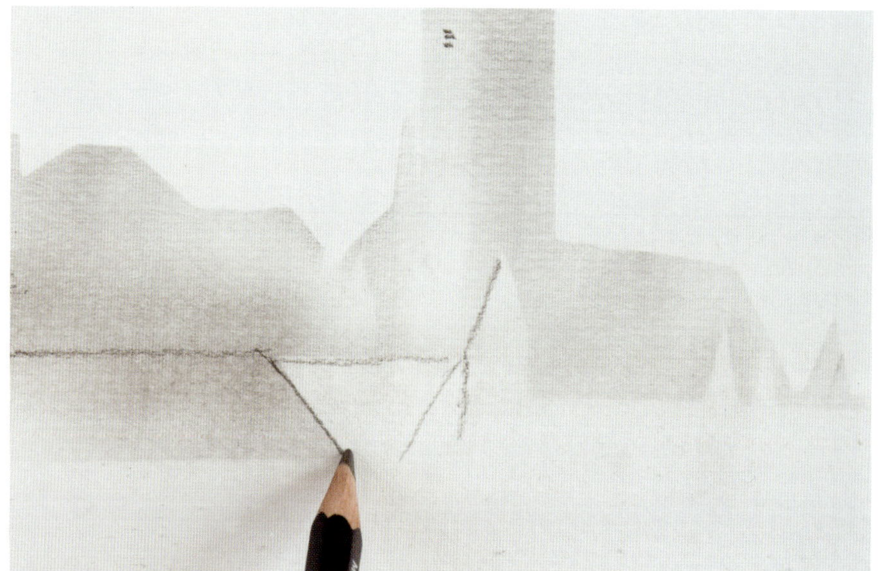

10 INDENTING WINDOWS AND SHUTTERS

Take a cocktail stick or clean matchstick and indent some horizontal parallel lines on the sides of the buildings. Three or four lines will do, quite close together. Add a central vertical indentation on each. These indentations will show up as white window woodwork at the next step.

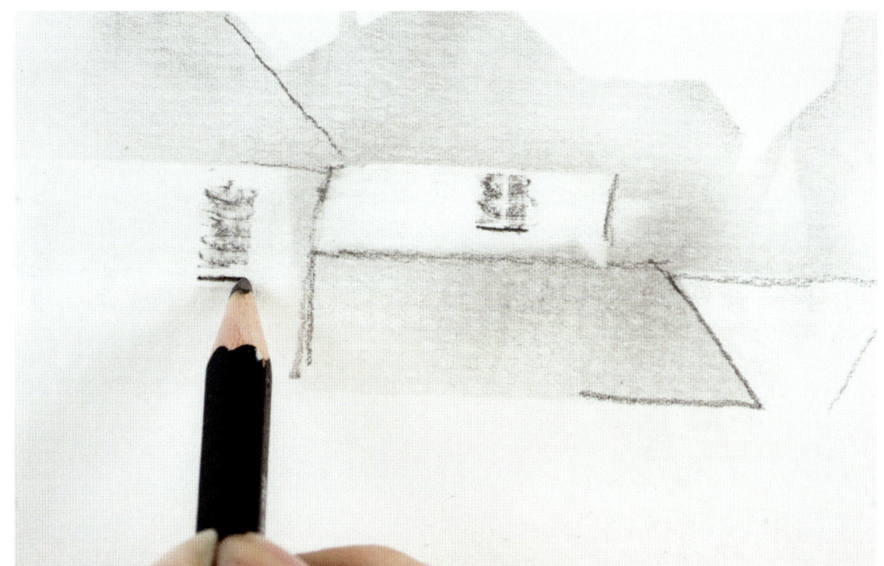

11 DRAWING IN LEDGES

Use the flat of the 4B pencil lead to shade in window rectangles where the indentations were made. Don't push too hard, or you'll obliterate the marks. Make more indentations to denote a white fence below the buildings. Use a 6B pencil and heavier pressure to draw over these. The darker tone will make the fence and hedge look nearer than the buildings.

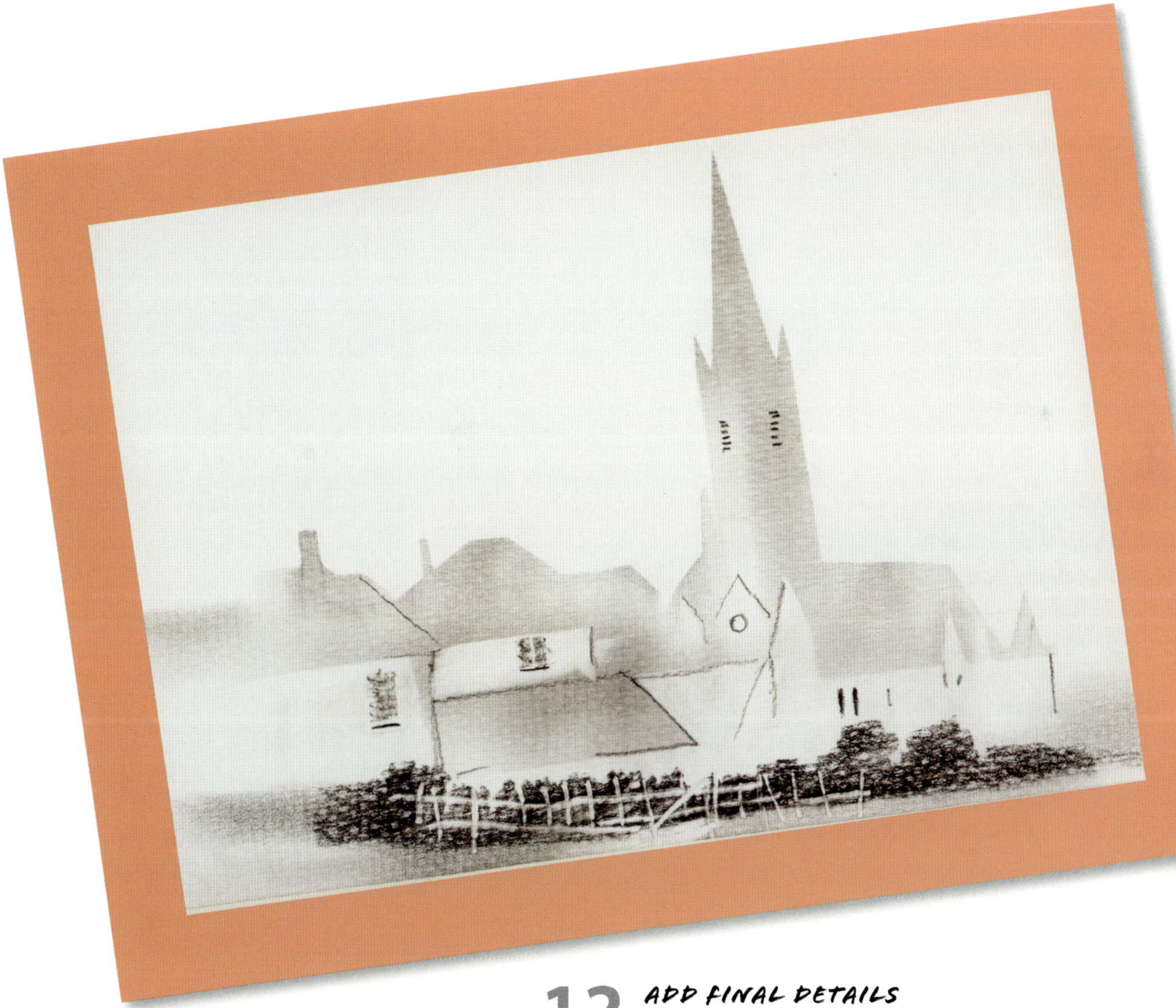

12 ADD FINAL DETAILS

To finish the image, add a couple of vertical lines to create thin windows in the spire, a few diagonals at its base to imply a porch structure, and use a finger to smudge down from the fence posts to add a little tone at the bottom. This method of scribbling and smudging is very versatile and can be used on almost any subject. Maybe you'd like to try this technique using a photo of your house?

PROJECT 3

QUICK & CLEVER

TREES IN A LANDSCAPE

PROJECT 3

Drawings don't have to feature just shades of grey; there is a wide range of colourful drawing media that we can use in our work. This project uses coloured pencils for drawing and indenting coloured lines, plus hard pastels to build up and blend the colours. Choose a bright blue pastel paper and you'll produce a vibrant, strong image. Before starting the drawing, take a little time to practise your indenting and blocking-in techniques. Remember, practice makes perfect!

YOU WILL NEED:

Coloured pencils: see swatches, below
Hard pastels: see swatches, below right
Blue pastel paper
Board to rest on
Note: I used the Derwent range of coloured pencils and hard pastels from the Cumberland Pencil Company for these projects; they are excellent value. If you use a different make, the names of colours may be different from mine, so match the colours using the colour swatches.

TREES AND A BARN

(SEE PAGE 77)

This drawing relies on the contrast between the fine lines produced by the coloured pencils and the softer appearance of the pastels. Have a go at layering, blocking in and indenting before starting on the image. But first, let's see how to simplify natural shapes, overleaf.

COLOURED PENCILS:

Silver Grey

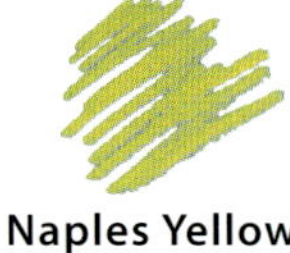
Naples Yellow

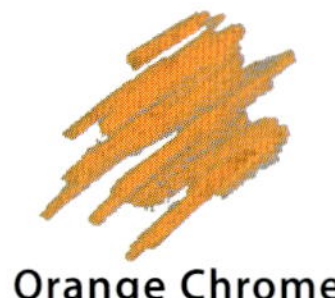
Orange Chrome

Burnt Umber

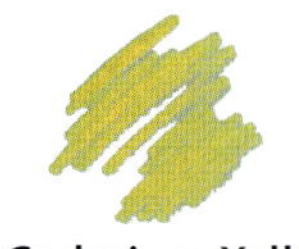
Cadmium Yellow

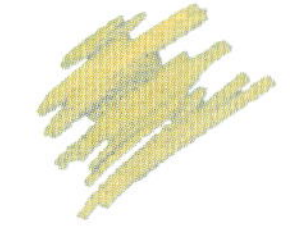
Yellow Ochre

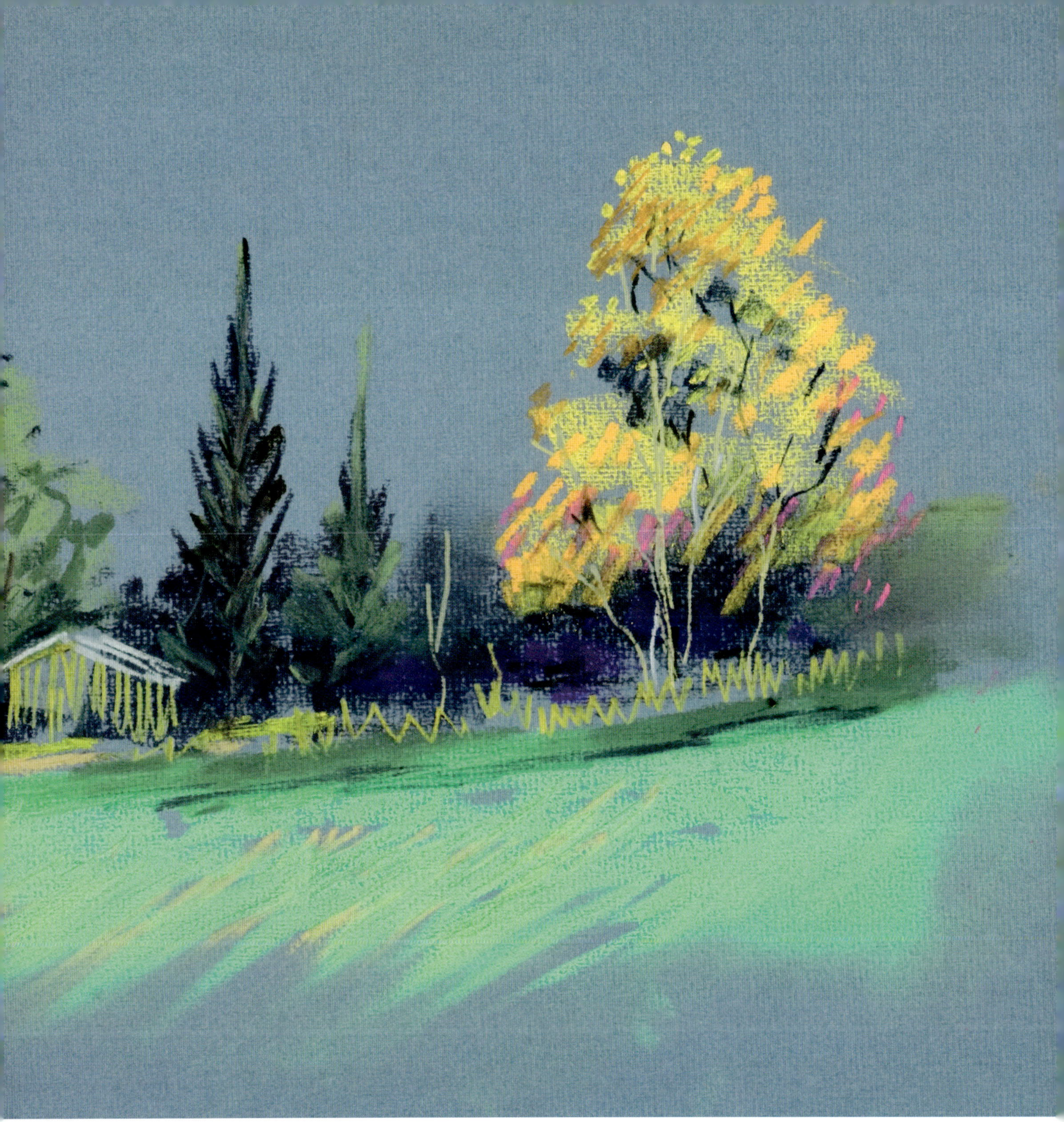

HARD PASTELS:

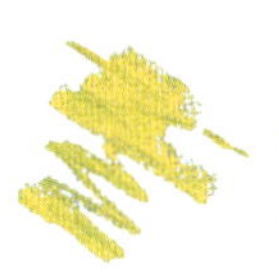
Mid-Yellow

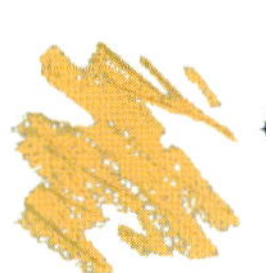
Orange

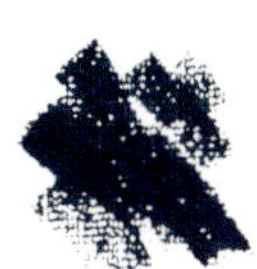
Indigo

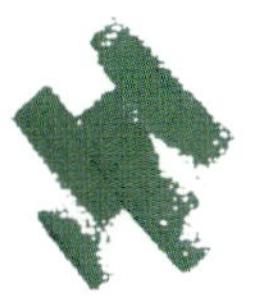
Olive Green

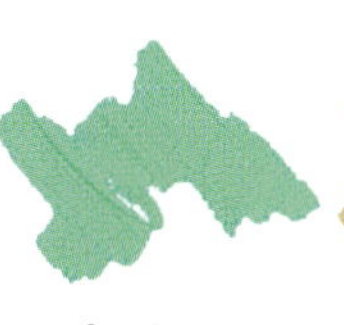
Pale Green

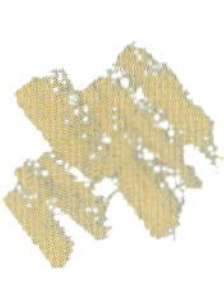
Buff

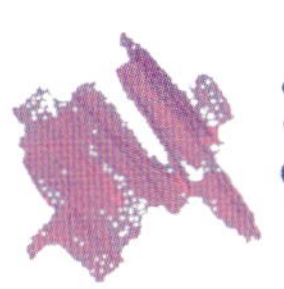
Magenta

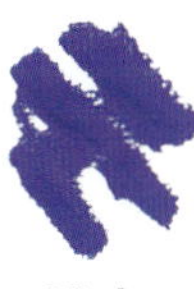
Violet

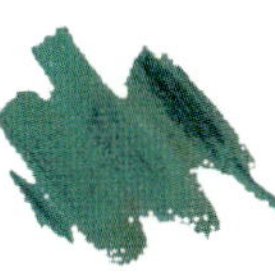
Sap Green

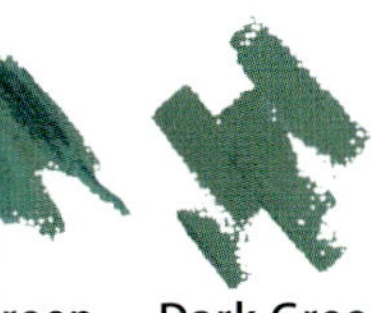
Dark Green

TECHNIQUE – SIMPLIFYING TREES

Trees are not too difficult to draw as long as you remember to concentrate on the masses of leaves, not individual ones. The tops of trees are usually lighter than the underneath, where the shadows dominate and combine with the shadows on the ground to impart stability and help to create a sense of perspective.

Natural shapes such as flowers are fairly easy to simplify, as long as you aren't distracted by small details. Keep the tones in mind, so you can emphasize light blooms against a darker background, or lighter masses of leaves against dark. Look for the geometry that underpins most natural shapes. Curved, flowing lines work well when drawing shapes such as flowers, while strong lines and angles are often more suited to branches.

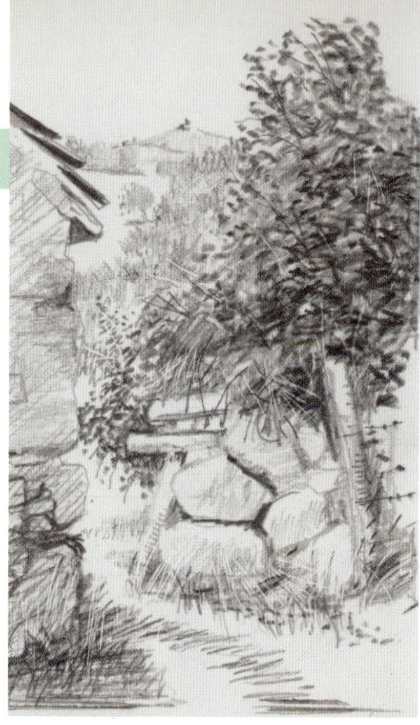

QUICK & CLEVER!

Assess tones more easily by screwing your eyes up almost shut and squinting. This helps to reduce the tones that you are looking at. Just don't let too many people see you doing it!

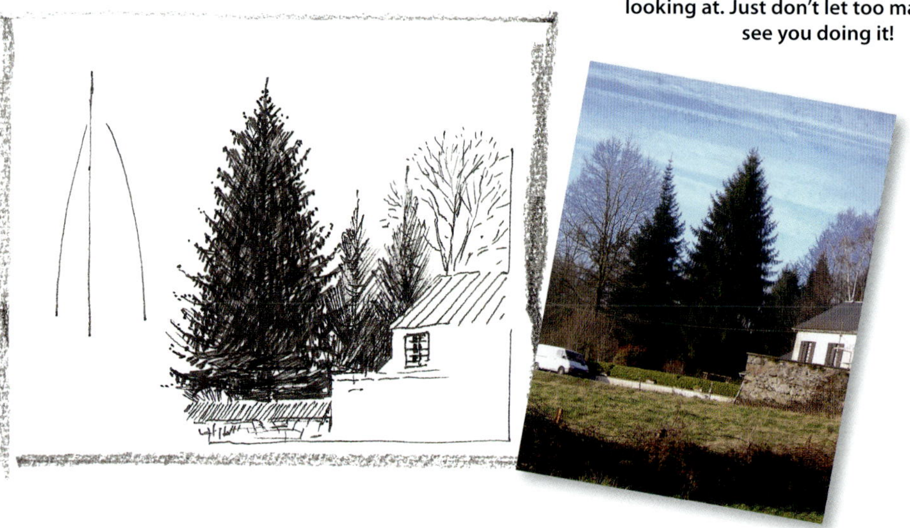

▶ *Coniferous trees are often almost triangular in outline, with branches coming off the trunk at regular intervals and tapering towards the top. It helps to draw the outline first, slightly smaller than the drawing of the tree will be, so the dark drawing hides it. If drawing distant trees behind the main one, make these lighter.*

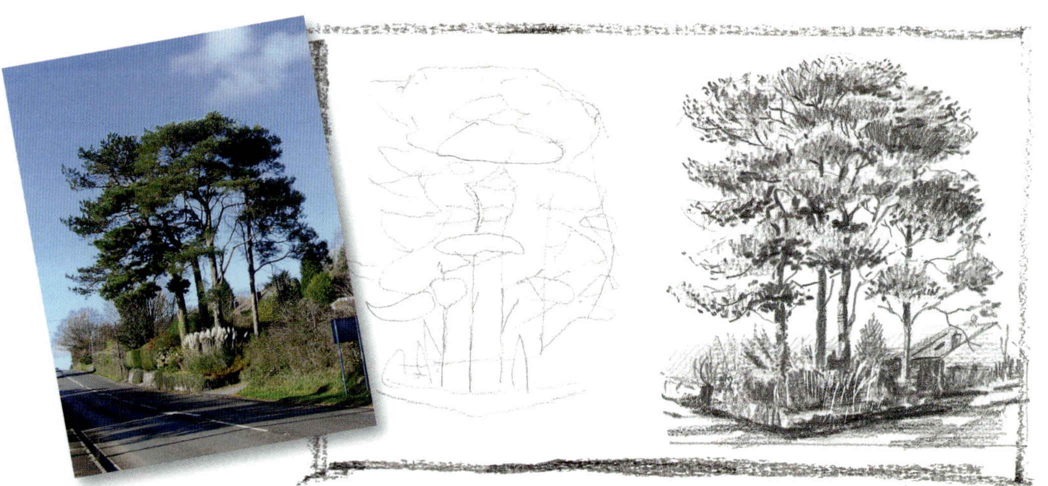

◀ *Groups of trees can be tricky, but are easily simplified if you draw around the masses of leaves, reducing them to simple outlines that overlap or interconnect. Where there are gaps in the foliage, known as 'sky holes', branches or trunks are usually visible silhouetted against the sky. These tie the groups of foliage together.*

▶ *It's good to practise drawing tree trunks and exposed roots. Look carefully at the tones and exaggerate the contrast if necessary, so that the drawing has strength. If using hatching lines to make tone, draw the line so that it follows the form – use curved lines for curved shapes, and so on. If the tree trunk has a clearly defined shape, practise this first.*

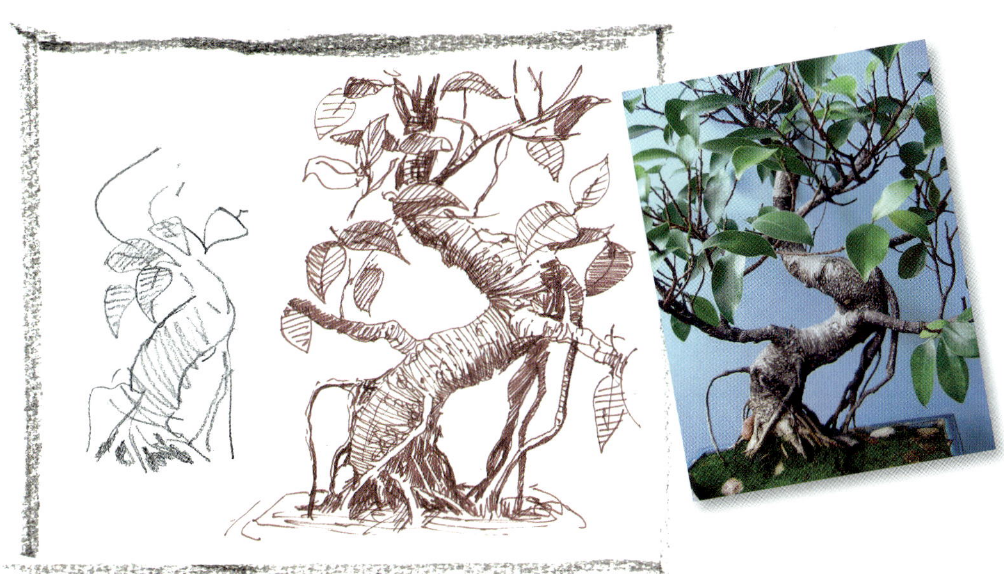

◀ *A good way to portray masses of leaves is to analyze the individual leaf shape, and then combine these in a drawing. Omit much of the detail and emphasize some of the leaves with an outline, or surround them with a darker or lighter area.*

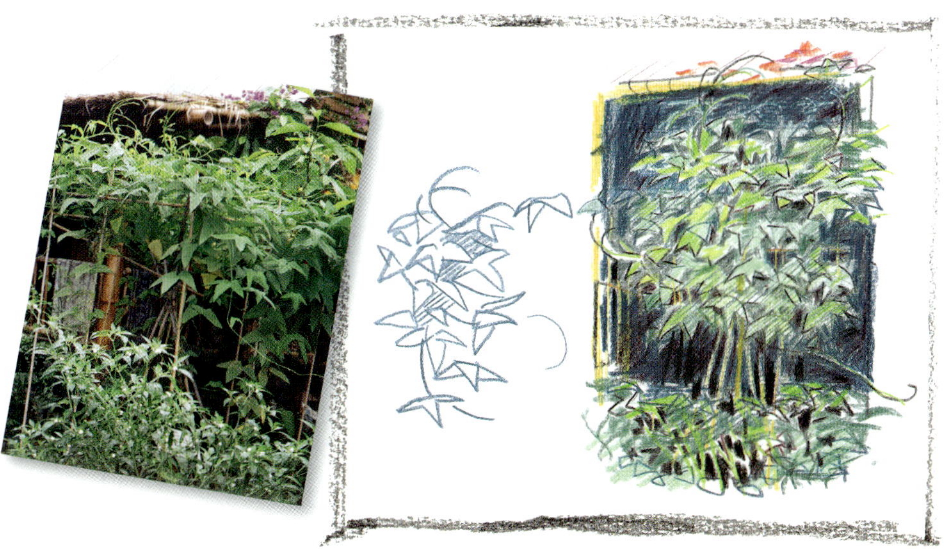

▶ *A complex bloom needs to be simplified. An easy way to do this is to draw centrelines for the petals before adding lines for the edges. Curved linear marks work well, and tonal changes should be very subtle. Pale flowers are easiest to draw if surrounded by dark colours such as leaves, which help to define the shape.*

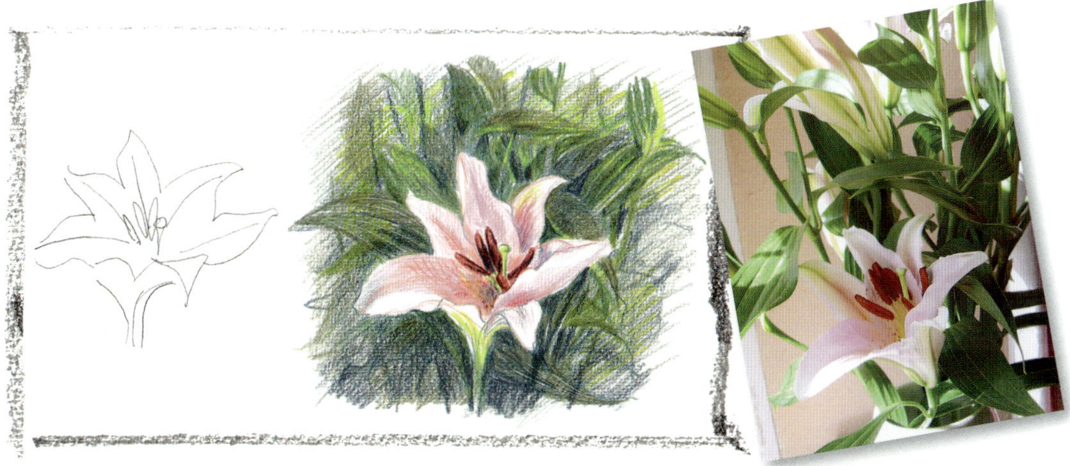

WORKING WITH COLOURED PENCILS AND HARD PASTELS

Before starting on the project, let's practise mark-making to get you accustomed to using and mixing colours. The techniques here rely on the difference between coloured pencils, which are quite hard and slightly waxy, and pastels, which, even if described as hard, are softer than pencils and don't make indentations. Use pale pastel paper for good effects.

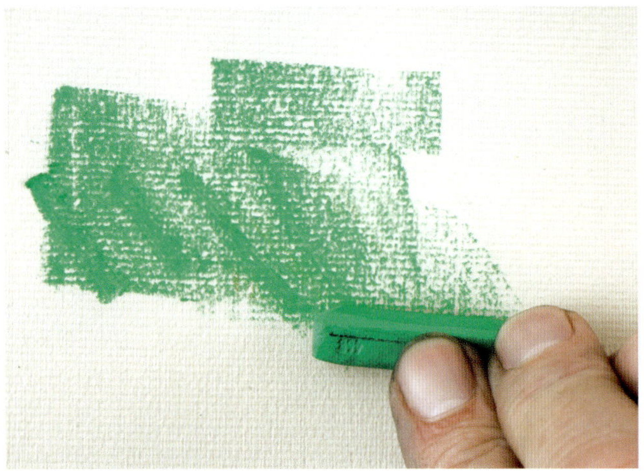

1 BLOCKING IN
By holding the pastel on its side, large areas can be covered easily, with distinctive angular marks. If your pastels are wrapped, it's best to unwrap them for this technique. Varying the pressure changes the tone, and breaking the pastel gives smaller shapes.

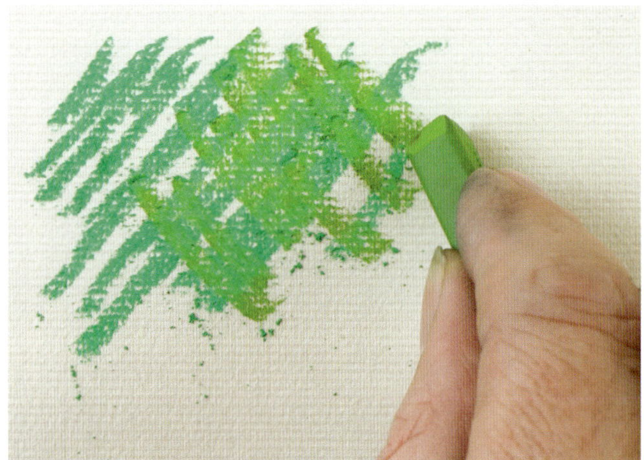

2 CROSS-HATCHING
A linear effect is obtained by using the same grip as for a pencil and drawing with the end of the pastel using short strokes. Varying the pressure gives thicker or thinner lines. Using a combination of diagonal lines helps to build up the density of colour.

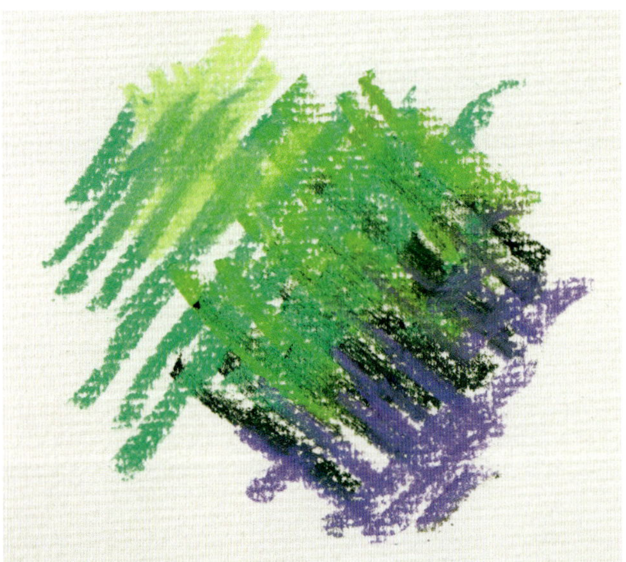

3 LAYERING
Adding one colour of pastel over another gives an interesting textural look, while using coloured pencil on top achieves a 'broken colour', as the coloured pencil tends to smudge the pastel and give a more blended effect. Adding little touches of bright colour using this method can produce a really vibrant look.

QUICK & CLEVER!

If your fingers get messy when using pastels, stop work periodically and wipe them with wet wipes or damp kitchen roll. Make sure your hands are dry before continuing.

4 INDENTING AND BLOCKING IN

Using sharp coloured pencils on paper produces an indentation at the same time as making a coloured mark. This can be used to good effect, and is especially useful for applying fence posts, branches, grass and so on. Push fairly hard, and use light colours such as pale brown, grey and yellow.

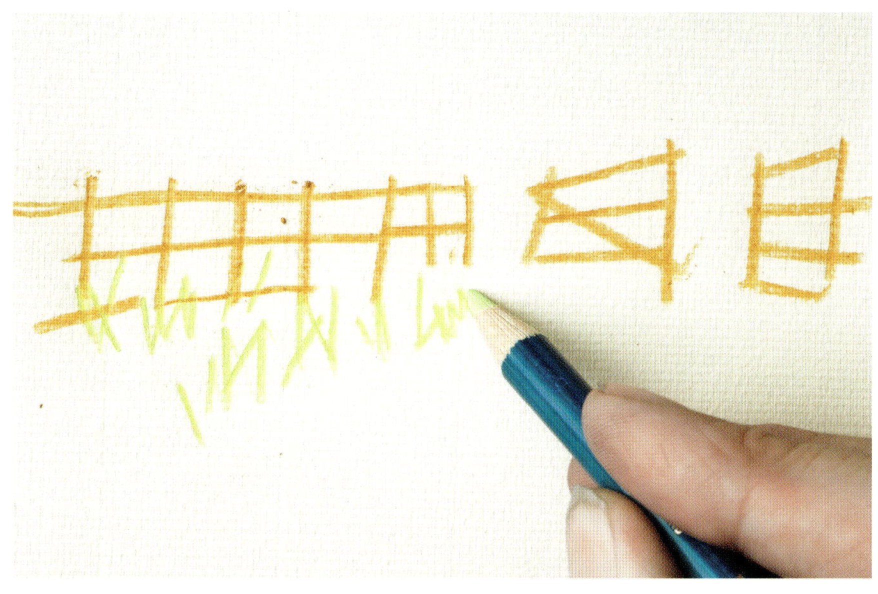

QUICK & CLEVER!

When using the indenting technique, place a piece of card under the paper to absorb the pressure. Otherwise, if using a pad, the marks will show on the pages underneath, and could spoil other drawings.

5 CONTRASTING COLOURS ON TOP OF INDENTING

Use the pastel on its edge with medium pressure. Working diagonally across the indented marks will produce clear, distinct lines, and the more contrast between the pastel colour and coloured pencil the greater the effect. For maximum strength, use several dark pastel colours such as green-blue and dark grey.

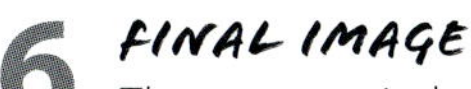

6 FINAL IMAGE

The contrast in both colour and line gives a spontaneous look, and is simple to produce. If you have difficulties making defined lines that stand out, try increasing the pressure, or using a softer paper. Pastel paper is good for this method. Remember to choose contrasting colours, using coloured pencils that are much lighter than the pastels that go on top.

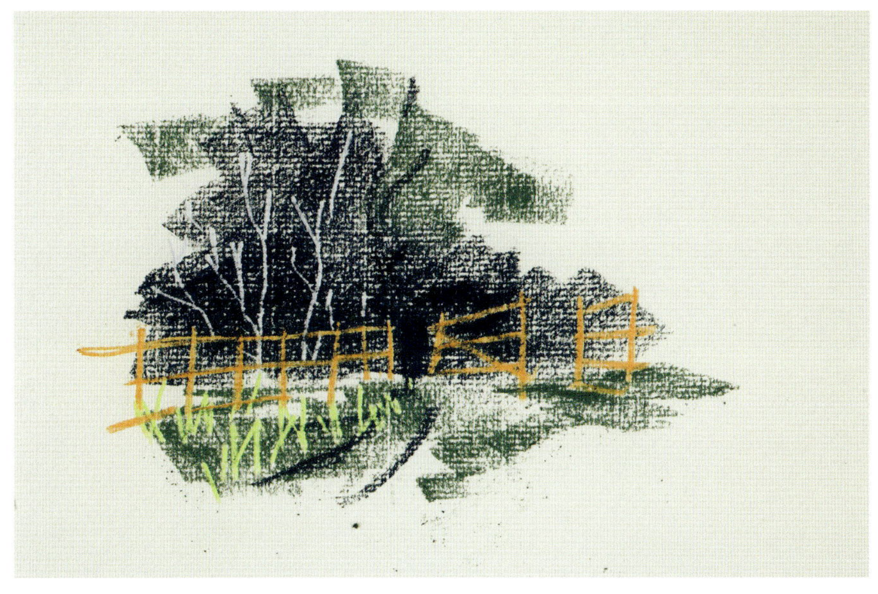

QUICK & CLEVER DRAWING

TREES AND A BARN

I hope you've now had a bit of practice using pastels for blocking in and cross-hatching and using coloured pencils for indenting coloured lines. I get really excited using these techniques – the end result is quick and clever, looks good, yet is actually quite easy to do. Now let's do a vibrant scene; your first coloured drawing!

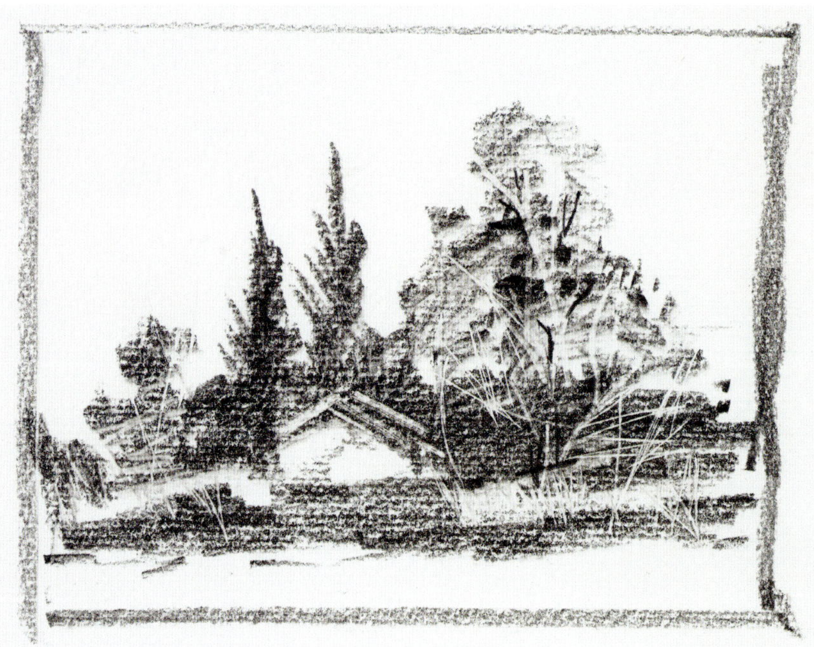

QUICK & CLEVER!

Before starting drawing with pastels or coloured pencils, select the colours you are likely to need and put them on an enamel or paper plate. Then you can carry on with the drawing without fumbling around looking for a colour.

1 START WITH A SKETCH

I've drawn a simple sketch to get you started. Use a brown coloured pencil, such as Burnt Umber, to draw the sketch lightly onto the pastel paper. Don't get too detailed; the simplest of shapes will do (see pages 68–69). Work at a size that you are comfortable with; 20 x 25cm (8 x 10in) would be plenty big enough.

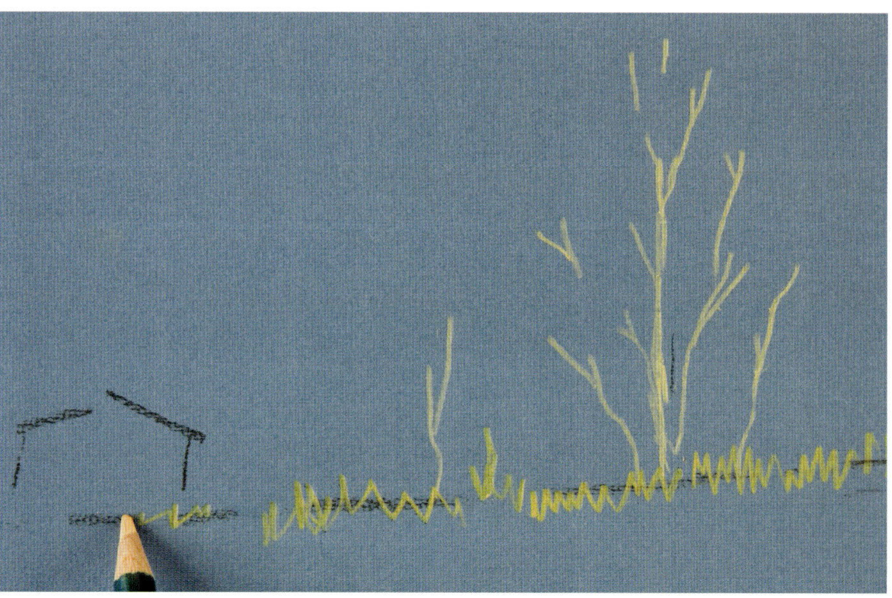

2 DEFINE TREE TRUNK AND BRANCHES

Taking a Naples Yellow coloured pencil, define the light-coloured lines of the tree trunk and branches. Use heavy pressure, and leave gaps here and there where the branches will be covered by masses of leaves. With a Yellow Ochre coloured pencil, scribble some lines to represent the grasses on the ground.

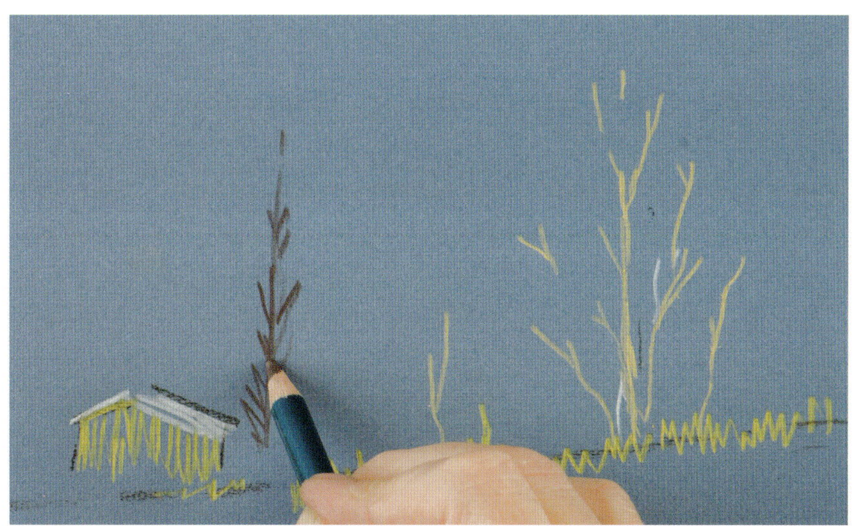

3 USE BURNT UMBER FOR BRANCHES

Use Yellow Ochre to apply the vertical lines on the side of the old barn, and Silver Grey for the tin roof. Use a Burnt Umber pencil for the darker trunks and branches each side of the barn. The pressure should be quite firm, so as to indent the colour into the paper. A few strokes of Cadmium Yellow add variety to the colour of the grasses.

4 BLOCKING IN WITH PASTEL

Break off a piece of Indigo pastel, and, using it on its side, block in some strokes at the base of the trees. Use a Dark Green pastel over and around this to produce a very dark green colour. Work diagonally over the indented branches and barn shapes with medium pressure.

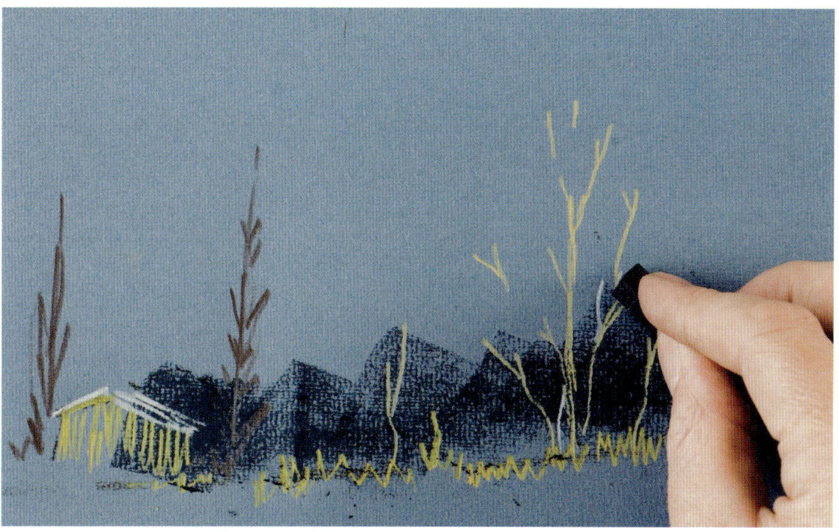

5 CREATING GAPS IN TREES

Use a piece of Mid Yellow pastel on its side for foliage masses, leaving gaps so the paper shows through here and there. Apply some of these strokes in the dark area at the bottom of the tree. Then draw some diagonal streaks with the end of an Orange pastel on to the yellow. Add a touch of Indigo under some of the foliage to give a shadow effect.

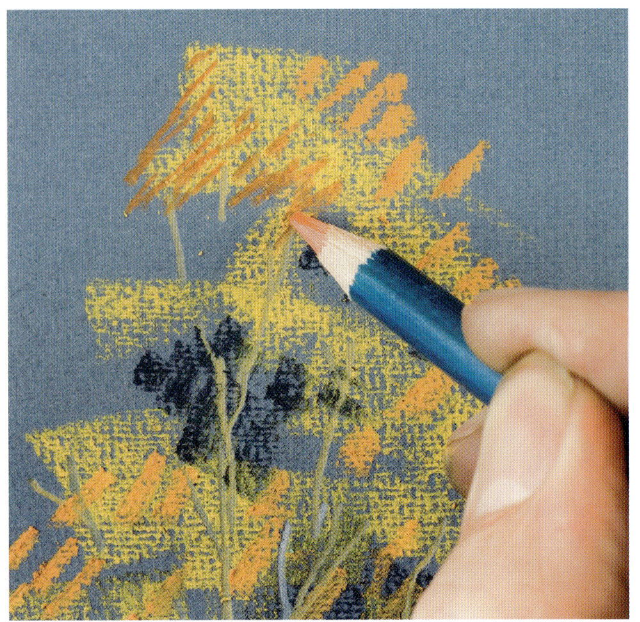

6 HATCH ON TREE

Apply short medium-pressure strokes of Orange Chrome and Cadmium Yellow pencil onto the yellow pastel, to impart colour and texture. Using diagonal strokes gives a more 'drawn' effect. Putting the yellow strokes at the top and the orange further down will give the impression that the top of the tree is receiving more light.

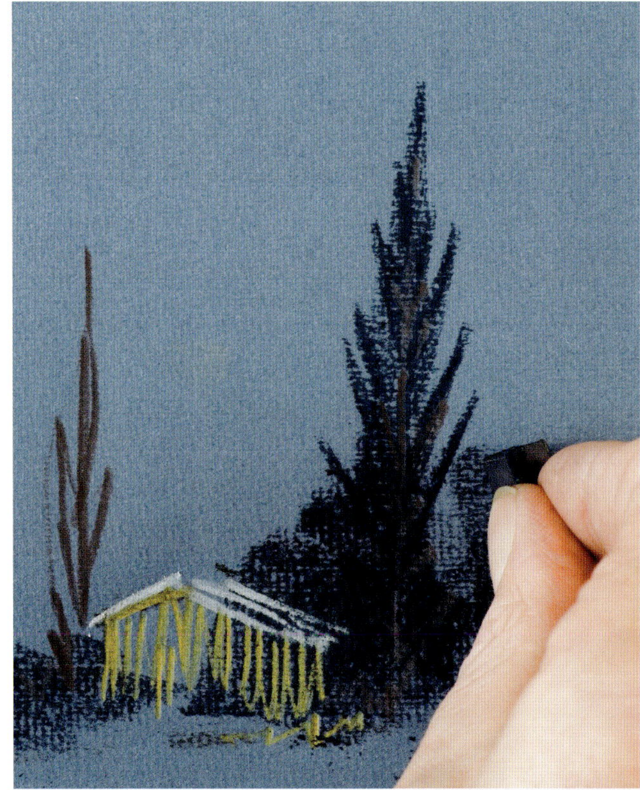

7 ADD MORE TREES

With the edge of a piece of Indigo pastel, draw a vertical line, then some diagonal angular marks coming out from it, getting smaller as they go higher up. Moving the edge of the pastel across the base adds a shadow area. Repeat the basic shape for a second tree.

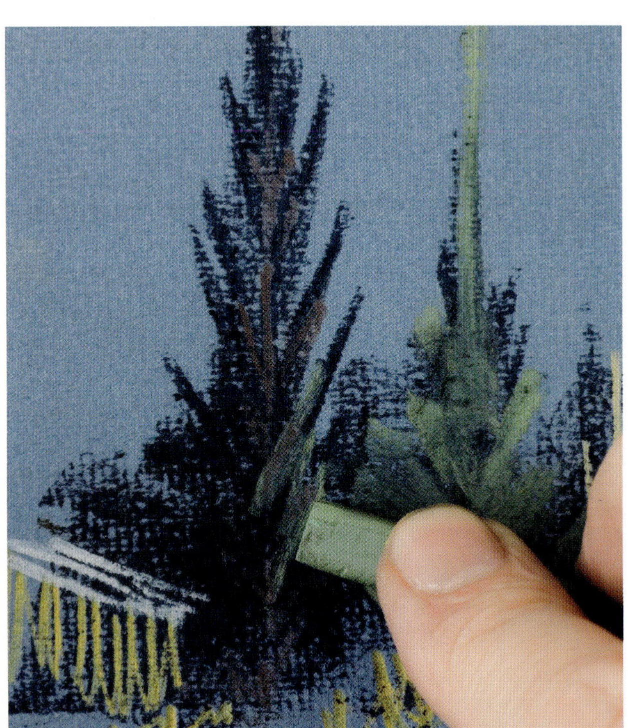

8 CREATE FORM IN THE TREES

Use a Sap Green pastel to add some lighter touches to the previously applied indigo. Work with the pastel end, to give a more linear effect, and make the lines follow the shapes of the conifer branches.

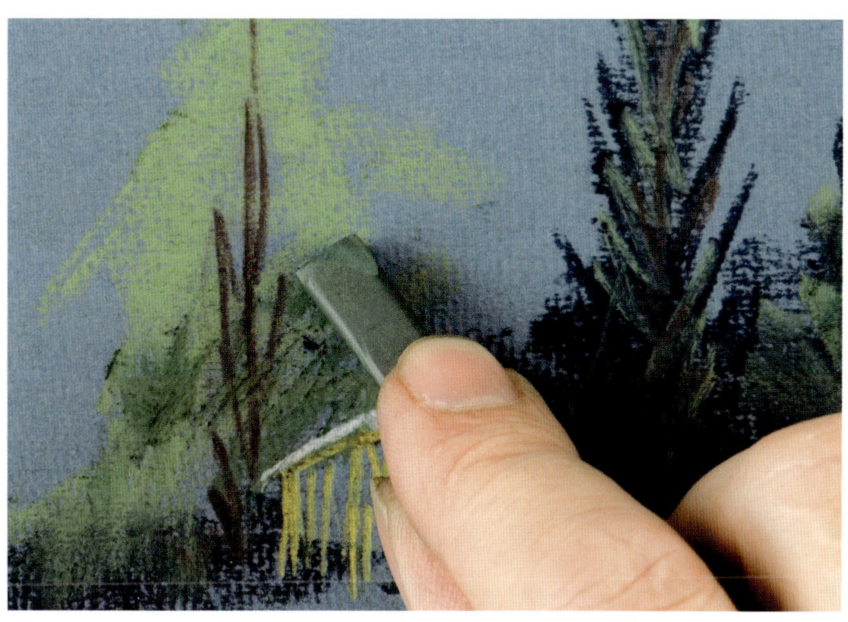

9 CONTINUE TO BUILD UP FOLIAGE

Add a few strokes of Sap Green on the left of the building plus the area behind it. Then use an Olive Green to add lighter touches to the top and one side of this tree, working over the previously drawn dark branches from step 7.

10 ACHIEVE A LEAF EFFECT

To give an attractive texture to the orange-coloured tree, add some further strokes with Orange Chrome and Cadmium Yellow coloured pencils. Very short movements, like little ticks and dots, will impart a leafy effect. Don't overdo this or the effect will be too busy.

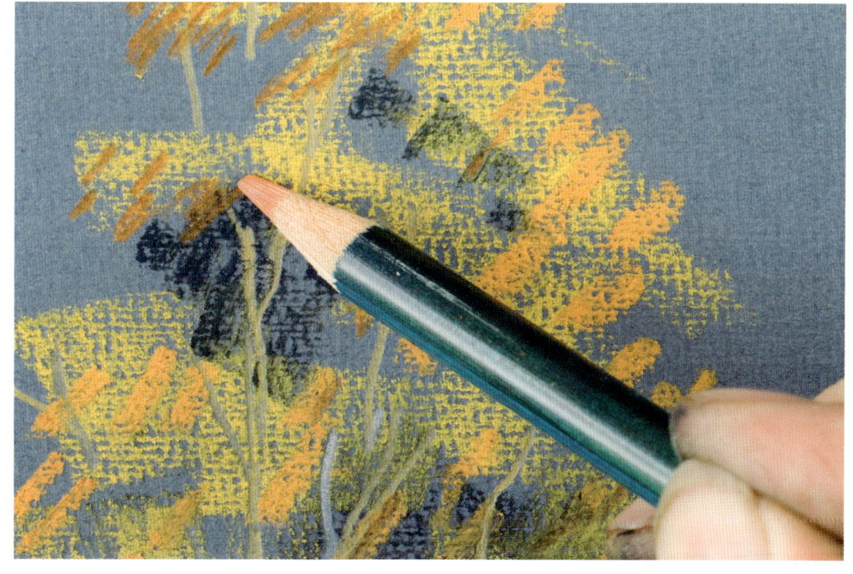

QUICK & CLEVER!

It's a good idea to sit back regularly, away from the drawing, so you can see how it is progressing. Don't work too close; it's uncomfortable and you will end up getting cramp.

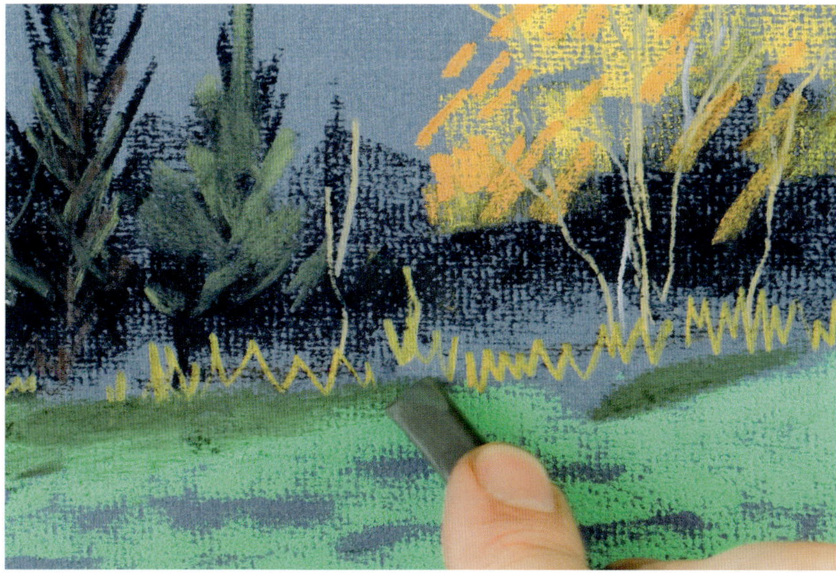

11 ADD A HEDGE

Use broad horizontal strokes of Pale Green pastel, with touches of Dark Green here and there in the hedge. Allow some little bits of the background blue to come through to help create a spontaneous effect.

PROJECT 3

12 EMPHASIZE THE BUILDING

Take the Indigo pastel, and use the end of it to stroke in some bushes in front of the tree on the left of the barn. Apply reasonable pressure to get this area quite dark, to add emphasis to the building.

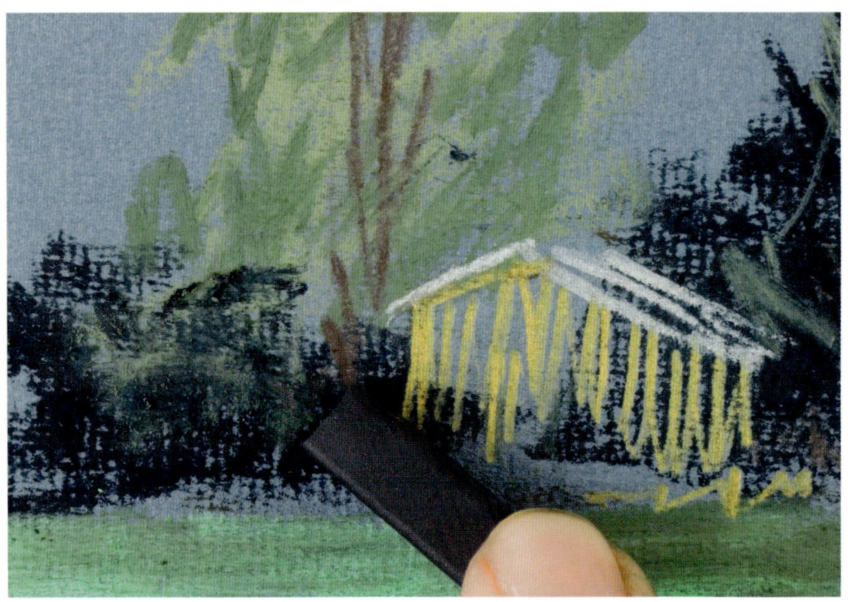

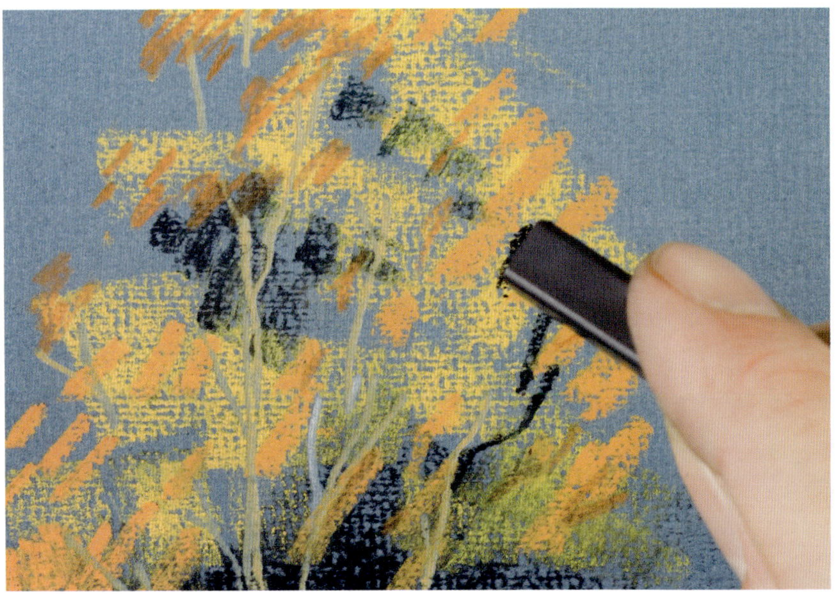

13 CONTINUE WITH INDIGO PASTEL

Use the corner of the Indigo pastel to draw some dark lines on the right of the tree, to give the look of branches in shadow. Don't make continuous lines; leave some gaps where the branches are hidden by masses of leaves.

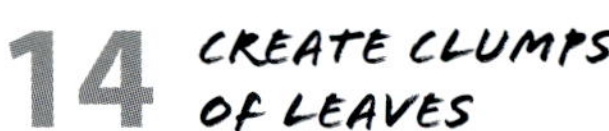

14 CREATE CLUMPS OF LEAVES

Carefully add some little dots around the tree behind the barn, with the corner of the Indigo, using light pressure. These will look like little clumps of leaves in shadow. We're nearly finished; it's time to sit back and admire your work!

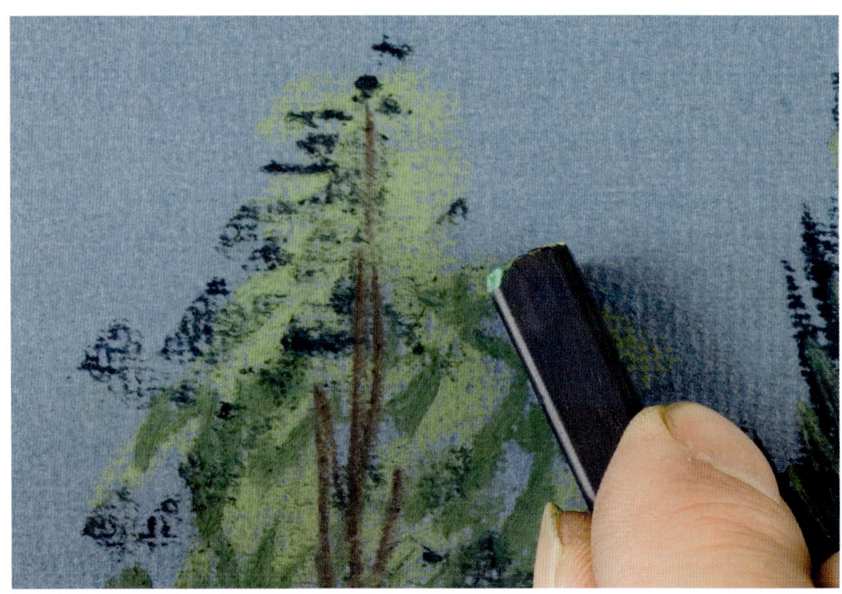

15 ADD A TOUCH OF VIOLET

Work some little strokes of Violet pastel into the dark shadow under the trees. Keep the strokes short and separate. This will add interest to the dark area and liven up the colour; violet and yellow work well together.

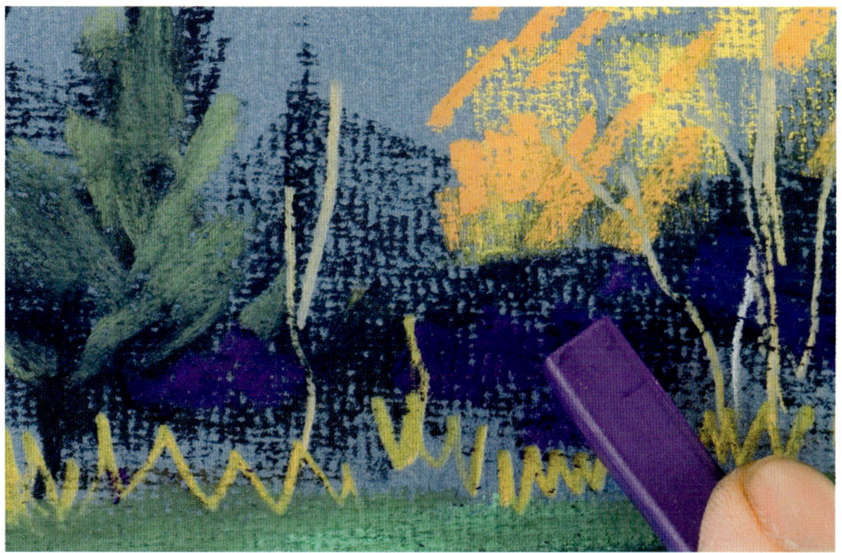

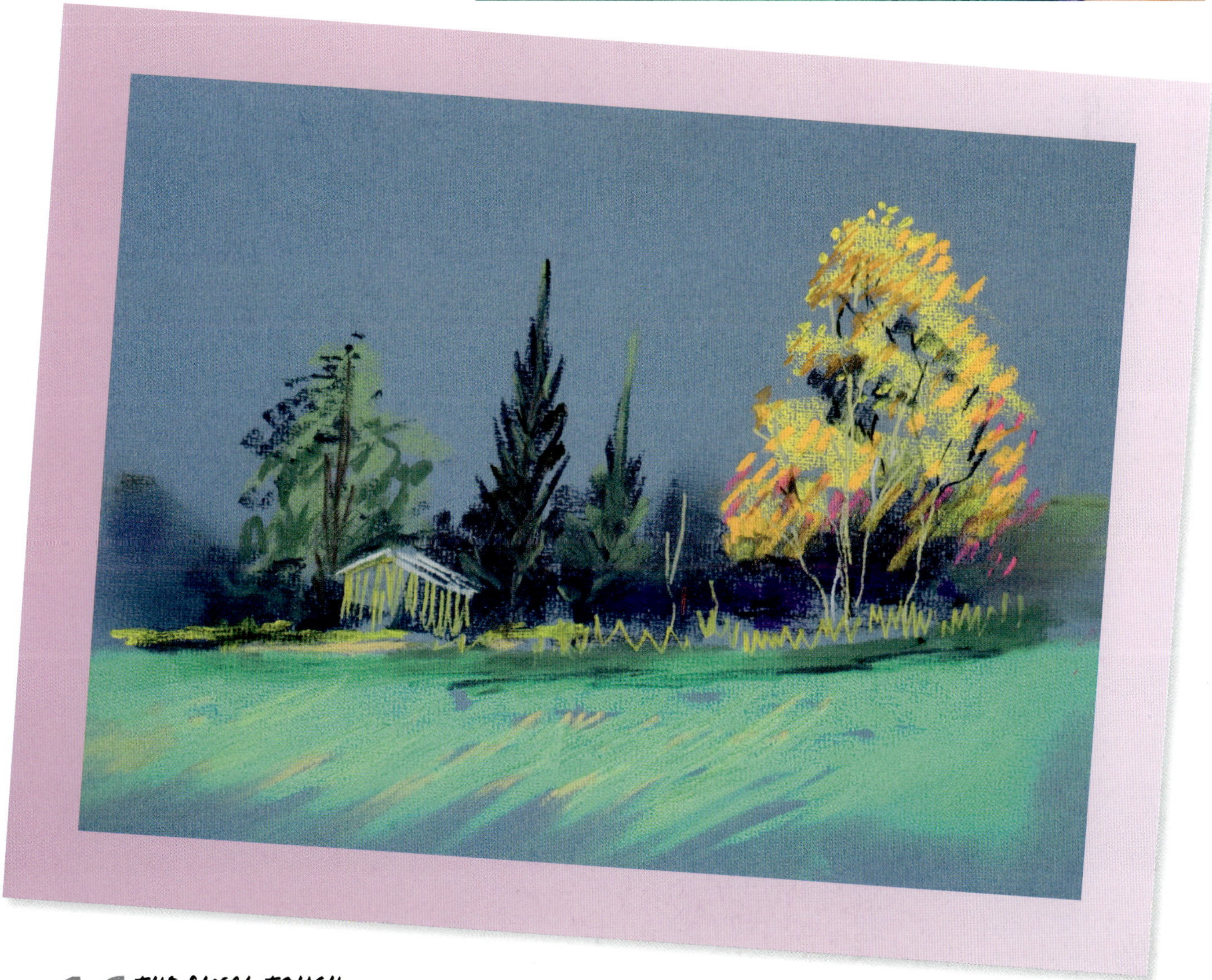

16 THE FINAL TOUCH

Knowing when to stop is the most difficult part! Putting in these tiny touches of strong colour at the end is always a delicate operation: too much and you spoil the image; not enough and the drawing could look a bit bland. Some tiny bits of Magenta pastel in the bright tree add vibrancy, while a few diagonal streaks of Buff pastel in the grass breaks the area up nicely. Well done!

PROJECT 4

QUICK & CLEVER

VENICE SCENE

Venice is a favourite subject of mine. Even though it's been painted so many times by so many famous artists, there's always something inspiring to draw or paint. In fact, drawing is the best way of capturing the place; if you set up an easel and start painting in Venice you immediately become a tourist attraction, but a small sketchpad can be more discreet. With a bit of practice you can even sketch the canals while eating a plate of pasta. Guess how I know that!

One of the most versatile of all drawing media is watercolour pencils. They can be applied dry on watercolour paper and wetted later; used dry as coloured pencils on cartridge paper; worked directly onto wetted watercolour paper; or dipped in water as you go. They are also light and easy to carry.

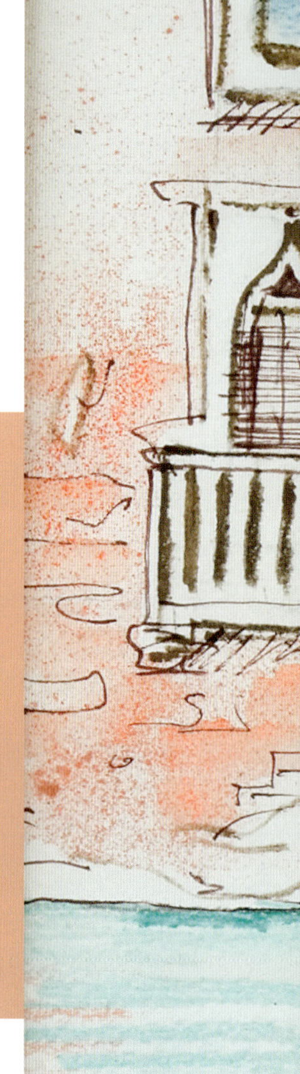

A LITTLE CORNER OF VENICE

(SEE PAGE 91)

I'll show you some interesting and quick ways of producing the texture in this drawing. Some of the techniques, such as dropping watercolour pencil 'dust' onto wet paper, give speckled effects. Others, like working over coloured lines with a wet brush, can be very subtle. Practise these separately, before you start on the actual drawing, and you'll have much more confidence when you start.

YOU WILL NEED:

Coloured pencils: see swatches below right
2B pencil
21 x 29.5cm (8¼ x 11½in) piece of 300gsm (140lb) watercolour paper
Piece of tracing paper
Pencil sharpener
Medium sandpaper
2 synthetic sable watercolour brushes: 1 flat 13mm (½in) and 1 No. 8 or No. 10

Note: I used Inktense watercolour pencils from Derwent (Cumberland Pencil Company). I have listed the colours used in the project by name, but if you use a different make from me the names of colours will most likely not be identical. Don't worry; just match the colours as best you can to the ones I've used. The end result will be slightly different; it could even turn out better!

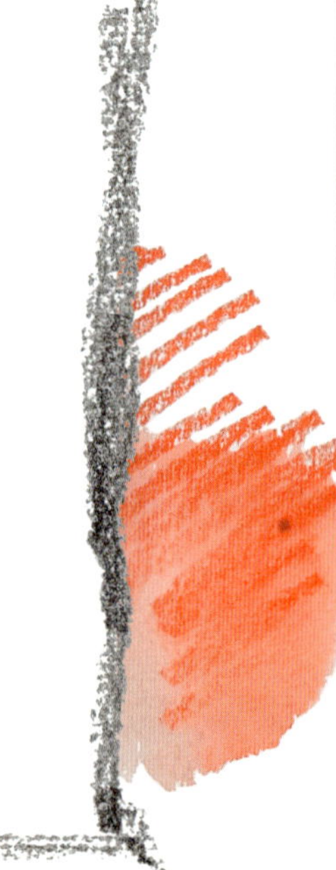

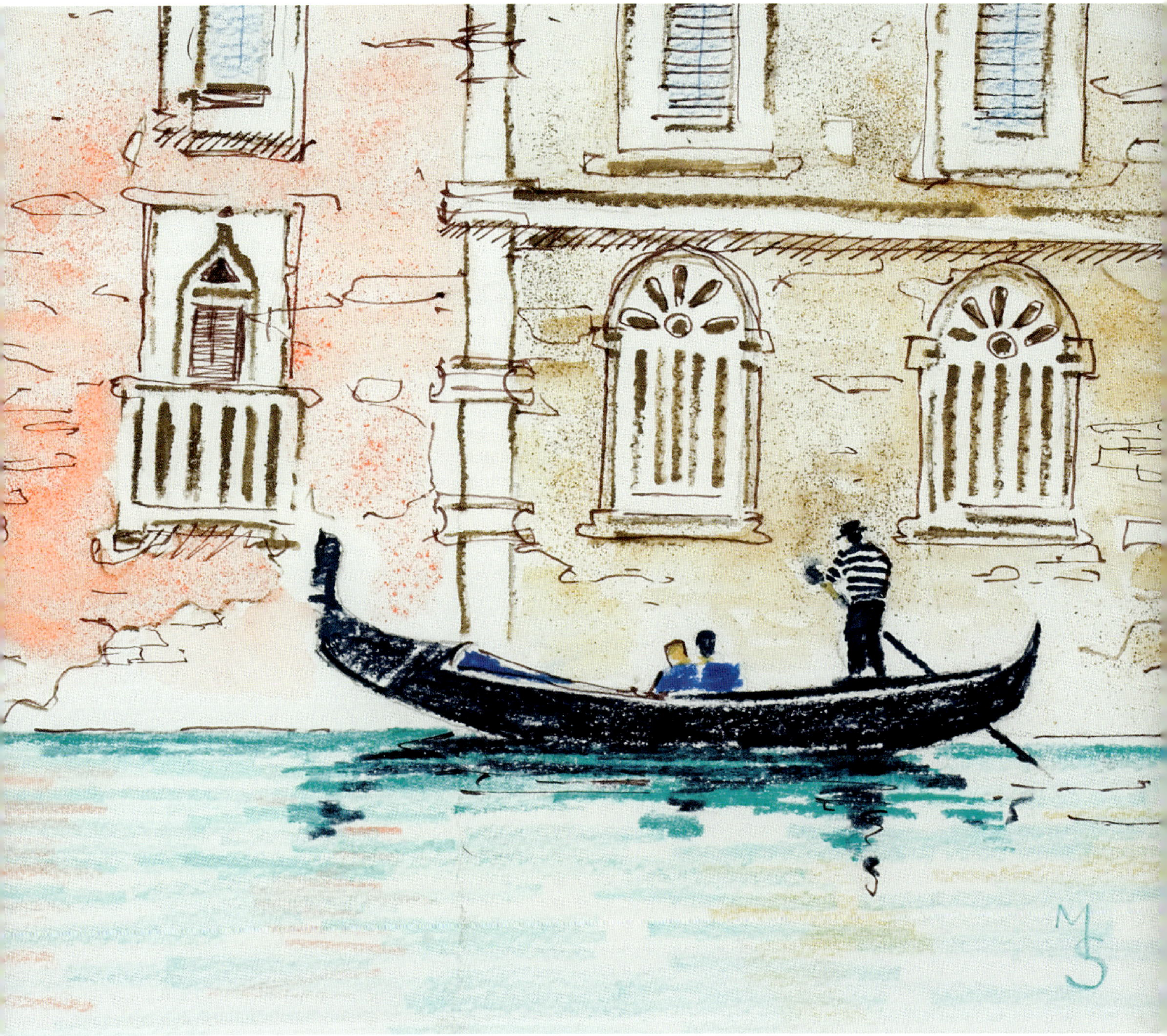

PENCILS:

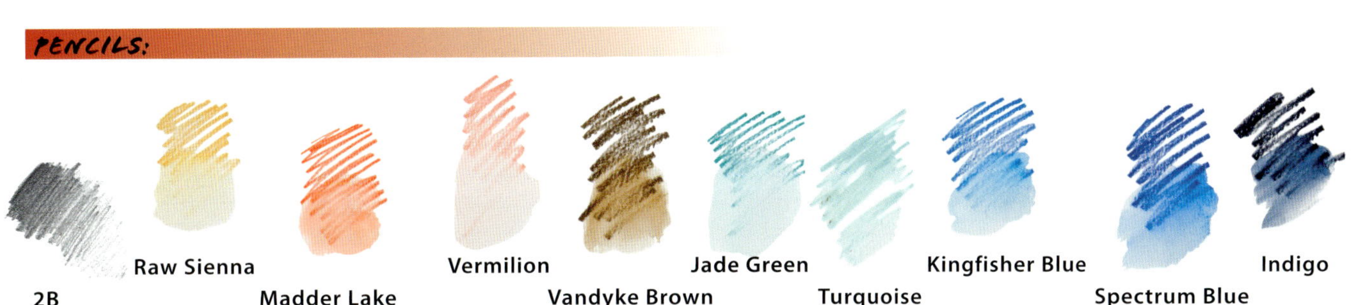
2B
Raw Sienna
Madder Lake
Vermilion
Vandyke Brown
Jade Green
Turquoise
Kingfisher Blue
Spectrum Blue
Indigo

PROJECT 4

TECHNIQUE – BOATS MADE EASY

Where would Venice be without gondolas? Yet lots of artists are reluctant to draw boats. In the groups I teach, there are usually about half who admit that they would like to draw boats but don't really know where to start. I show them this 'beginning boats' exercise.

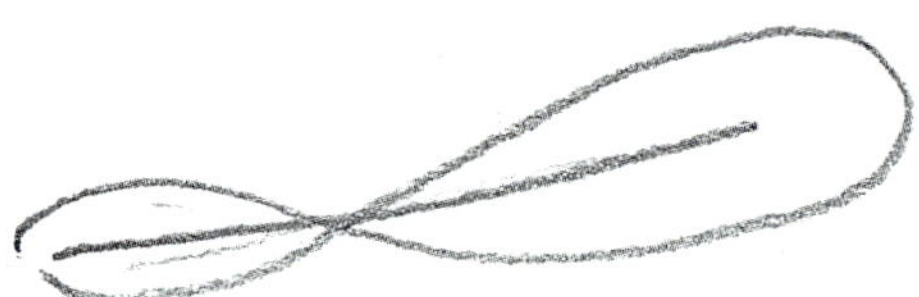

1 DRAW A LINE

The first step is really simple; just draw a line! Don't use a ruler; it's good practice to do as much freehand drawing as you can. Make the line about 8cm (3in) long (just guess it), sloping up slightly to the right, like this.

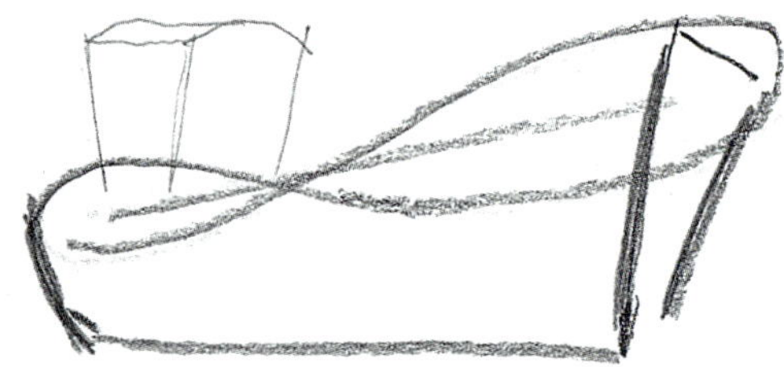

2 STRETCHED FIGURE OF EIGHT

Now draw a stretched figure of eight, on its side, with the right-hand 'bowl' bigger than the left. Don't make it too squat or dumpy, or this won't work. Drawing curves like these is also good practice, so you're getting your money's worth on this exercise!

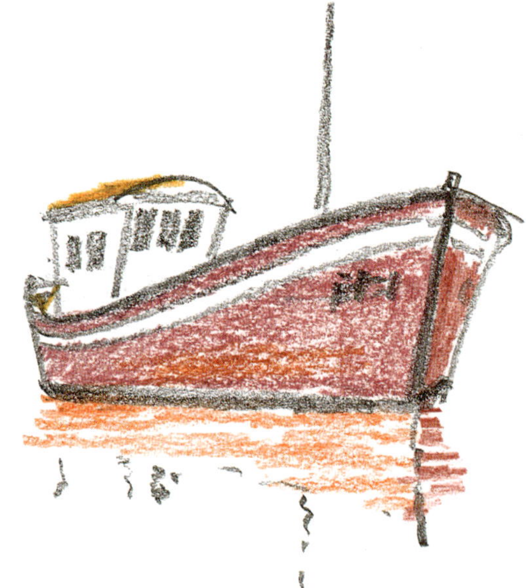

3 ADD THE CABIN

From the left-hand edge of the bowl, draw a short curved line down, and a straighter one from the right-hand edge, as I've done. See the boat shape appearing? The cabin can be added, and any unwanted lines rubbed out afterwards.

LOOKING DOWN ON A BOAT

The method below works for a three-quarter view of a boat; if you are looking down at one, from a harbour wall for instance.

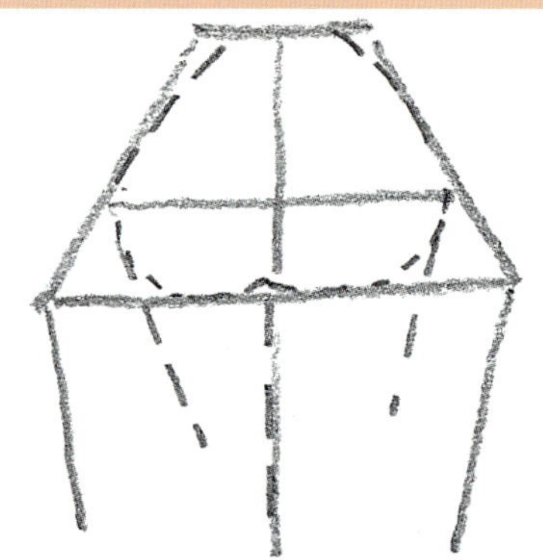

1 DRAW A BOX

Imagine the boat you are going to draw is inside a transparent box, touching the sides. Draw the box like this, so that it tapers slightly as it goes away from us. Add a centreline for reference, and another line across, about a third of the way back.

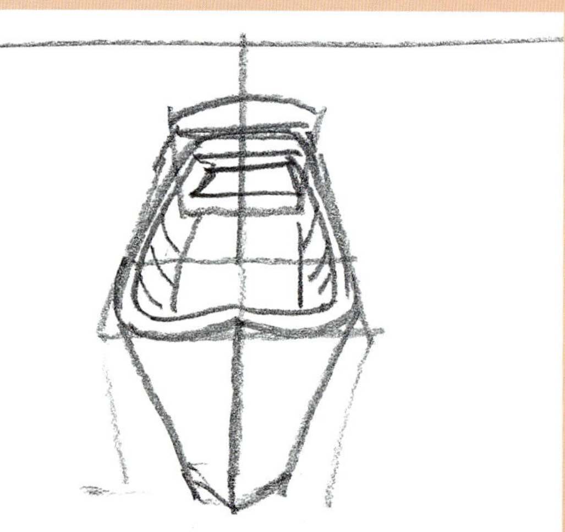

2 ADD DESCENDING LINES

Draw a curved line along one side, then a similar curve along the other side. Add some short descending lines front and back (sorry, bow and stern!) and you can see the boat shape developing. When you're happy with the shape, rub the 'box' lines out, and add a cabin.

TECHNIQUE – SIMPLIFYING FIGURES

Figures look good in a drawing; they lend movement and human interest, imparting a sense of scale and creating involvement. Most beginners are afraid of drawing figures because of the apparent complication. I often find this at the classes I run! When starting on figures, remember that they don't have to be recognizable as individuals. There is a big difference between figures in a setting like a landscape or a town, and a full-length figure study of a particular person.

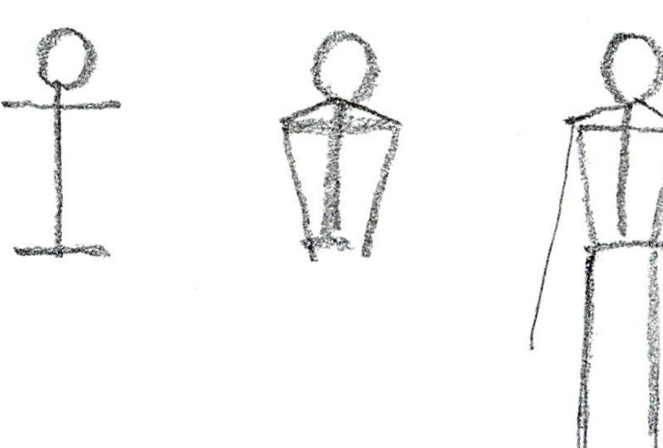

1 START WITH GUIDELINES

Draw a small oval shape for the head. Add a tapering rectangle for the body, then a centreline for each of the arms and legs. These guidelines can be removed or worked over later. It's easier to make your figures too thin initially and build out to the correct size than to try to make them the correct size and have to erase the wrong bits. Putting colour on with coloured pencils or watercolour pencils will bring them to life. Try drawing these for practice. Don't forget the guidelines! Make sure you draw the legs long enough; beginners often make them too short.

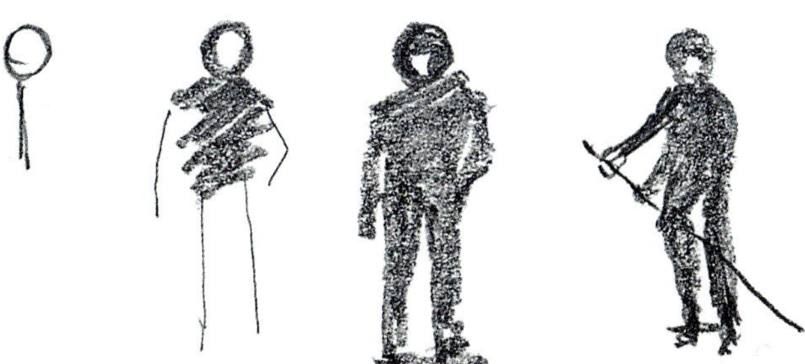

2 ADD SOLIDITY

As with many of the subjects you will be drawing, the figure is best started as a set of guidelines. Draw them faintly so that they can be erased later. Putting in a centreline to start with will enable you to divide the figure into sections: head, torso and legs. For an adult, the head will be about one-sixth of the overall figure size. The legs are longer than the torso. Practise the figures as silhouettes; it's easier.

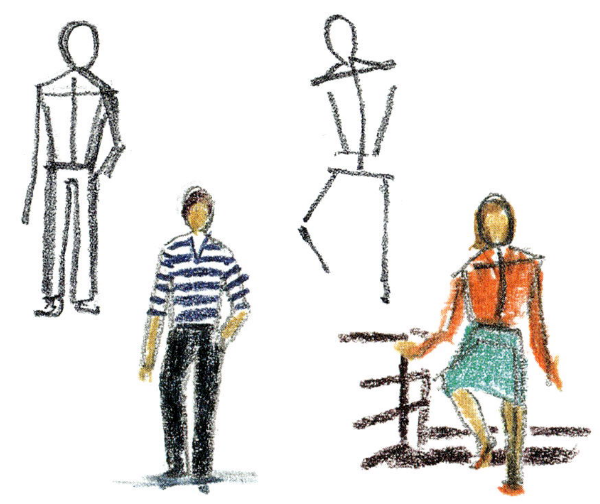

3 IMPLY MOVEMENT

Figures need to be studied carefully. They should be drawn in their natural environment; it makes them look more believable if they are doing something, even if it's sitting or talking on the phone. I take a little sketchpad everywhere; if I have a few spare minutes, I draw figures. People move, of course, but often they will repeat the same movements over again. Someone selling tickets, or rowing a gondola, will often adopt the same pose regularly. This means you can draw them bit by bit!

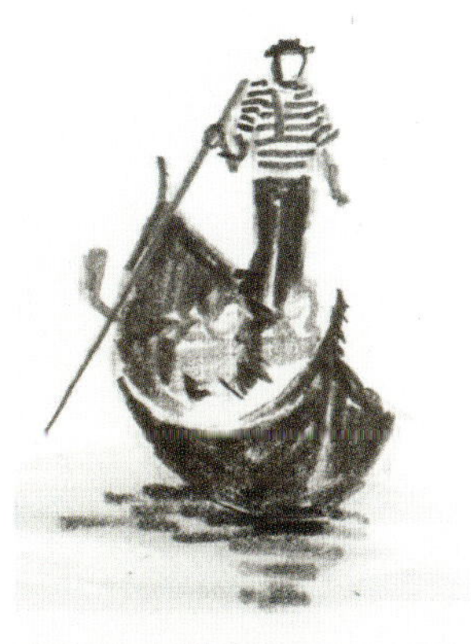

QUICK & CLEVER!

Draw people whenever you get the chance. If you're shy, hide your pad behind a newspaper and no one will know what you're up to!

One of these gondoliers is leaning as he pushes on the oars; the other is resting between strokes. Notice how the folds in their trousers and striped shirts add realism.

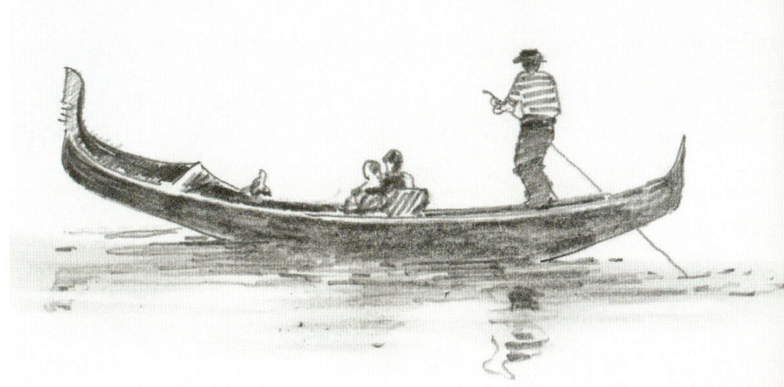

TECHNIQUE – WATER AND REFLECTIONS

Deep water has a moving, reflective surface. The thing to remember is that it's mainly flat and horizontal, apart from occasional ripples and waves. So make most pencil strokes horizontal, and add water with a brush in the same direction. Soft blending of one colour into another helps impart a fluid look. Don't press too hard when applying watercolour pencil for reflections, or you may find the lines won't blend easily.

1 SCRIBBLE IN THE BASE COLOUR
The look of still water is very atmospheric. Colours need to be from the cool end of the spectrum: blues, greens and greys. To make the water look flat, the strokes must be mainly horizontal, otherwise the effect will be like a waterfall. Leave gaps between the strokes to imply ripples.

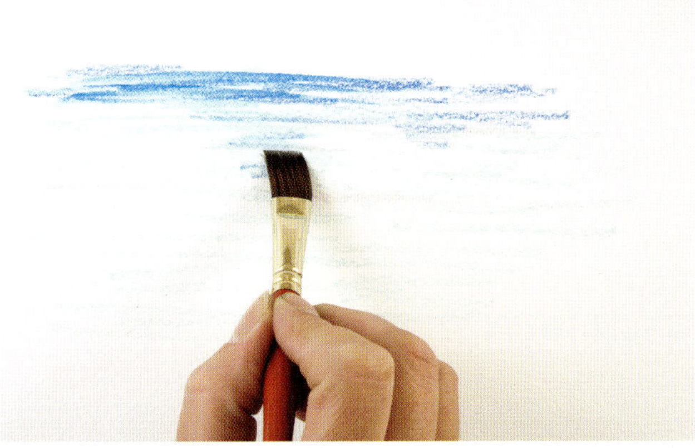

2 BRUSH WATER OVER WITH A FLAT BRUSH
Take a wet 13mm (½in) watercolour brush and blend some of the lines, making sure to keep the strokes horizontal. Bringing the brush down with an irregular zigzag shape will make realistic-looking shadows.

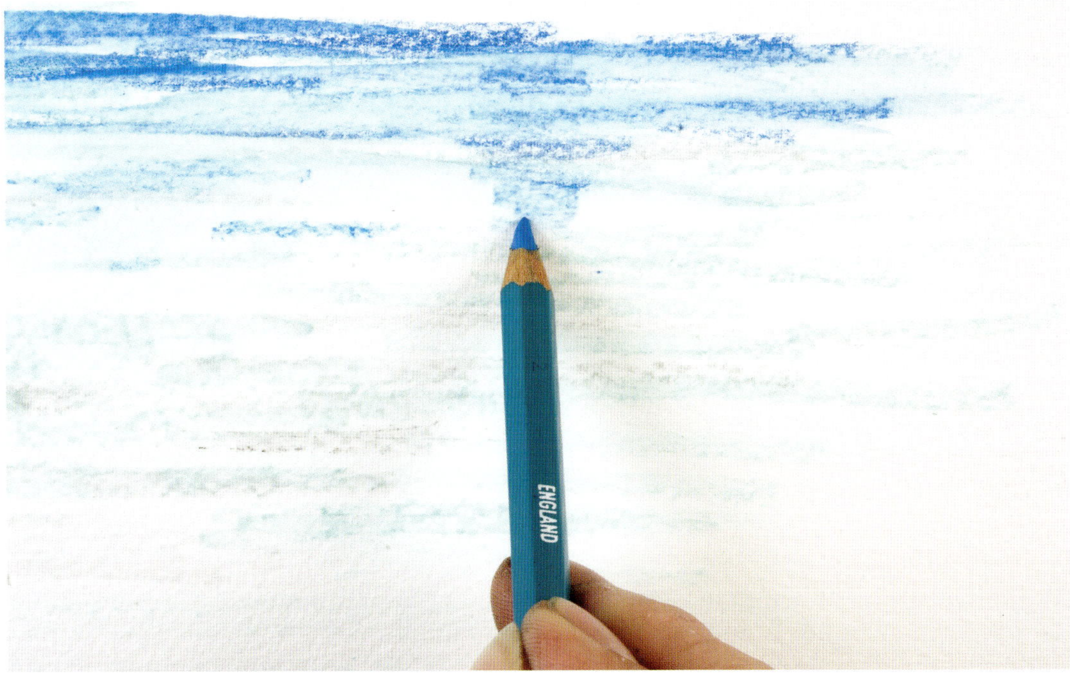

3 ADD REFLECTIONS AND RIPPLES
While the paper is still damp, work back in with darker blues or greens to add impact and strengthen the look of reflections. Working with watercolour pencils on damp paper will give a harder, more defined line.

TECHNIQUE – EASY WAYS WITH TEXTURE

Old crumbling buildings, with flaking plaster and soft brickwork, need some special techniques. One of my favourites, and an easy technique to learn, is using pigment dust. This is made by scribbling watercolour pencil on sandpaper and letting the dust fall onto damp paper. Where the paper is wet, the pigment sticks and gives a light speckle, almost like airbrushing. Where the paper is dry, simply blow the dust away, and you're left with white paper.

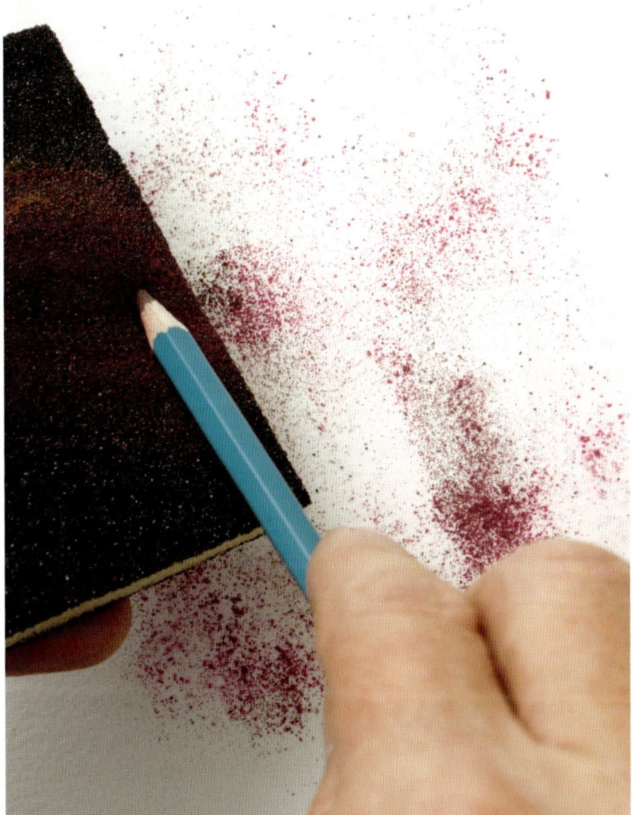

1 SAND COLOURED PENCIL ON TO WETTED PAPER

Wet the paper with a brush where you want the dust to stick. Cross shapes look good for buildings, because the white rectangles that are left can be turned into windows. Take some medium sandpaper and, while the shapes are still wet, scribble on the sandpaper so the dust falls onto the image. The more you scribble, the darker the effect will be. Try combining several dark browns and reds.

2 BLOW OFF EXCESS COLOUR

Blow gently across the paper and you will get some speckled areas, while other areas (where the paper is dry) will be left completely white. This can form the basis for more layers of different colours, or be left as it is, to be worked on when dry. If you're trying this technique when working in a group, be careful who you blow your pigment dust at!

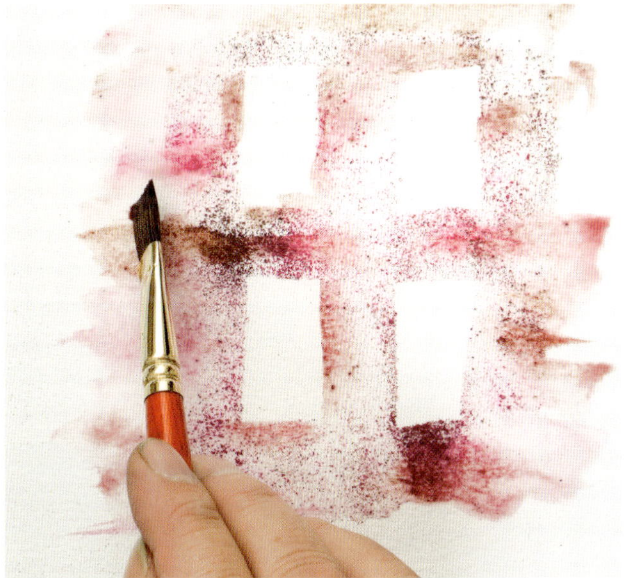

3 ADD WATER TO BLUR COLOURS

When the pigment is dry, you can blend or soften the effect by working over it with a wet brush. This will often give changes in colour as the pigment dries in thinner layers. Be warned; this technique is addictive. I know several people in my groups who make complete paintings in this way. They get through a lot of sandpaper!

QUICK & CLEVER DRAWING

A LITTLE CORNER OF VENICE

I hope you've had a bit of fun practising the techniques; now you're going to start using them! The image is based on several photographs that I took while on a trip to Venice, combined together to produce an interesting composition. The overall impression of the photos is one of complexity, so our first job is to simplify.

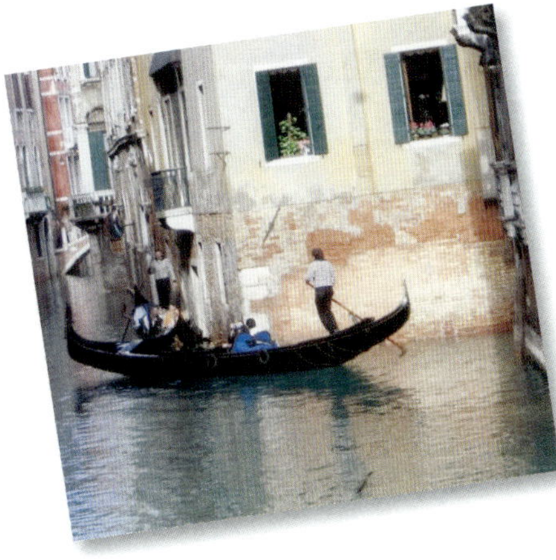

One of these photographs has a complete gondola, which is a nice shape, but the background looks rather dull. Another has nice-looking colours, so we'll combine the two to make a good drawing. Placing the gondola so it's coming into the image, not going out of it, will make it look more attractive.

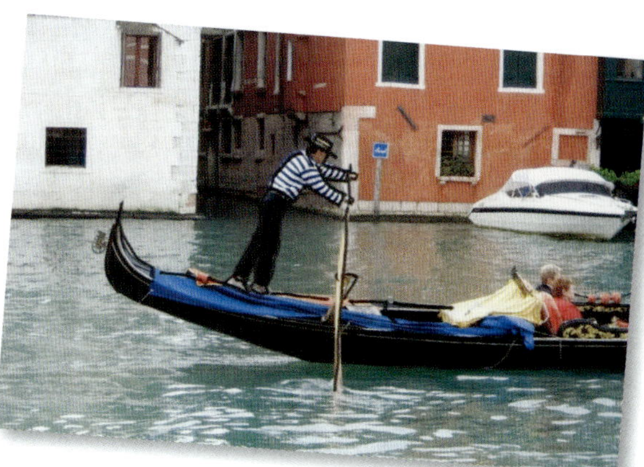

1 START WITH A SKETCH

Do a thumbnail sketch (remember those?) to plan the drawing. It shouldn't be detailed, or too big. This is not far from actual size. Don't skip this bit! It's only by planning our work that we know how to proceed. Divide the sketch into four sections with guide marks, to help with enlarging.

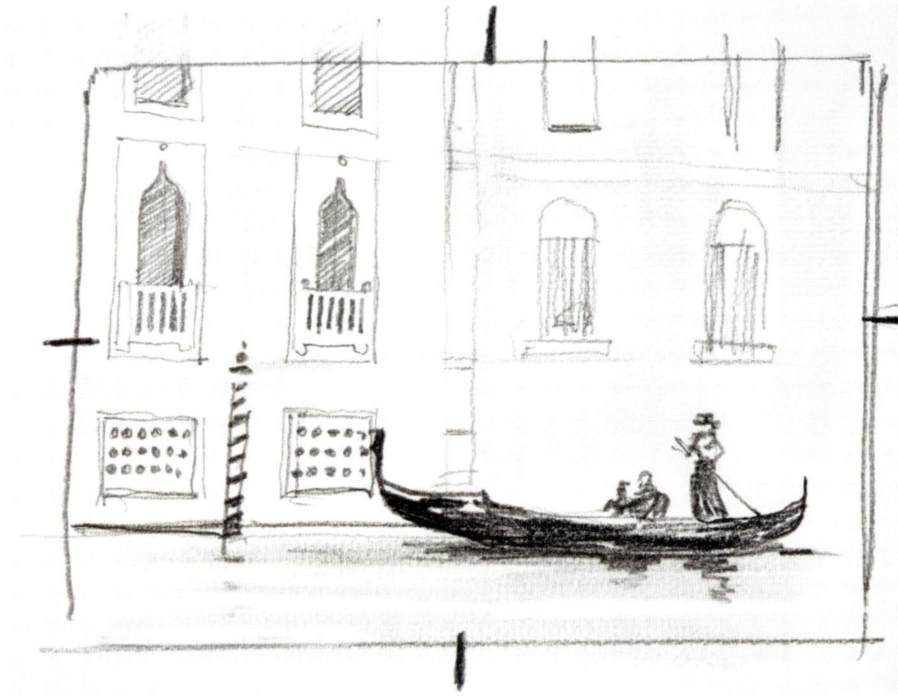

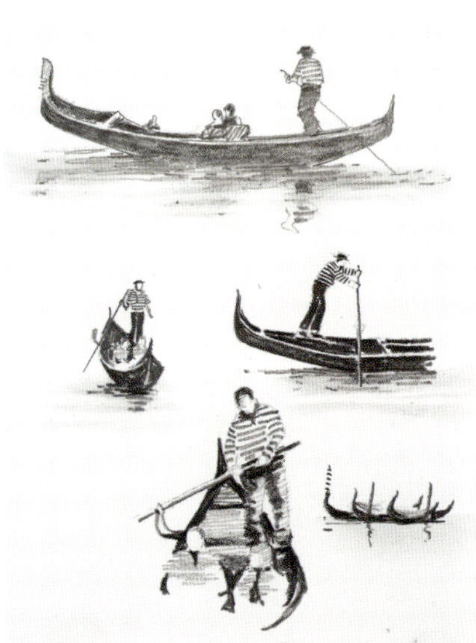

2 PRACTISE SOME GONDOLAS

Before proceeding, it's worth practising some gondolas on a separate piece of paper. Do several, like this, and see which looks best. If you like one, but maybe it's too small for the larger drawing you are going to do, don't worry; simply scan or photocopy it and enlarge it to the size you want. Then you can trace it out. Lots of illustrators work like this.

3 DRAW IN GUIDELINES

Using the thumbnail sketch as a guide, draw the image onto a piece of watercolour paper with a 2B pencil. Use light pressure and faint lines. If it helps, you can draw a simple grid first (see page 59 if you've forgotten how).

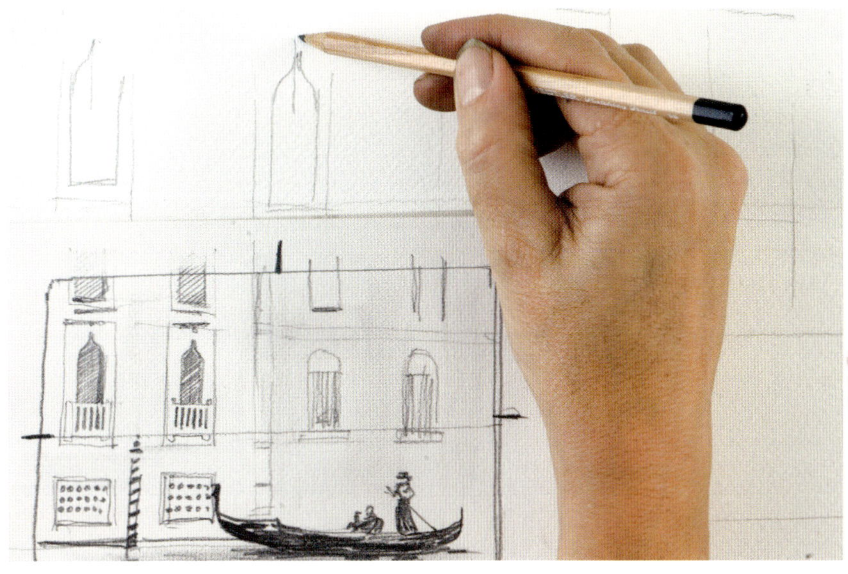

4 SKETCH IN SOME WINDOW SHAPES

Keep the pressure light, and draw simple lines. Don't try to put everything in; detail will come later. While doing the enlarging I decided that the stripy mooring pole to the left didn't add anything to the composition, so I left it out. Feel free to put it in if you want.

5 TRANSFER YOUR GONDOLA TRACING

If you've made a gondola tracing, here's an easy way to transfer it. Turn it over and use the 2B pencil to scribble on the back, covering the image. (Don't rest it on the drawing in progress to do this; it will transfer lines.) Scribble dense lines of graphite, with no gaps.

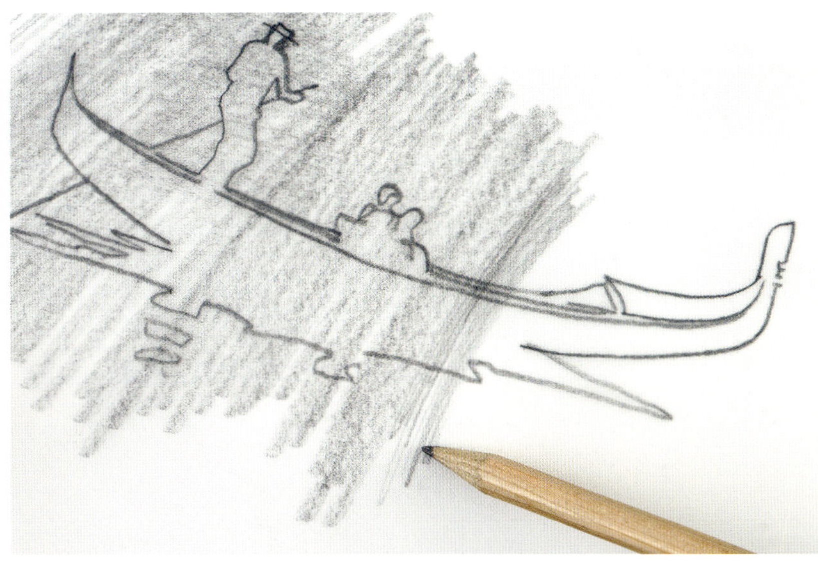

6 DRAW OVER THE OUTLINE

Place the tracing where you want the gondola to be, scribble side down, taking care not to put it right in the middle (you don't want to be boring, remember). Then, holding the tracing firmly so it doesn't move, draw over the lines of the gondola again, with firm pressure.

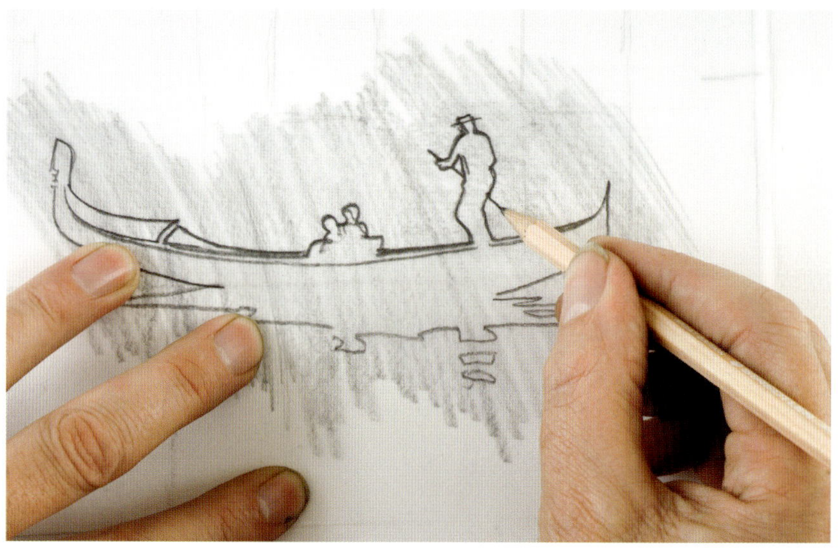

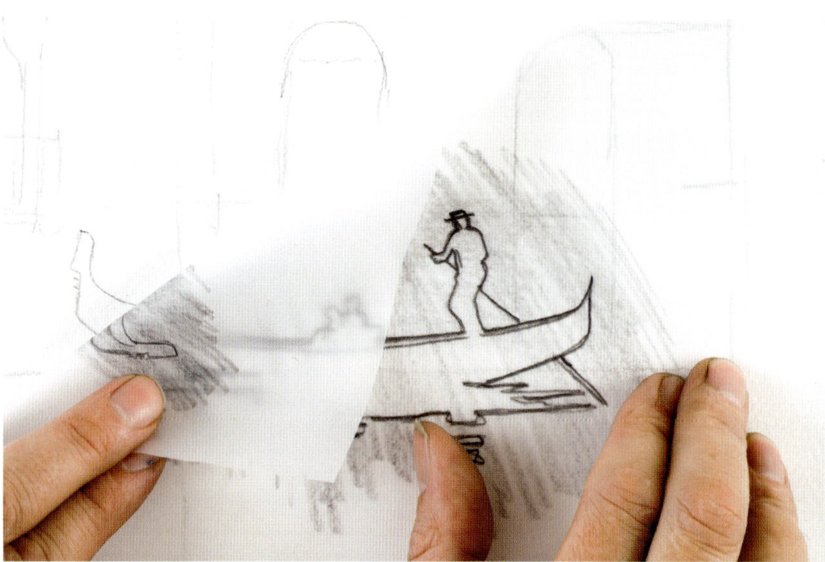

7 CHECK TRACING

If you need to check on the progress of your tracing, carefully lift one side while making sure that the paper doesn't move. If it does, you'll end up with several gondolas!

8 COMPLETED SKETCH

The next step involves adding colour, so take some time now to check that everything in the drawing is OK; it will be difficult to change once you start using watercolour pencils because they aren't easy to rub out.

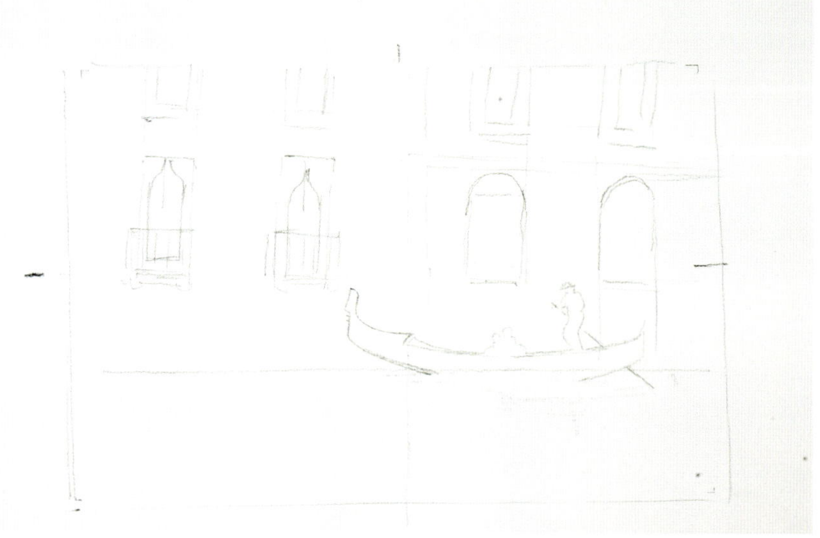

9 ADD COLOUR

Now it gets colourful! Wet all around the windows on the left-hand building with the 13mm (½in) brush. Don't wet the window shapes, the canal or the gondola and figures. Leave some dry irregular shapes at the bottom of the building. Take a Madder Lake watercolour pencil and scribble onto the sandpaper, letting the dust fall onto the left-hand building. Add some Vermilion in the same way.

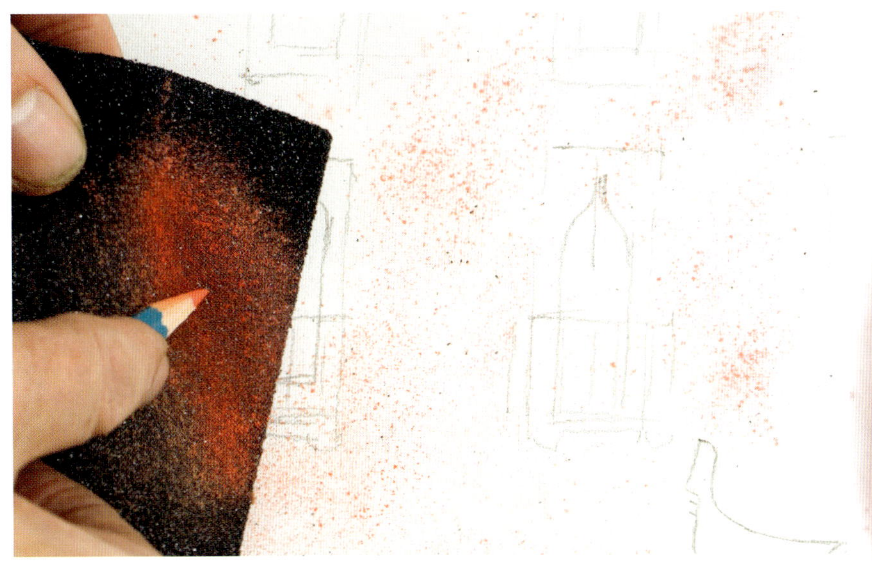

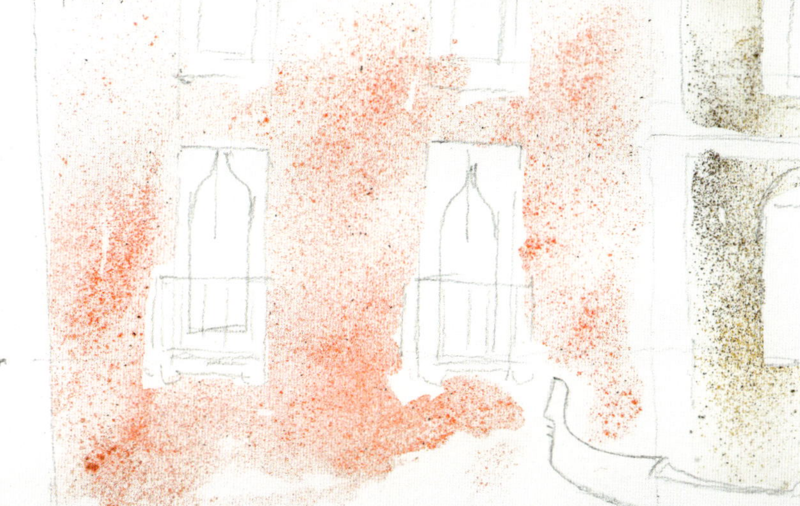

10 BLOW OFF EXCESS DUST

Gently blow off the excess dust, so the speckled image remains. If your image is not defined enough, you didn't use enough dust; add more water and do more scribbling until you're happy with it.

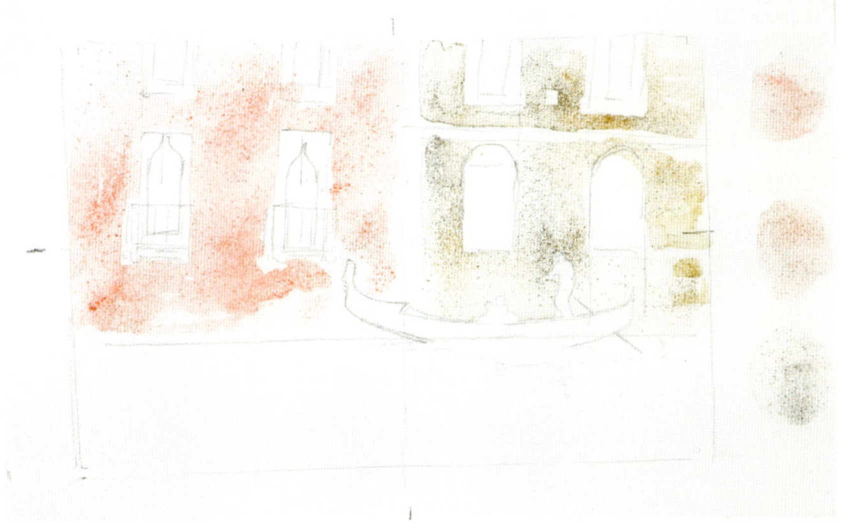

11 REPEAT TECHNIQUE

Use the same wetting-and-scribbling-on-sandpaper technique (I really must invent a name for this!) for the rest of the buildings. Remember not to cover any windows or figures with water; carefully paint round them. Use Vandyke Brown and Raw Sienna; you can try the colours using a piece of scrap paper, or on the side of the image, as I've done here.

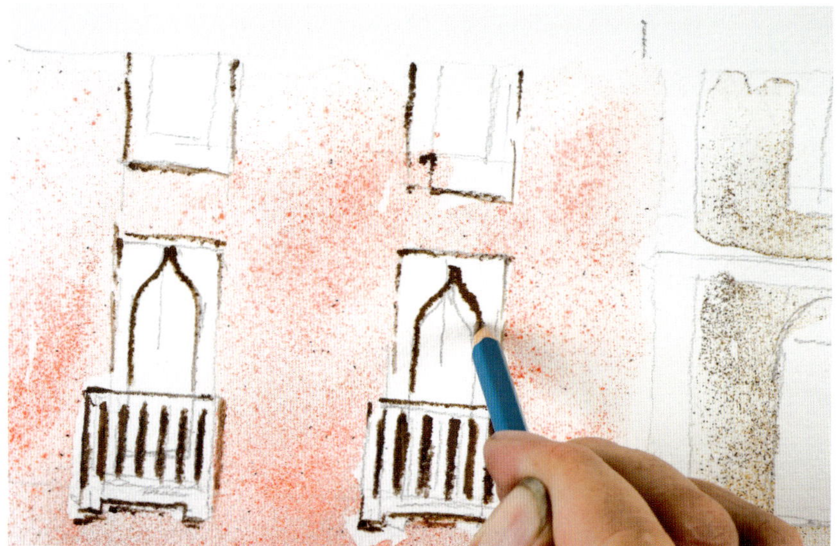

12 OUTLINE WINDOWS

Use Vandyke Brown pencil dipped in water to give a strong outline to the building detail. Define the windows, and place some short verticals beneath the windows in the pink building to make the balconies. To create an old, weathered look, it's best to avoid straight, heavy lines.

13 DRAW CRUMBLING PLASTER

At this stage you should be developing a textural look to the buildings, with some definition on the windows. Don't worry if your lines are a bit wobbly; so are many Venetian buildings! Use Vandyke Brown to show the edges of some of the crumbling plaster.

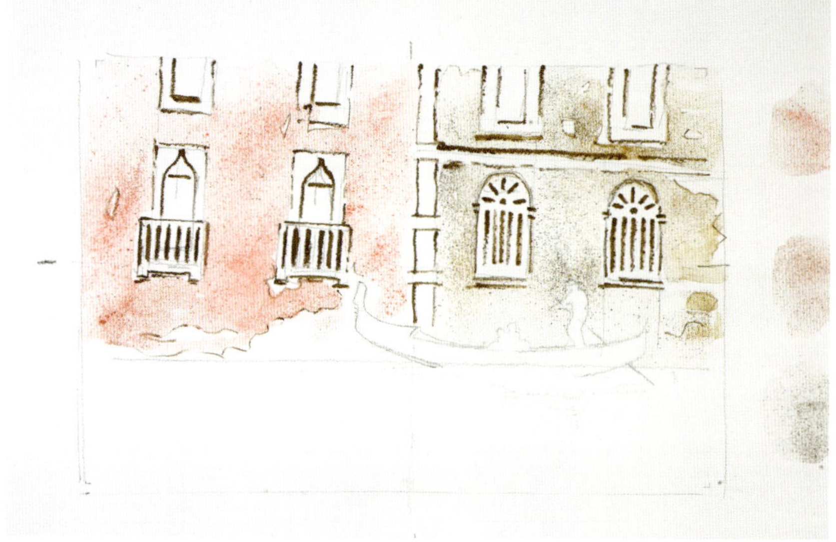

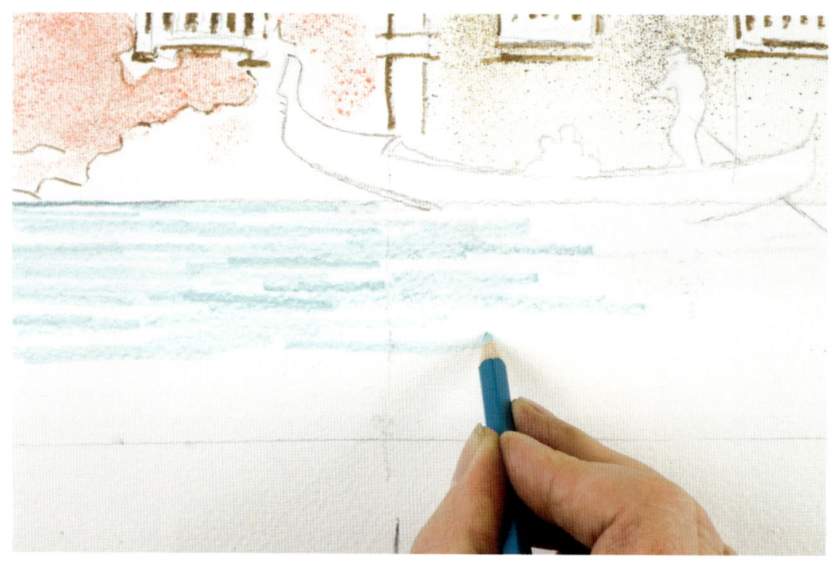

14 APPLY WATER STROKES

Apply short horizontal strokes of Kingfisher Blue, Turquoise and Jade Green for the water. Leave plenty of gaps; you can add more later, and you'll need some white paper to apply the reflected building colour on.

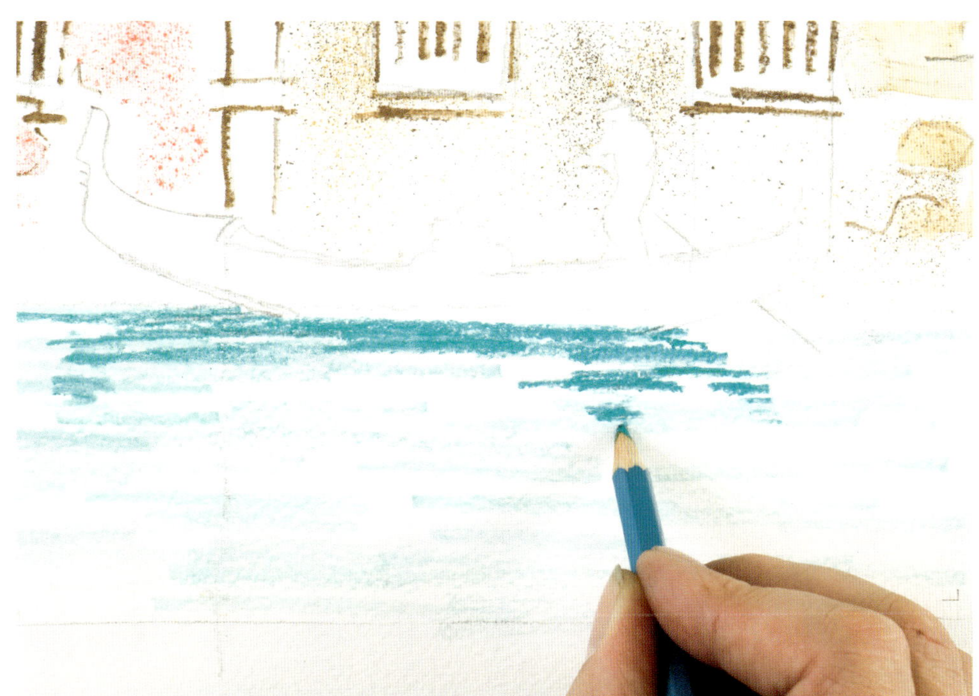

15 INDICATE THE SHADOWS OF THE GONDOLA

Use Jade Green dipped in water for a stronger application of colour under the gondola. This will become the shadow of the gondola. Sometimes it's easier to apply shadows and reflections first and then put the object causing them in afterwards.

16 BLOCK IN THE WINDOWS

Add some Kingfisher Blue to the shutters along the first-floor windows. Using similar colours throughout a drawing imparts a sense of unity.

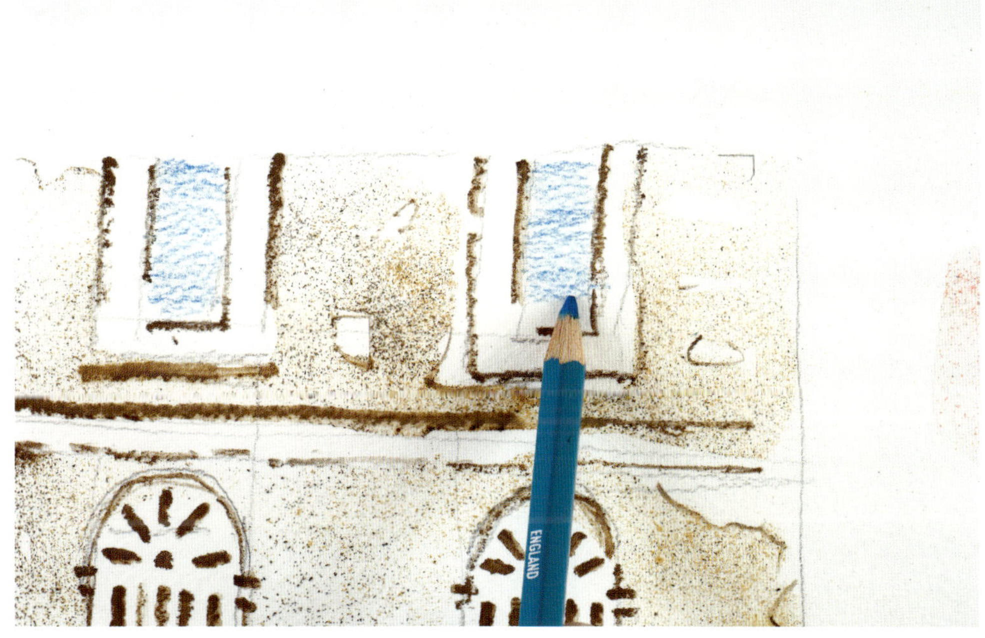

17 ADD REFLECTIONS OF THE BUILDINGS

Take some Madder Lake and use it dry for the reflections on the left. Add the colour to the white paper between the blues and greens. Repeat with Raw Sienna in the water beneath the other buildings.

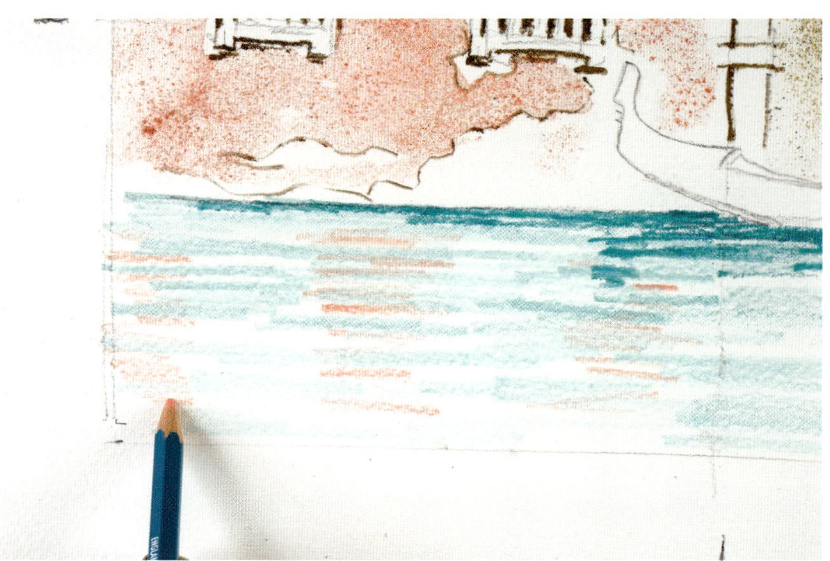

18 BLOCK IN THE GONDOLA

Use an Indigo pencil to block in the gondola. Leave some thin lines to show the edge of the boat. Add a few horizontal touches of this colour to the shadow under the gondola to tie the shadow in; this makes the boat appear to float on the water. (If you don't have Indigo, use Black.)

19 DRAW IN THE GONDOLIER

Sharpen the Indigo pencil to a fine point, then dip it into some water. Use this to draw the gondolier. Practise first on a separate piece of paper. You can show his shirt by simply drawing in the stripes. Be careful; don't make the head too big. Put the oar in, using the same colour.

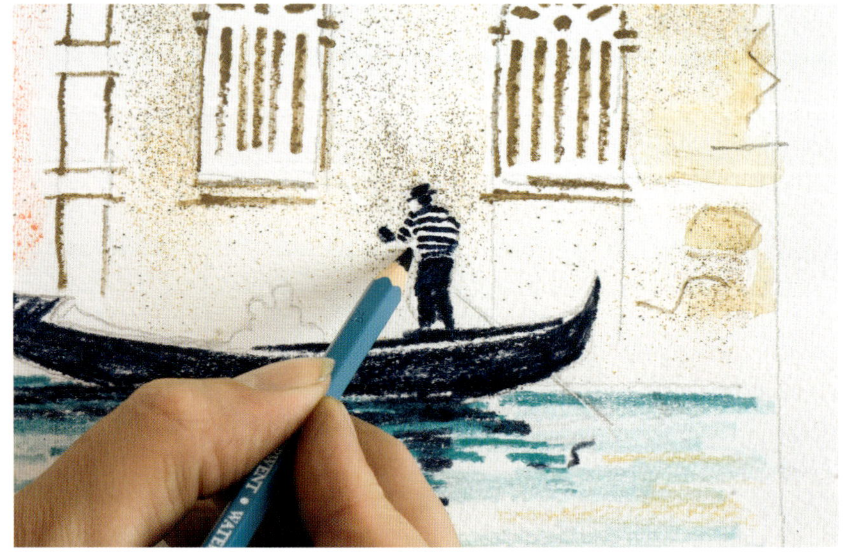

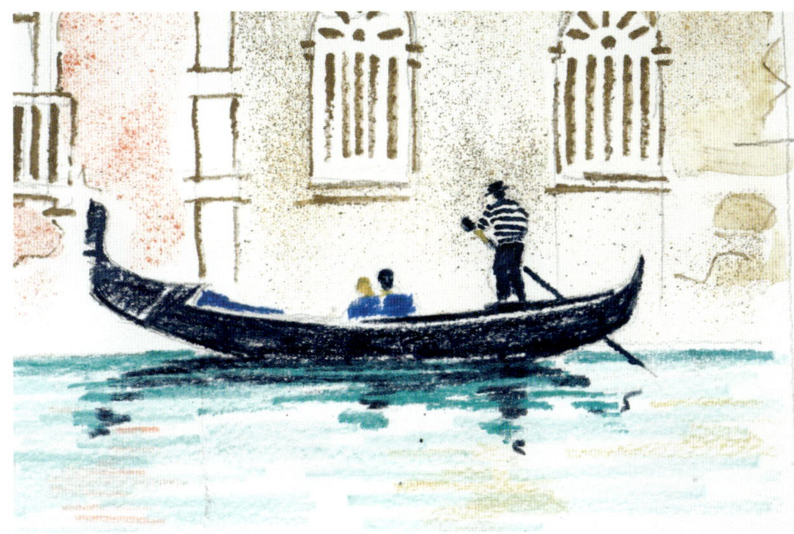

20 ADD THE PASSENGERS

Take a Spectrum Blue and draw in the seats and the blue section at the front. Use Indigo to apply one of the passenger's heads, and Raw Sienna the other. Once again, guard against making the heads too big; it's a common error!

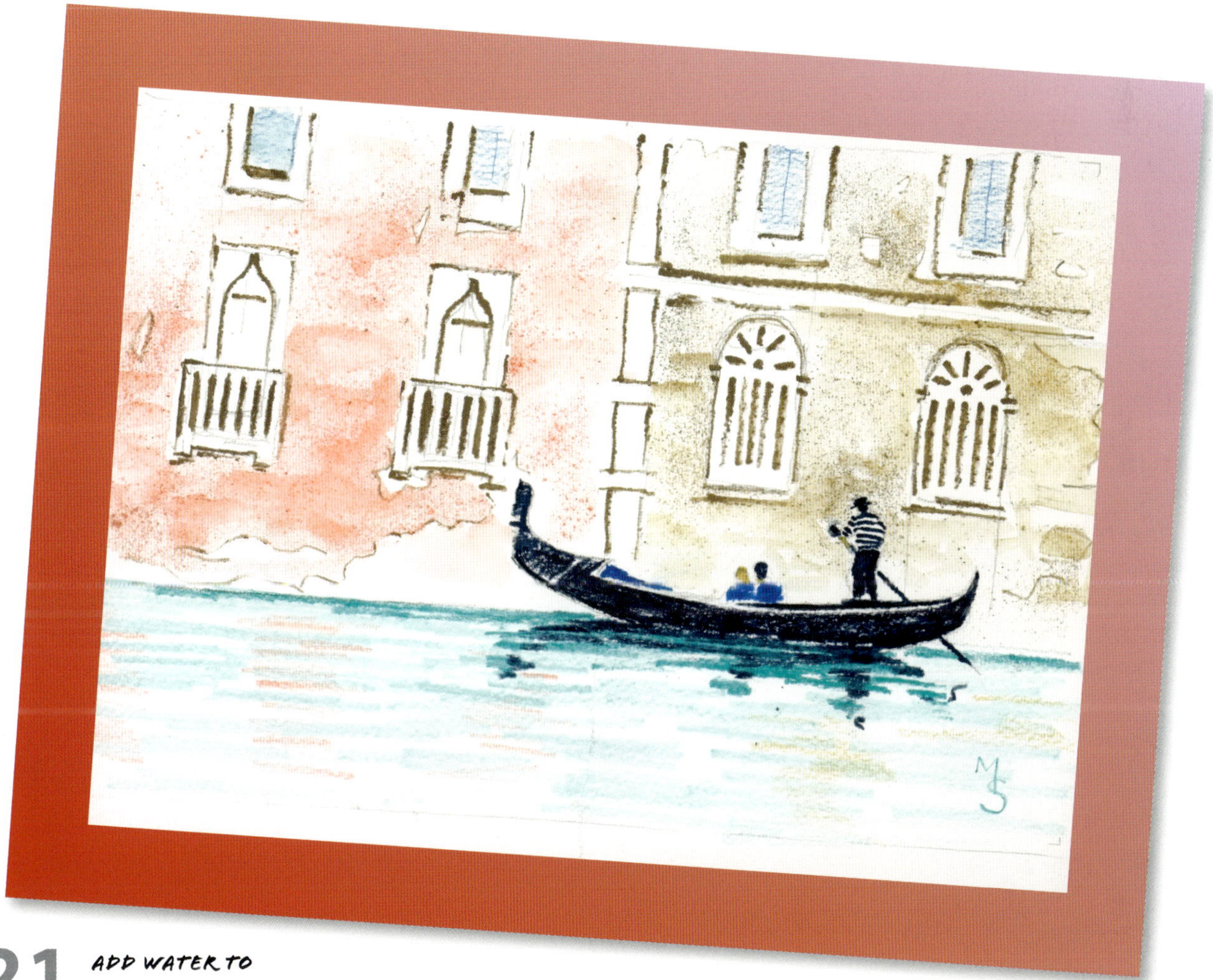

21 ADD WATER TO SPECKLED COLOUR

Adding a few brushstrokes of water to the buildings here and there gives an irregular brick or stone effect, especially if a 13mm (½in) brush is used. The image is light and the texture adds a weathered look.

PROJECT 5

QUICK & CLEVER

SPANISH SCENE

This subject is from an area of Spain I've drawn and painted often. High in the foothills of the Pyrenees, the monastery of St Pere de Rodes stands remote and solitary. Reached via a turning and twisting road, the buildings encapsulate more than 1,500 years of history. This image is of one corner and features the medieval church associated with the now-derelict village. It's always a popular spot with any art groups I bring here, and is a very good subject for pen drawing. Working in pen encourages the artist to be bold, once they overcome the nerves of making a start! So, before you make a start on this pen project, some practice would come in useful. Try some of the exercises: building texture with pen, and enhancing pen with colour.

YOU WILL NEED:

Watercolour paper
Brown or sepia waterproof drawing pen
Watercolour pencils: see swatch below right
No. 10 synthetic sable watercolour brush
Pencil sharpener
Board to rest on
Note: I used Inktense pencils from Derwent (Cumberland Pencil Company). Other makes may use different names, so use the closest you have to the colours shown on the swatch

HIGH IN THE PYRENEES

(SEE PAGE 105)

One of the easiest ways of making a drawing that has 'depth' is to put blues into the background and warm colours like reds in the foreground. This image is quite simple to do. It combines pen and watercolour pencils, and you will be able to see how the blue distance recedes and the red poppies look close. Have a go at the preliminary techniques before tackling this drawing.

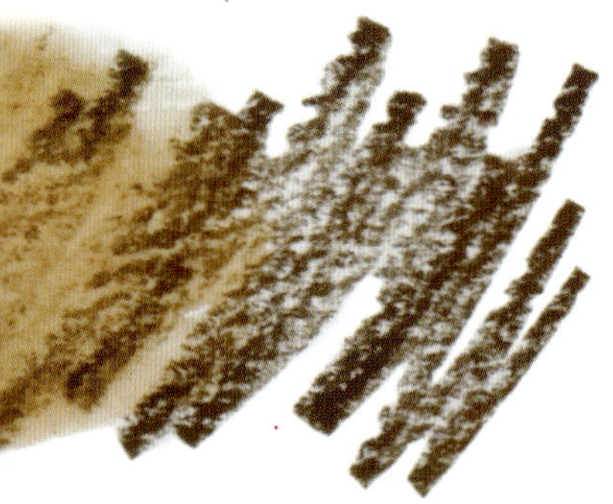

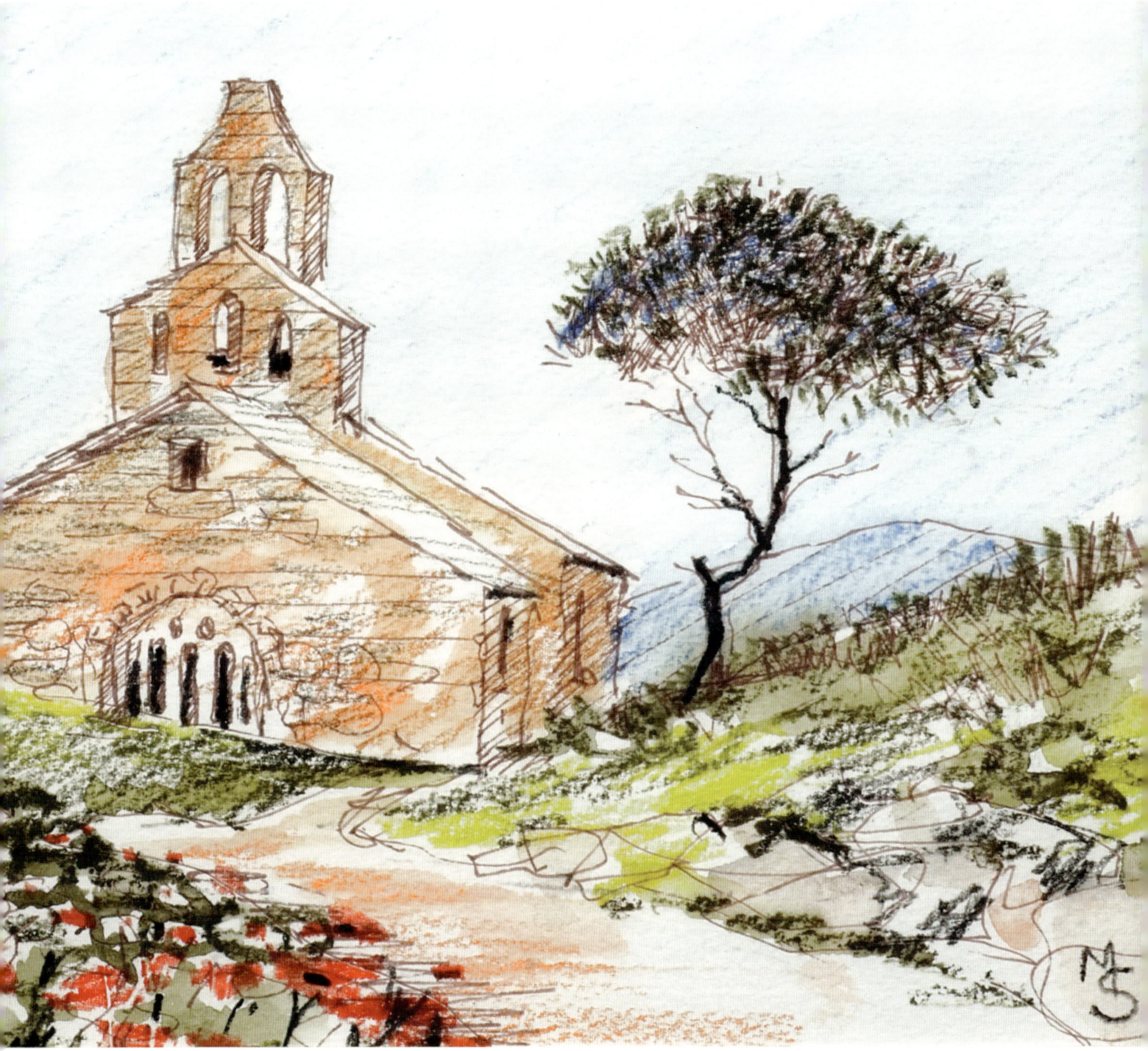

WATERCOLOUR PENCILS:

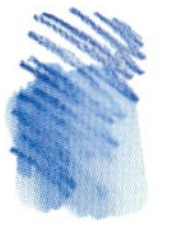
Iris Blue

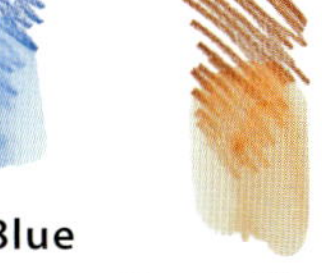
Burnt Sienna

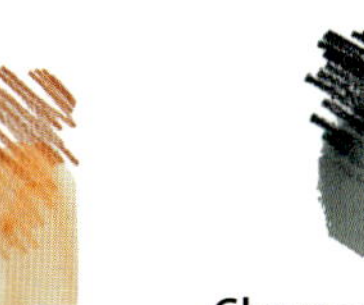
Charcoal Grey

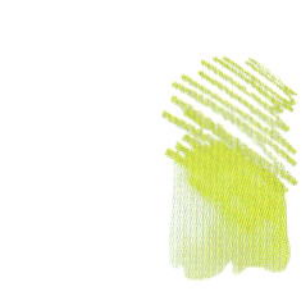
Lemon Yellow

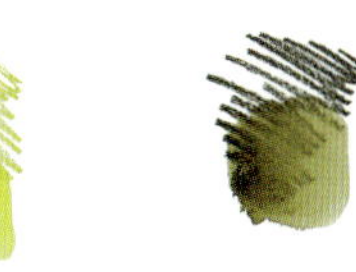
Leaf Green

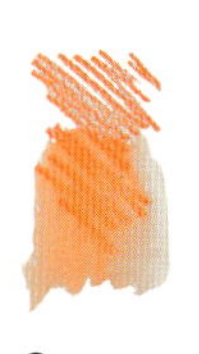
Orange

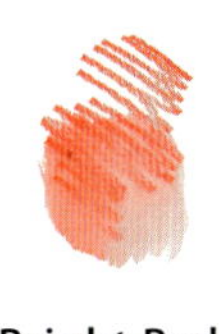
Bright Red

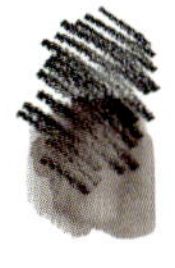
Burnt Umber

TECHNIQUE – BUILDING UP TEXTURE WITH A PEN

A drawing pen produces a unique look. With practice you will become familiar with a variety of drawing pens and what they can achieve. Unlike pencils, the pressure on the pen doesn't really change the eventual tone. For example, if you scribble hard with a pencil, the lines will make a darker area. With a pen (at least with a ballpoint or fibre-tip), the line remains the same however hard you press. So, in order to make areas darker, you have to put more lines in. These lines can be applied in a variety of ways to imply different textures. Experiment with some of these marks to see which suits your subject best. Let's look at foreground rocks and shrubs.

SHARP LINES

▶ *Sharp angular lines that criss-cross give a solid, sharp stone or rocky look. Add more lines on one side to impart shadows. Shadows will make your drawings look three-dimensional. Make sure that all the shadows are on the same side, otherwise your image won't look real.*

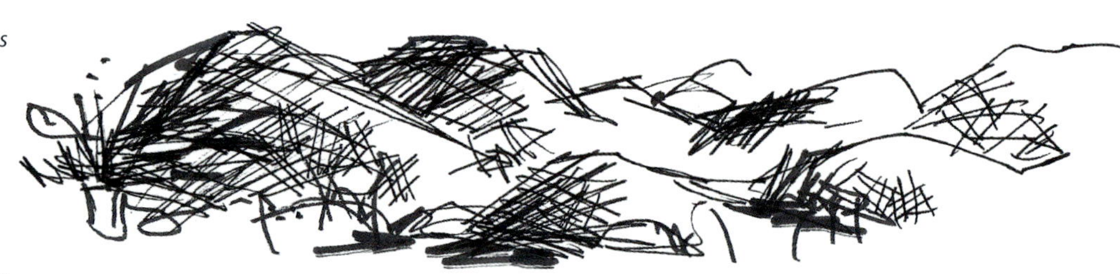

CURVED LINES

▶ *Curved lines give an appearance of weathered boulders, dry-stone walls and pebbles. Short curved verticals around the bases give the impression of grass. Remember, the further away the stones are, the smaller they appear to be. Diagonal lines superimposed on the curved ones will add shadows on one side.*

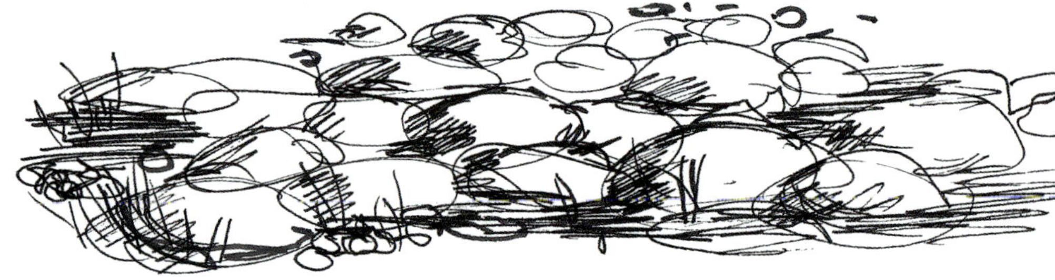

IRREGULAR SCRIBBLES

▶ *Tight, irregular scribble shapes are useful for applying dense foliage, especially if interspersed with dots or short dashes to look like individual leaves. Scribble more on one side than the other, and at the base, to give a shadow effect. Where there are gaps, draw in some branches; thicker at the bottom and thinner higher up.*

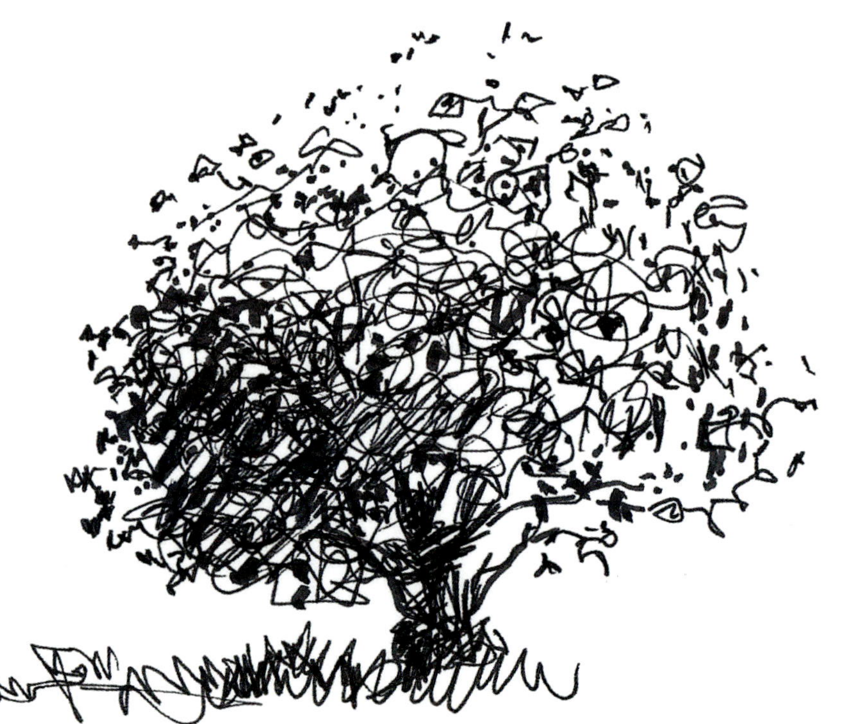

TECHNIQUE – TRANSFERING PERSPECTIVE LINES

Sometimes, when drawing from a photograph, angles on buildings are difficult to judge. Here is a method that I use often. It's simple to do, uses no maths or complicated techniques, and is pretty accurate. All you need are two straight edges. Here I've used a couple of pencils.

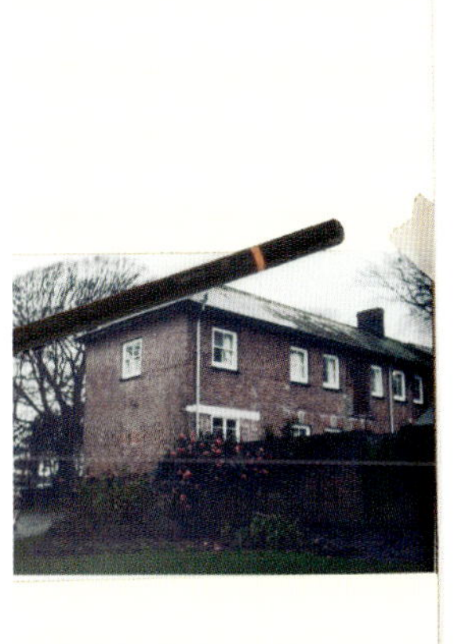

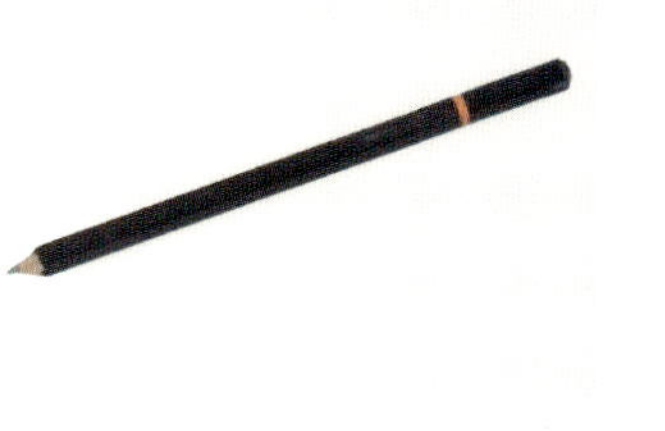

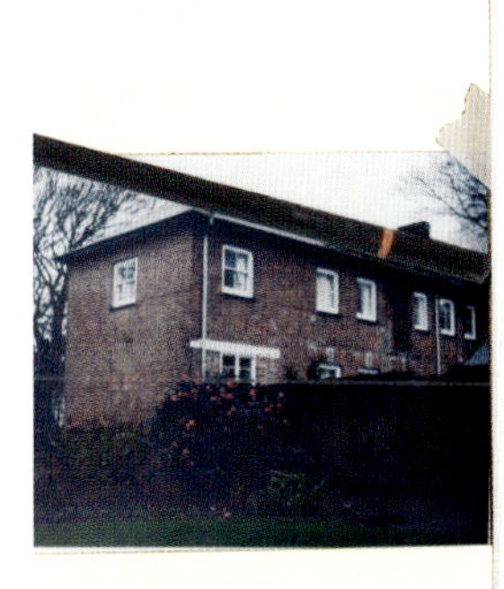

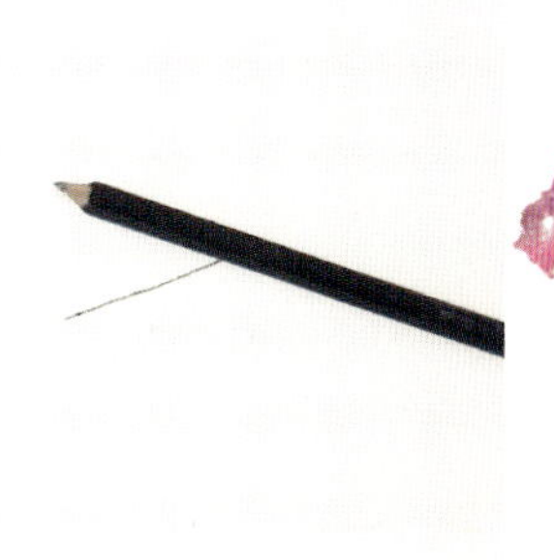

1 CREATE THE ROOFLINE
Put a straight edge along an edge on the building in the photo. I have started with the edge of the roof. Now, place your other straight edge on the paper, where you want to draw the building, ***so the two straight edges are parallel***. The pencil on the photo is at the same angle as the pencil on the pad. Can you see that? Draw a line at this angle on the paper.

2 ADD THE SECOND STRAIGHT EDGE
Next, put your straight edge along another part of the roof. Again, looking down from above, place your second straight edge ***parallel to the one on the photo***. Make sure you do not move the photo or the sketchpad. Can you see that my pencils are parallel? Excellent! Now draw that angle on the paper.

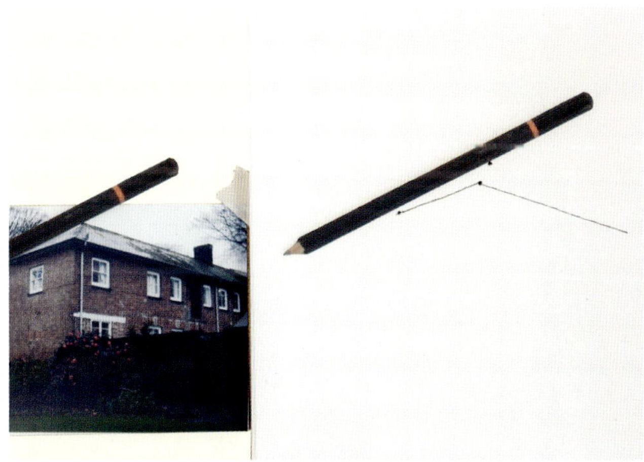

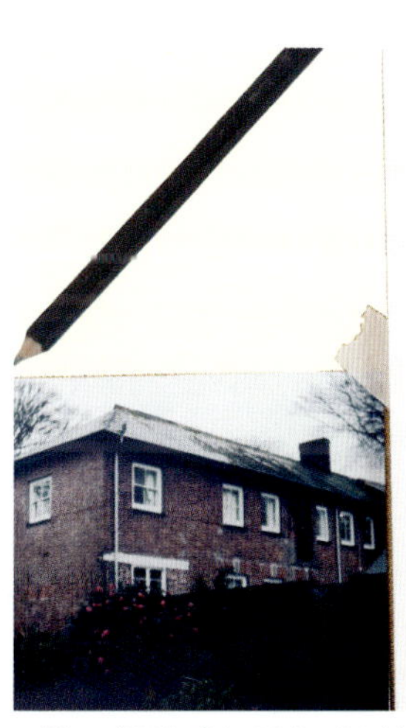

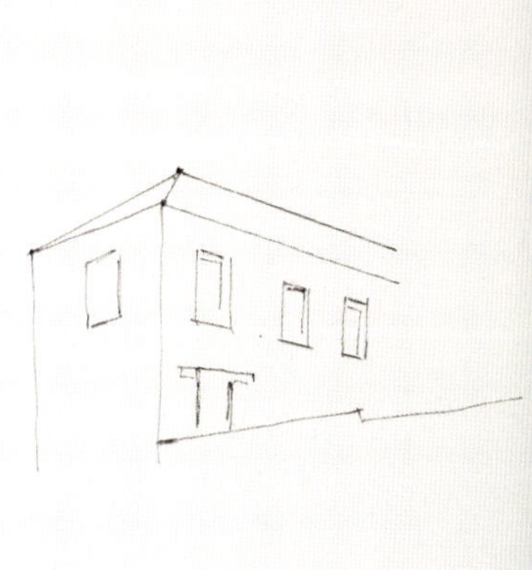

3 ADD FURTHER ANGLES
I shall do the smaller end section of roof next, and by then you will have the hang of it. ***Can you see the pencils are parallel?*** Well done.

4 THE FINAL TOUCH
I have done a bit more, using the method to get the angles of the tops and bottoms of the windows, and the top of the wall. Now find a photo of your own, and follow the steps for your own image. You will see that it is not as difficult as you probably first thought.

TECHNIQUE – USING TEXTURE AND TONE TO ENHANCE A LINE DRAWING

Old buildings work especially well with line and colour, especially if the lines used are not too straight; if you have a shaky hand, this is the subject for you! Broken and wobbly lines add a more spontaneous look, too.

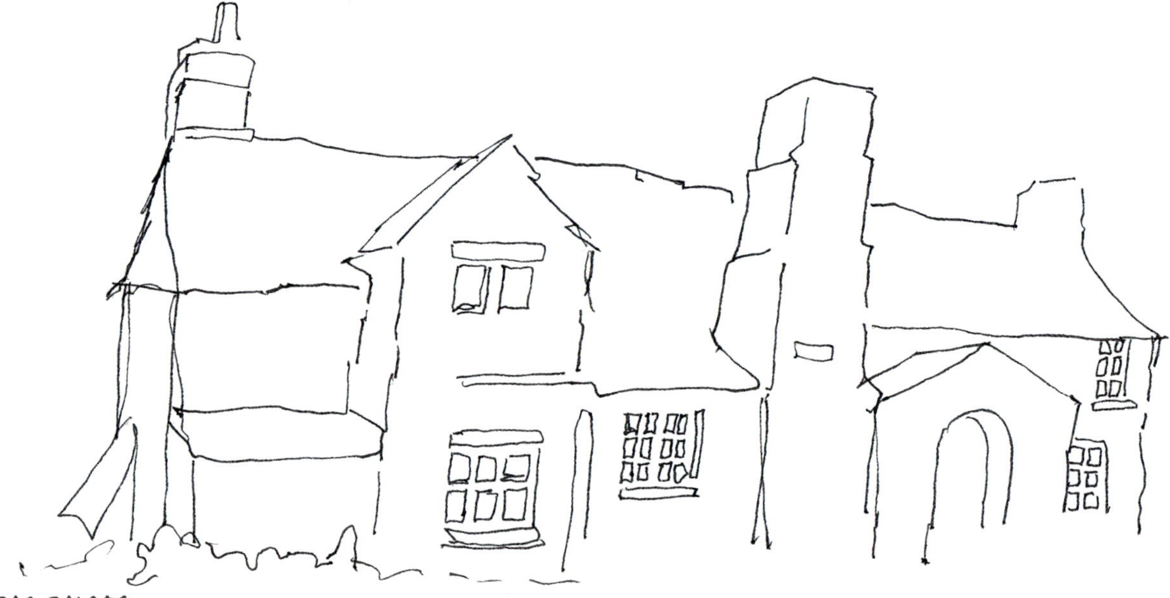

BASIC SHAPE

▲ *Line on its own can portray the basic shape of the subject, but without adding tone there is no real solidity. Tone is needed to impart form, or the illusion of three dimensions.*

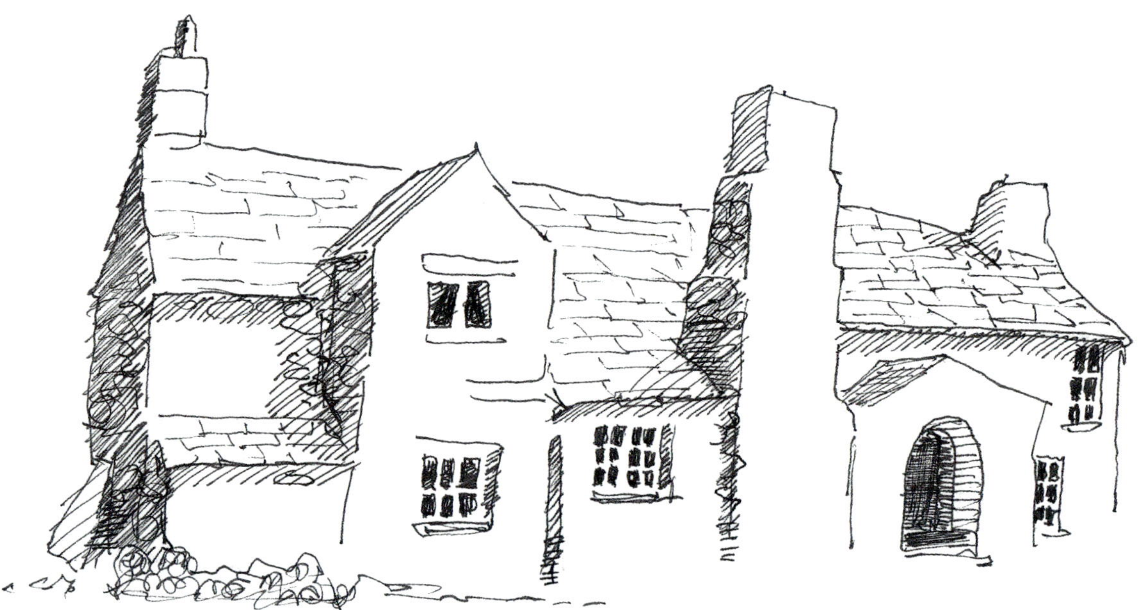

ADDING TEXTURE WITH CROSS-HATCHING

▲ *With a little cross-hatching, the building becomes more believable, and now looks more solid. Further lines have been added to give the subject more texture. Notice how this alters the appearance and changes the mood. Scribbled lines worked over the shadow areas give a feel of rugged stone. Cross-hatching and scribbling are used to good effect.*

TECHNIQUE – USING COLOUR TO ENHANCE A DRAWING

Any drawing that is made with a pen can have colour added to it. The process needs careful planning, because too much colour could spoil a nice, fresh drawing. Often just some light touches are needed.

When colour is added, the three-dimensional look can be enhanced still further. Watercolour pencils can be applied dry, and wetted in certain areas to add to the stony look. Where the pencils are wetted they change colour slightly, which adds to the effect. Notice here how the image, which has been drawn again in brown ink, looks different from the black one on the preceding page.

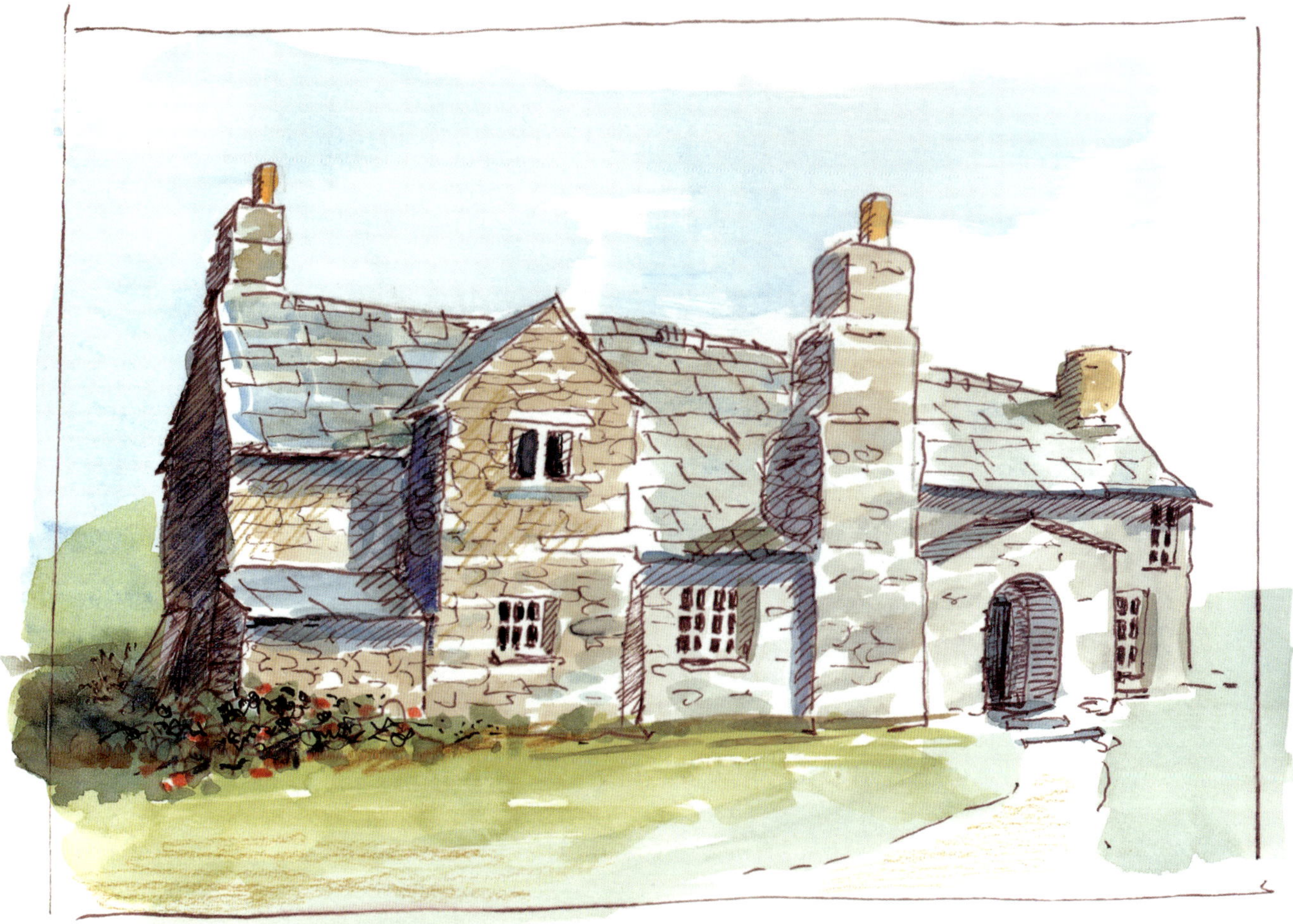

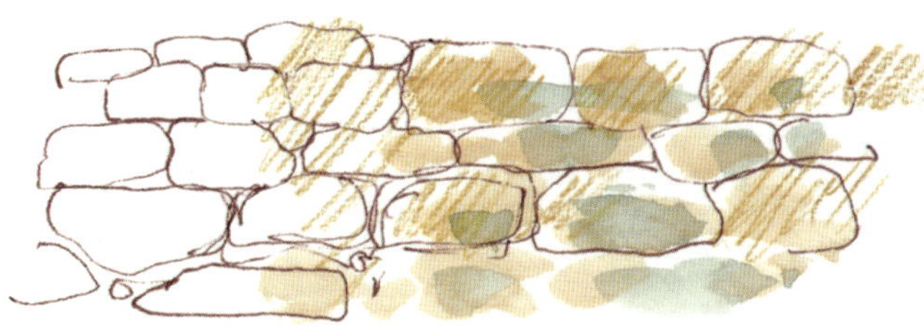

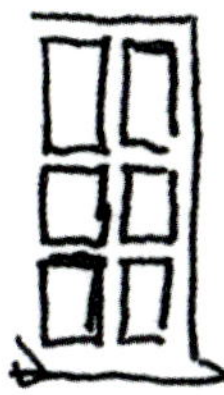

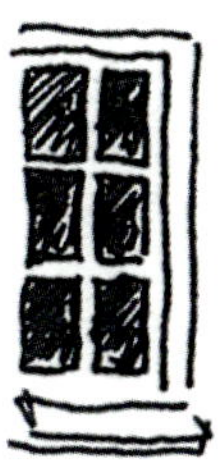

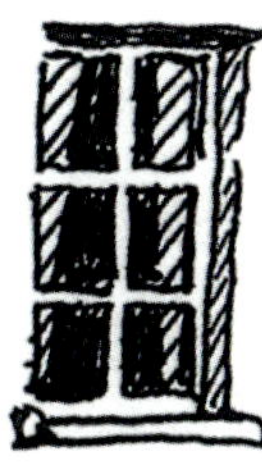

▲ *Stonework can be enhanced by little touches of brown or grey watercolour pencil. When wetted, this looks very effective.*

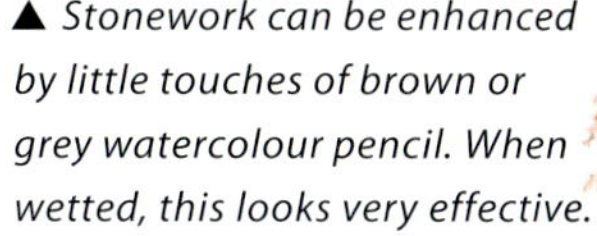

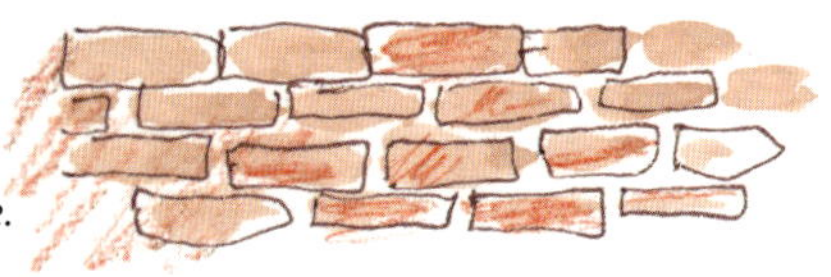

▲ *Windows can be drawn simply. Just draw some rectangles, very close together, and fill them in. The gaps between them will be the window woodwork, so it's important that the gaps are very thin. With practice, you can shade part of the window rectangles with a lighter tone; this will look like curtains when the darker middle part is filled in.*

QUICK & CLEVER DRAWING

HIGH IN THE PYRENEES

I hope you have enjoyed doing some of the practice pen exercises. You are doing the practices, aren't you? Good. Remember; practice makes perfect. The more pen drawings you do, the better you will become. Let's start on the project now, and you can see your new skills being put to good use.

PROJECT 5

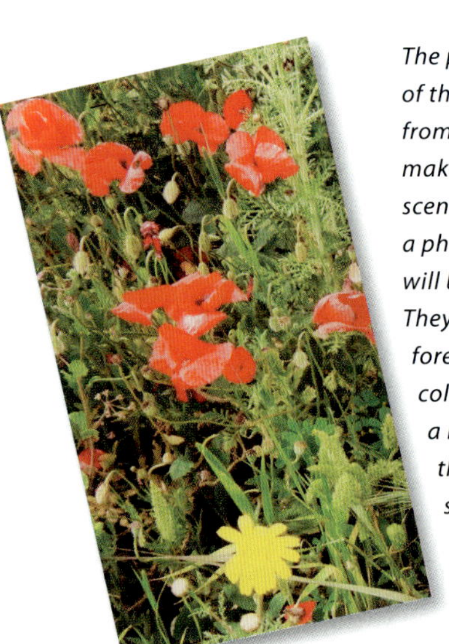

The photo shown right is the view of the corner of the church, taken from slightly above. The tree makes a nice addition to the scene. I've included a portion of a photo of some poppies, which will be used for reference. They will look good in the foreground and add a bit of colour. Now we need to do a little sketch to plan how things will look. Don't skip this bit!

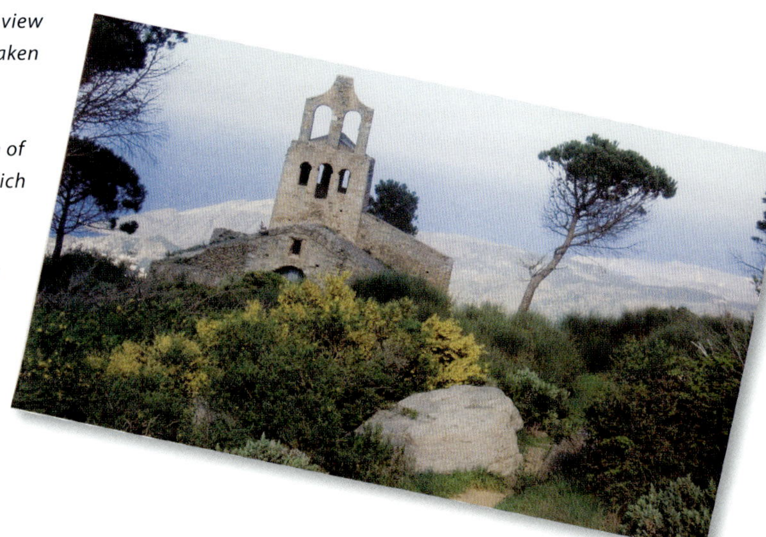

1 PRELIMINARY SKETCH

The thumbnail sketch has been divided into four with a simple grid, and so has the larger piece of paper. Various things have been changed: the tree has been moved nearer the building; the treetop behind the building has been omitted; and a pathway has been added, among other things. Use the simple grid to put in faint guide marks so you know where things go.

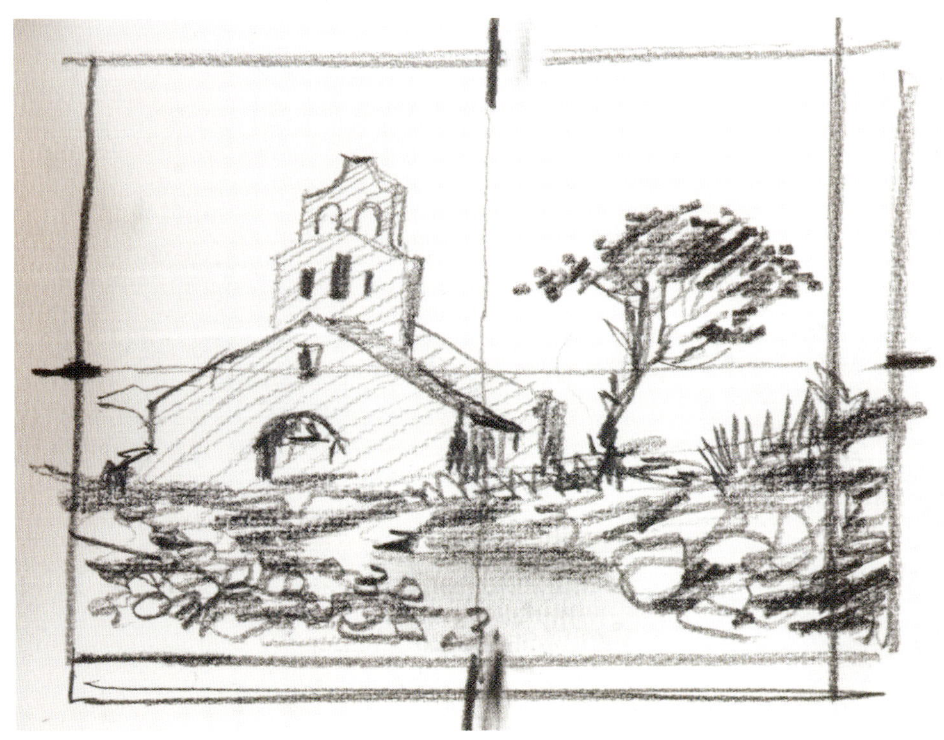

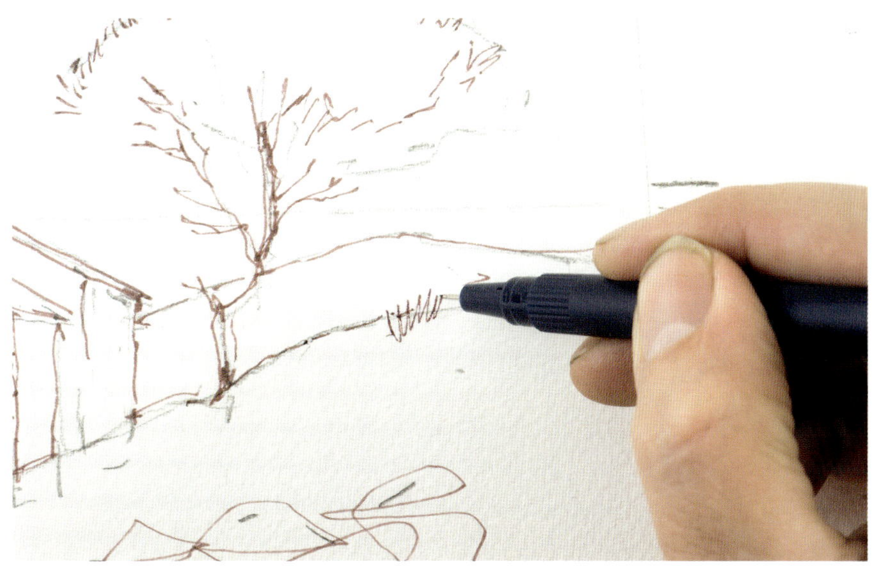

2 PEN DETAIL

Using a brown sketching pen, work over the pencil lines, adding more detail. Broken and wobbly lines on the building look more interesting and authentic than making them too straight and regular. Use simple shapes for the door and windows, and irregular shapes to imply stonework.

3 DON'T ADD TOO MUCH DETAIL!

The basic pen drawing can be quite delicate; it's not necessary to put in too much detail, because colour will be added next, and tone can be included then. The shaded area on the side of the church makes it look more solid, and the lightly drawn stones give stability.

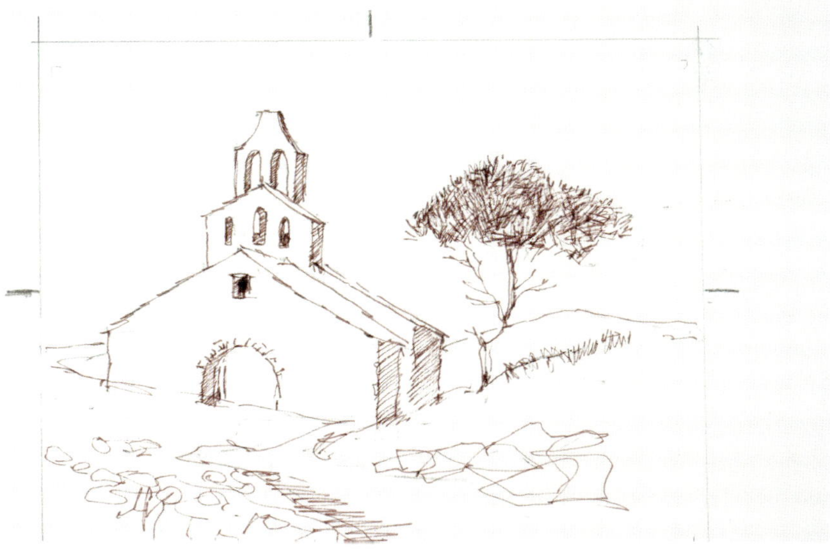

4 START TO SKETCH IN THE SKY

Now we'll add some colour! Take an Iris Blue watercolour pencil and, using light pressure, work some diagonal strokes into the sky. Work over the tree, but leave the building and landscape.

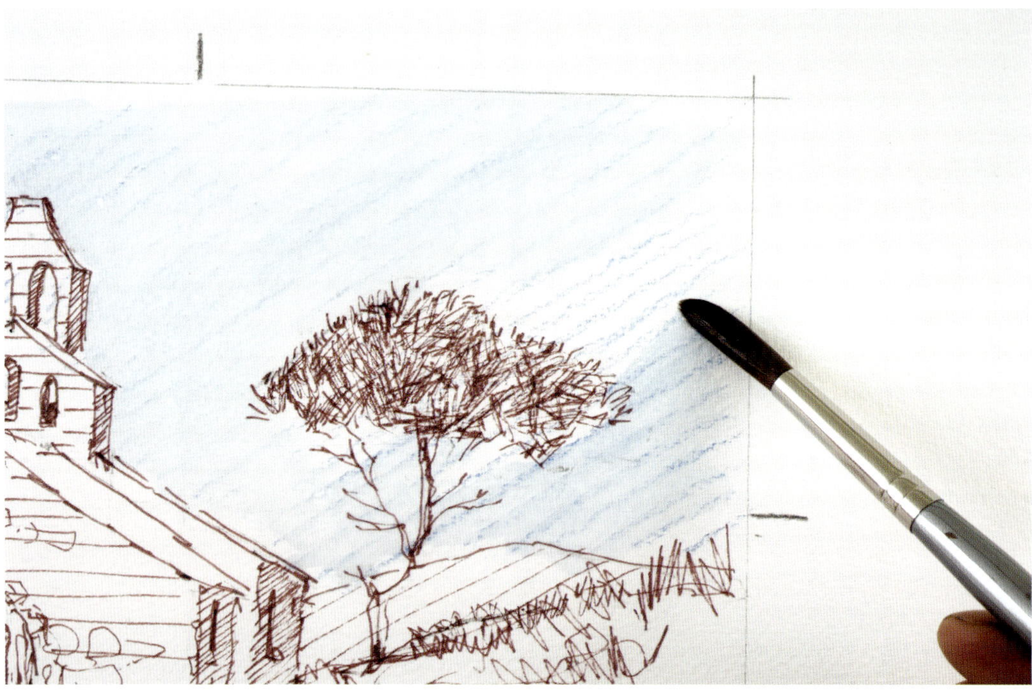

5 ADD WATER TO THE SKY

Use a no. 10 watercolour brush to add water to the sky, working along the diagonal lines to soften them. Then work the other way, across the lines, so they more or less disappear.

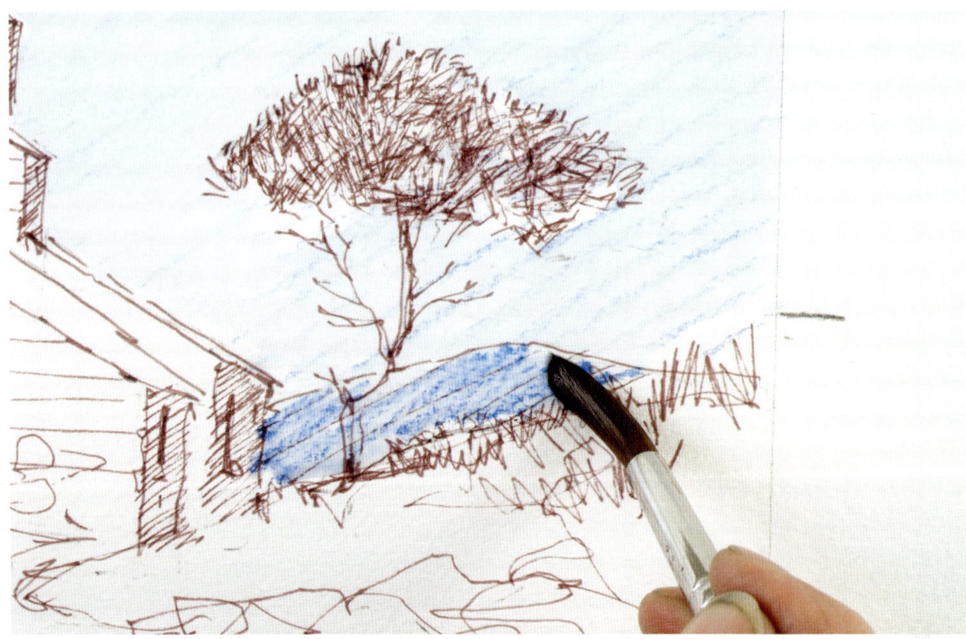

6 ADD COLOUR TO THE HILL

When the sky area is dry, use the same Iris Blue, with firmer pressure, to colour the distant hill on both sides of the building, and then paint water on it, to make a darker blue than the sky. Add a few light touches of this colour to the tree, also.

7 ADD COLOUR TO THE SCRUB AREA

Use Leaf Green, dipped in water for a more intense effect, to add colour to the scrub area to the right and below the church. Add Charcoal Grey, lightly, below the front of the church and to the area of boulders below the scrub.

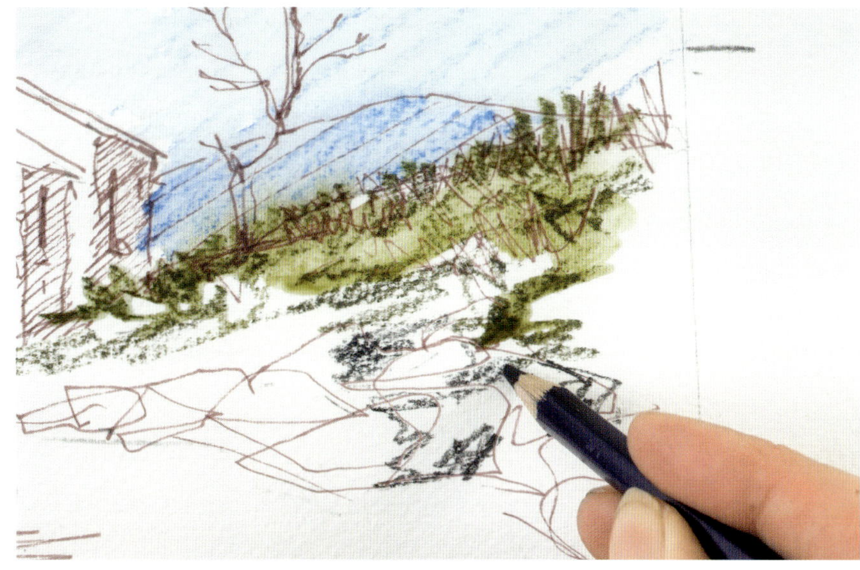

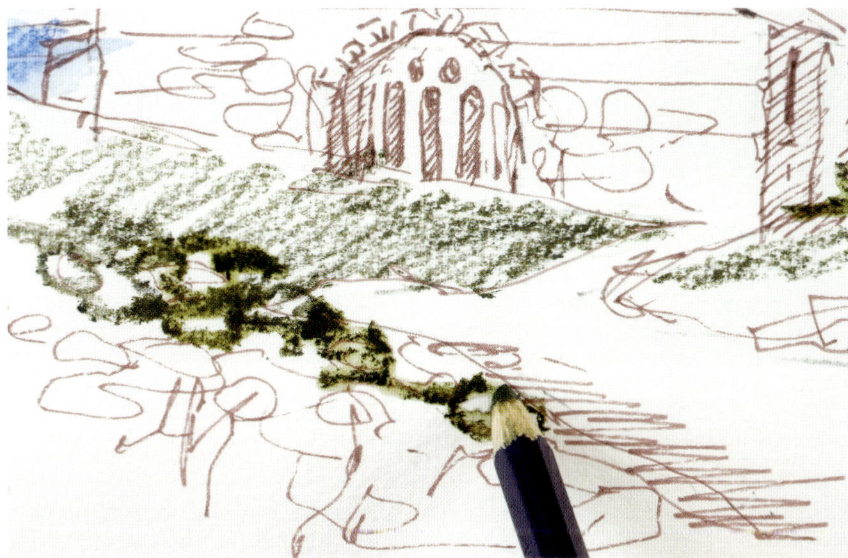

8 DELINEATE FLOWER SHAPES

With a Leaf Green, dipped in water, work around the area where the poppies are going to be, leaving gaps so that the poppies can be applied later. This is a good time to take the pen and add any detail to the church door, also. Set aside to dry.

9 INDENT AREAS FOR STALKS

Use a cocktail stick to indent onto the paper where the poppies are. When colour is applied to this, the indentations will look like stalks. Don't use too much pressure, or you may tear the paper.

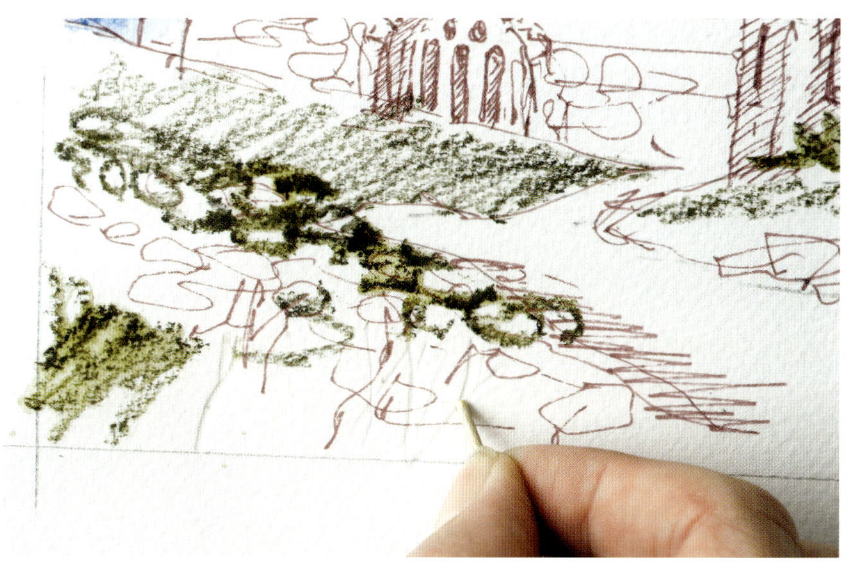

10 LIFT COLOUR OFF THE PENCIL

Lift some colour off the end of the Leaf Green pencil, and use this diluted colour to add to the area below the poppies. This will be paler than the colour applied previously, as it's more dilute.

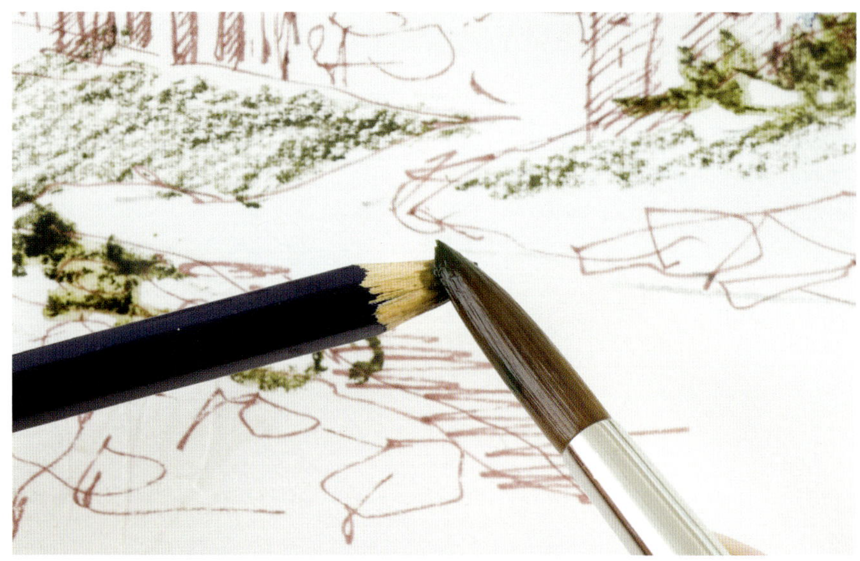

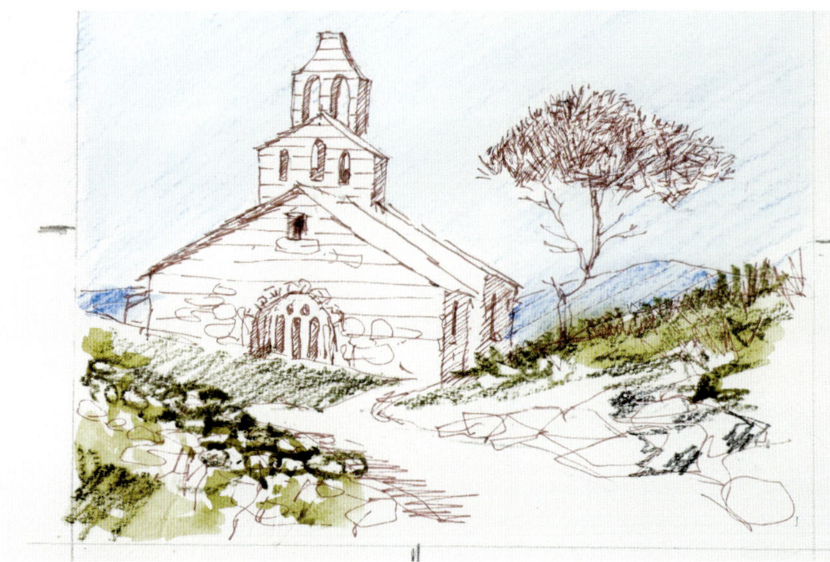

11 TAKE A BREAK!

Have a break now, while things dry. It's important when drawing to sit back regularly and take an overview of how the image looks. This is a good time to go back to the pen and add details that you feel might enhance the image. A touch more detail around the door, some additional stonework on the wall, and so on.

12 ADD LEMON YELLOW

Gently scribble over the scrub area on the right with a Lemon Yellow watercolour pencil, carefully avoiding the rocks near the path. Add some brushstrokes of water here and there to dilute the yellow.

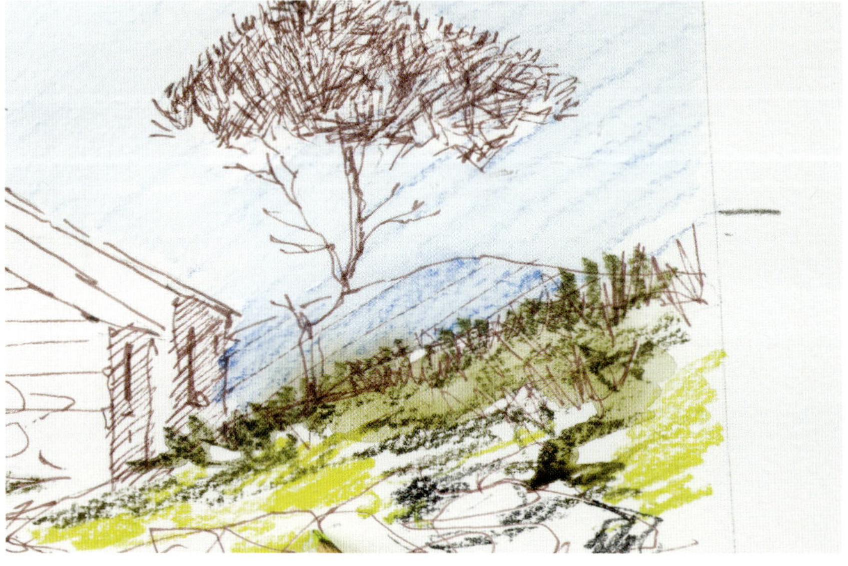

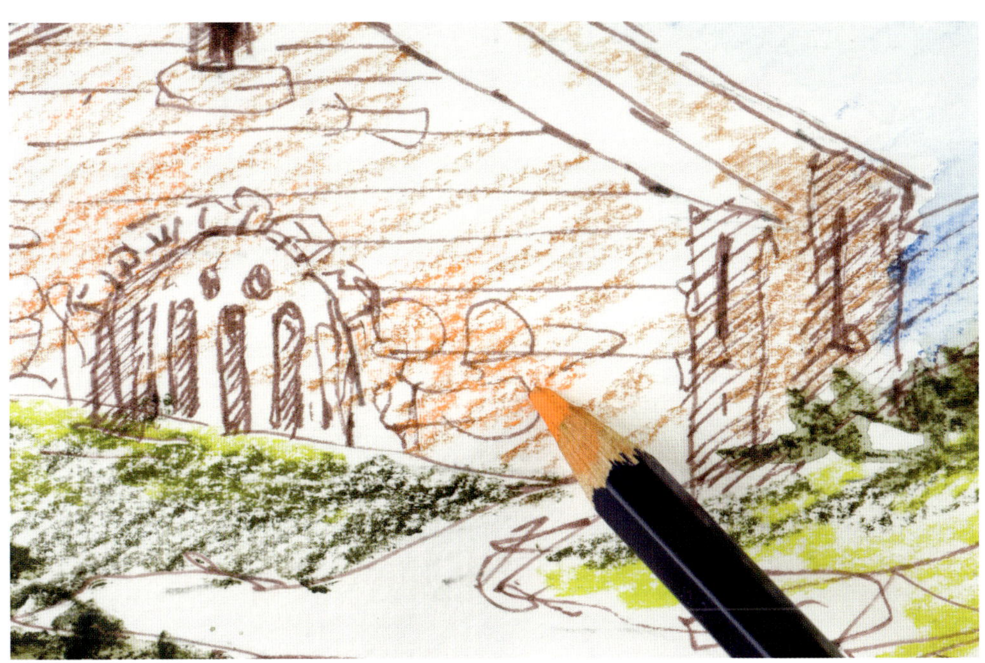

13 ADD ORANGE TO THE CHURCH

Use a Burnt Sienna pencil to stroke some colour onto the church tower and the wall. Be careful that you don't get any on the sky. Take an Orange watercolour pencil and apply a few gentle strokes to the front wall, and some horizontal ones to the path.

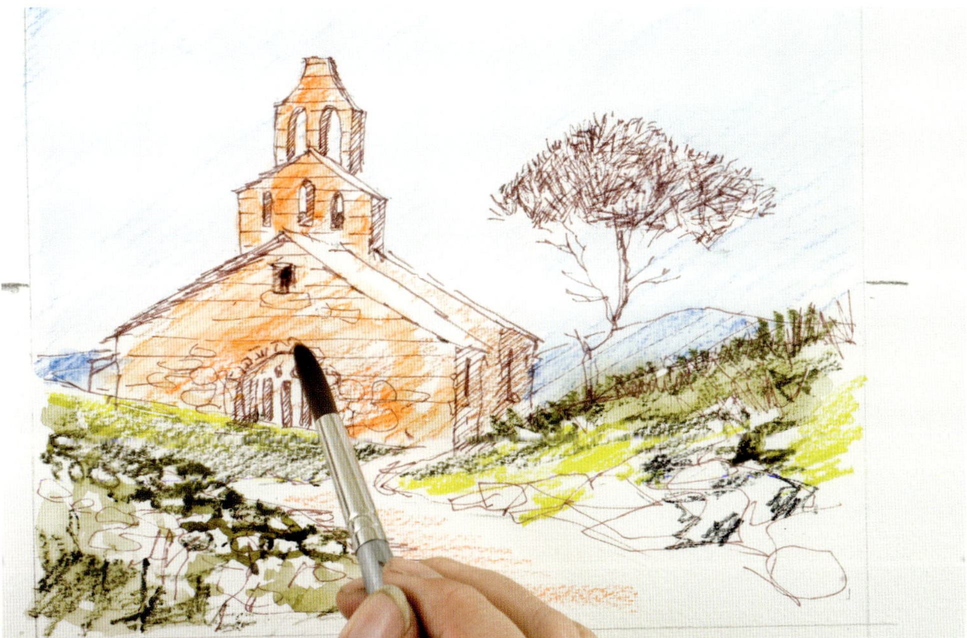

14 BRUSH OVER THE COLOUR

Leaf green is added to the Lemon here and there, on both sides of the path, to impart a greenish tinge. Brush clean water over the building and path; avoid adding too much of this wash on the roof. Leave some of the stones unwetted, to give a textural effect.

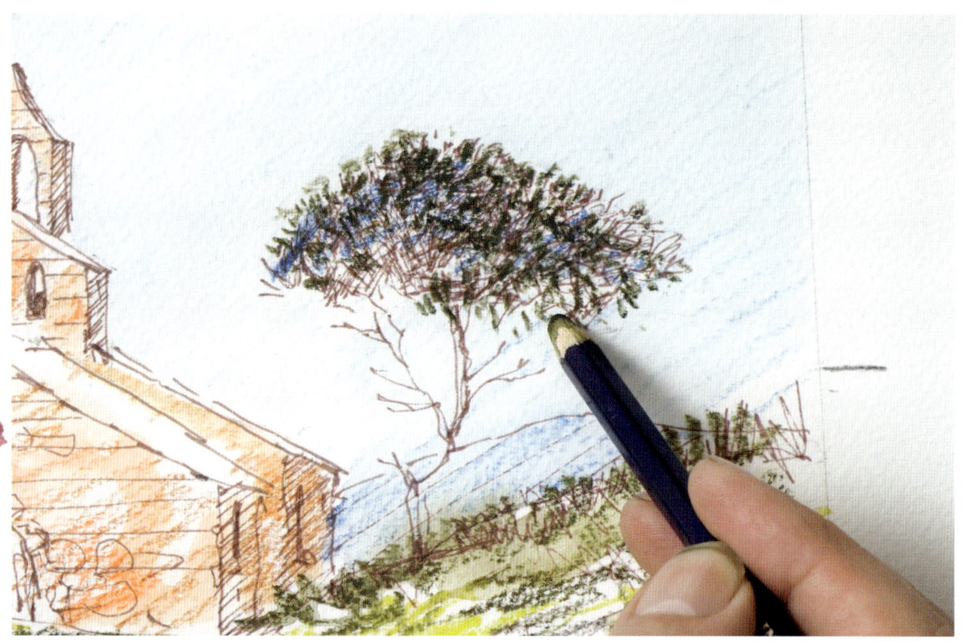

15 STIPPLE LEAF GREEN ON THE TREE

Stipple some Iris Blue onto the tree, using dots and short strokes. Stipple some Leaf Green in the same way.

16 DRAW IN POPPY PETALS

Draw in the poppies with a Bright Red, dipped in water. Overlap some of the red shapes, and avoid making all the blooms the same size and shape; some of the distant ones can simply be dots of red. Add some stalks and dark centres with Burnt Umber.

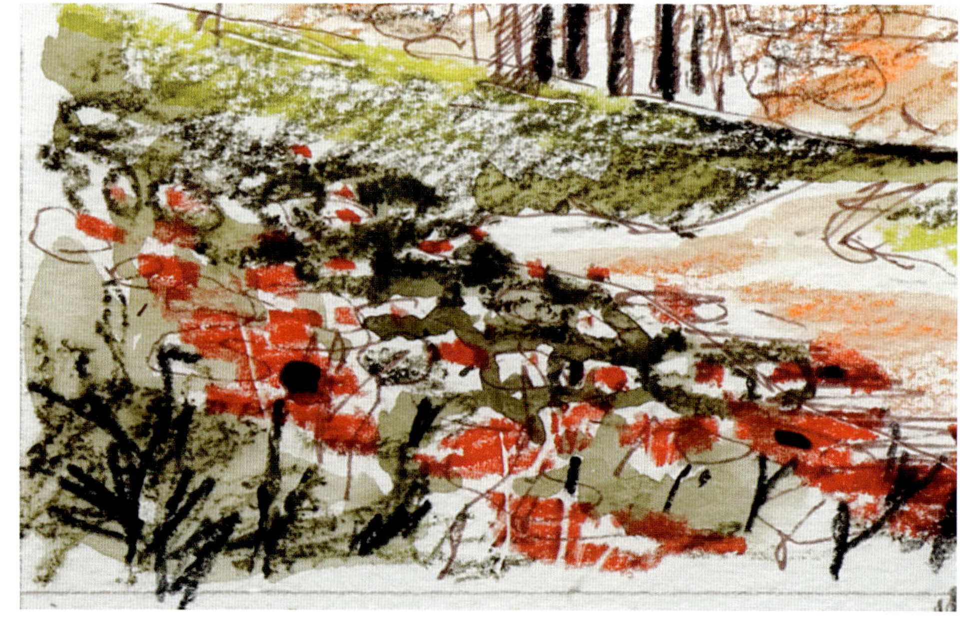

17 ADD STONEWORK EFFECT

Use a Charcoal Grey to gently scribble over the orange front of the building to give more of a stonework effect. Use very light pressure and work on a few of the stones, not all of them, to give an irregular appearance.

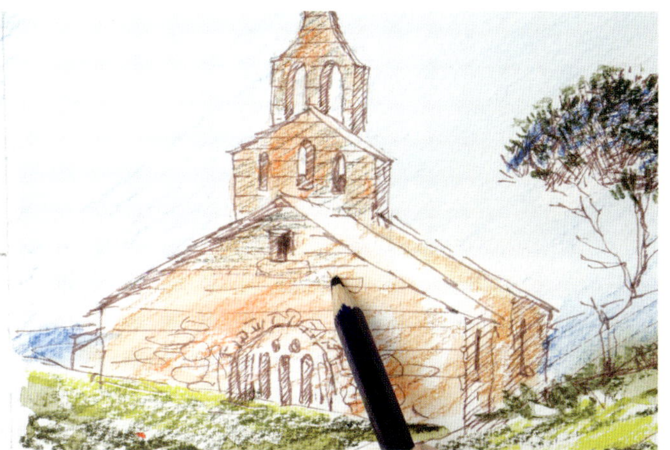

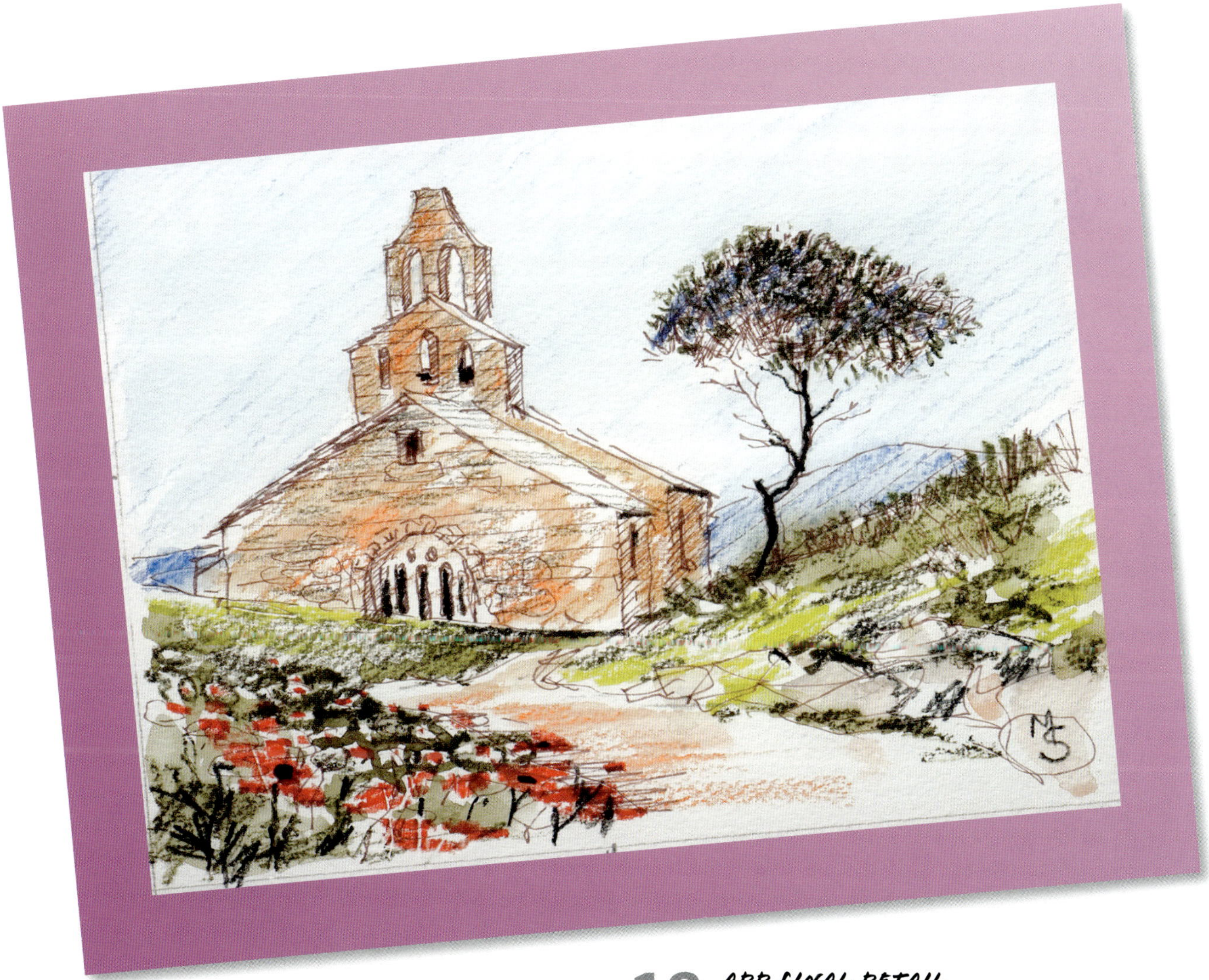

18 ADD FINAL DETAIL

Take a Charcoal Grey dipped in water, to strengthen the shapes of the branches, and add some additional shadows under the tree and beside some of the boulders. The same colour is used dry on the tower and under the gutter, to darken those areas. Now sit back and enjoy the look of a nicely coloured line drawing. Why not try these techniques on your own choice of image next? Remember, old buildings, rocks and landscapes all work well with this method.

PROJECT 6

QUICK & CLEVER PORTRAIT

I've used a combination of pastel pencils and tinted charcoal for this self-portrait. Tinted charcoal is a relatively new drawing medium, and gives a soft, feathery stroke with good blending. If tinted charcoal isn't available in your local art shop, you can use similar colours of pastel pencil. Portraits are one of the most fascinating subjects that you can get involved in! Practising drawing faces can seem very daunting for a beginner – what happens if it doesn't look right; what will the subject (the 'sitter') say; how can you get anyone to sit for you? All of these challenges can be solved if you join the distinguished group of artists who have developed their skills by drawing themselves to create a self-portrait. The term 'self-portrait' conjures up an image of someone sitting immobile in front of a mirror, face fixed in a concentrated expression, but it doesn't have to be like that. I regularly do self-portraits, and often use a photo as reference. This has several advantages: it isn't as tiring as sitting still for a long time; you can be more relaxed; and you can control the lighting for the photo and thus for the portrait.

For this project, you are going to work along with me on a self-portrait. Now, because I don't know what you look like, we're stuck with drawing me. Kim, who did the photography for this book, kindly took a photo of me for us to use. First, let's practise some techniques that you'll find useful. Although we're going to do a portrait, let's have a look at drawing figures; the two are connected, after all!

YOU WILL NEED:

- A set of pastel pencils (some manufacturers produce a set specifically for portraits)
- Tinted charcoal pencils (if you have difficulty finding these, use equivalent colours of pastel pencils)
- A small set of hard (square) pastels
- Soft 4B pencil for drawing onto photo
- Pastel paper; green-grey or similar cool, dark colour
- Torchon or stump, for blending
- Board to rest on
- Sharpener for pastel pencils
- Pair of dividers or compasses
- When you come to do your own self-portrait, a large three-quarter view head-and-shoulders photograph, lit from the side

PORTRAIT OF THE AUTHOR

(SEE PAGE 119)

I used a combination of pastel pencils and tinted charcoal for this self-portrait. Tinted charcoal is a relatively new drawing medium, and gives a soft, feathery stroke with good blending. If tinted charcoal isn't available in your local art shop, you can use similar colours of pastel pencil.

PASTEL PENCILS:

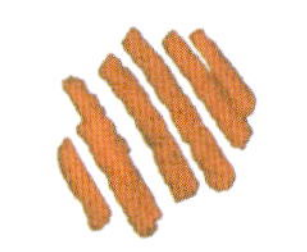

Dark Terracotta

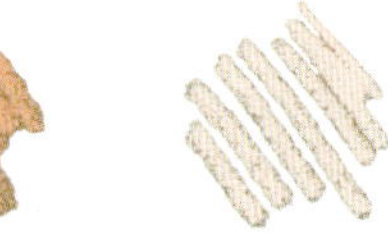

Medium Terracotta

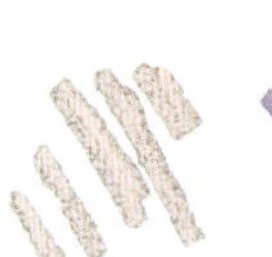

Light Terracotta

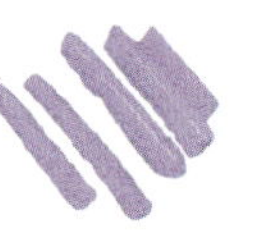

Spectrum Orange

Dark Violet

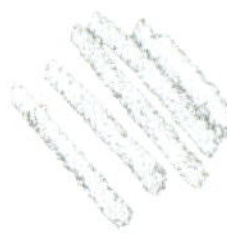

Burnt Carmine

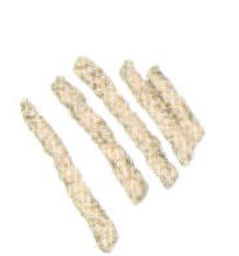

White

Peach

Burnt Umber

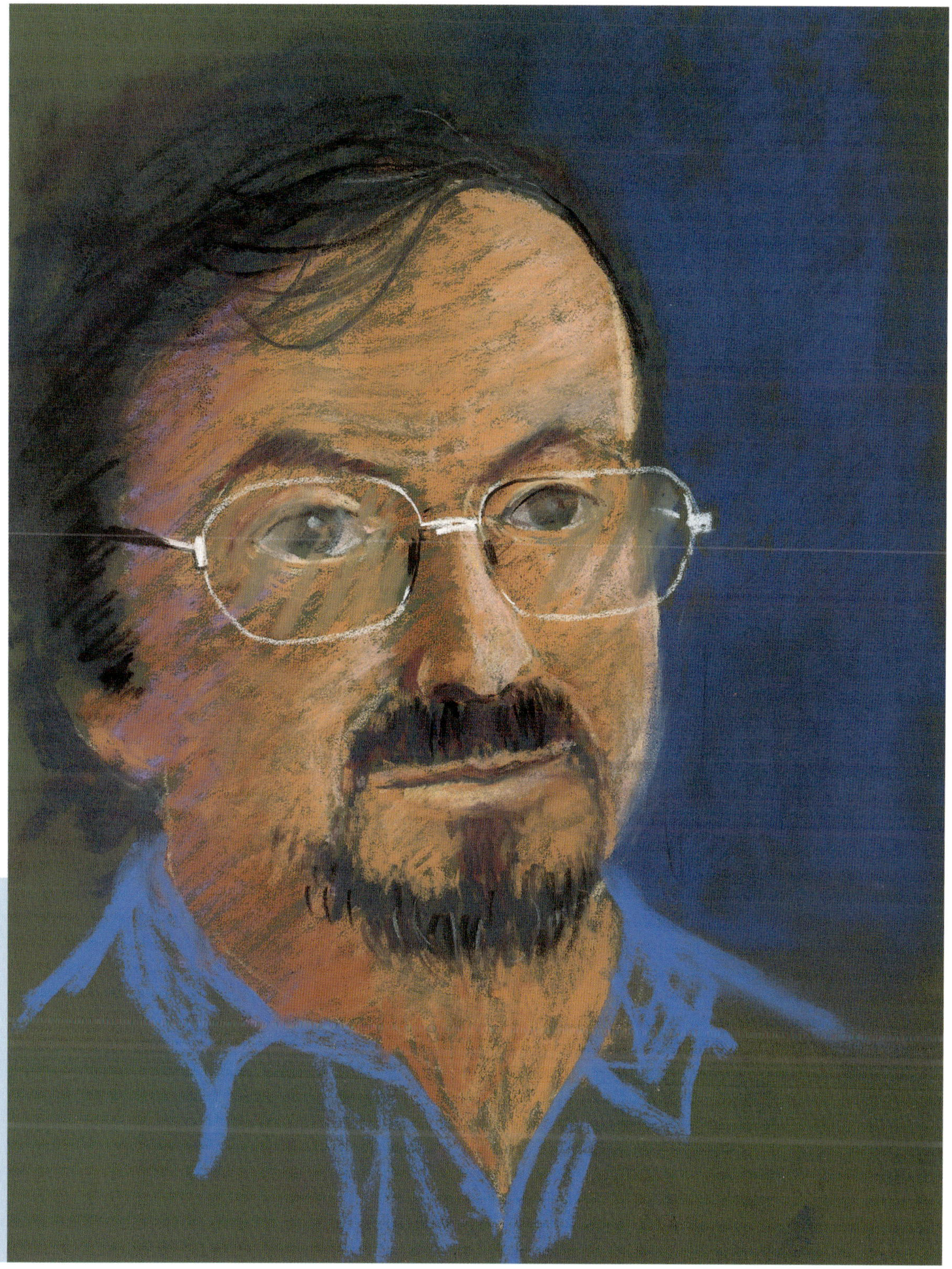

TINTED CHARCOAL

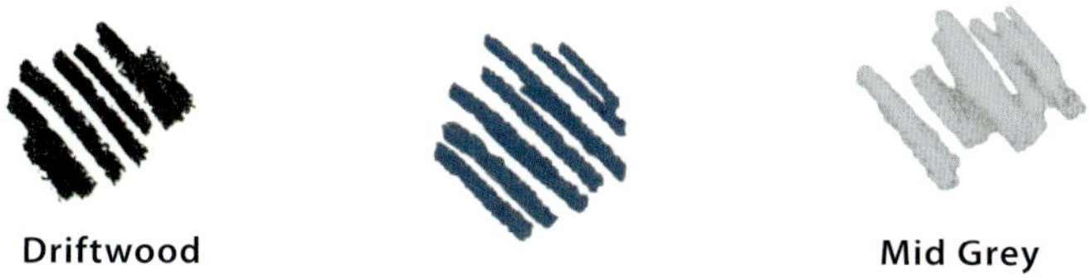

Driftwood

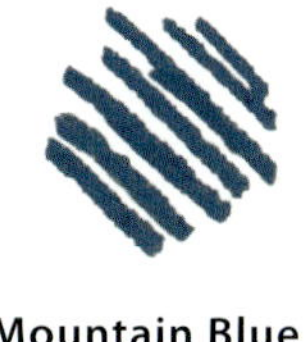
Mountain Blue

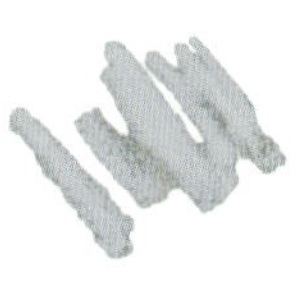
Mid Grey

HARD PASTELS

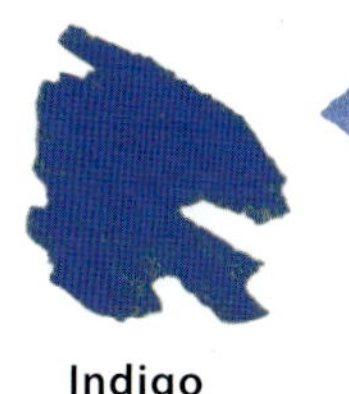
Indigo

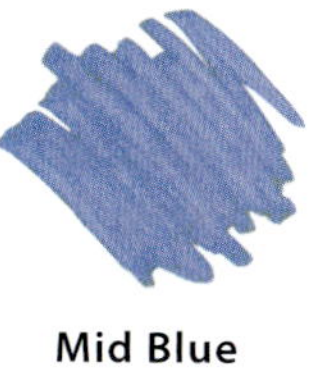
Mid Blue

TECHNIQUE – FIGURES AND PROPORTION

We did a little bit of figure practice earlier in the book, and now we'll take it a step further. The best way to learn how to draw people is by observation from life. Studying photos of figures can also help, especially if you want to draw people in action, such as athletes. Here I give you a general guide, along with a few tips.

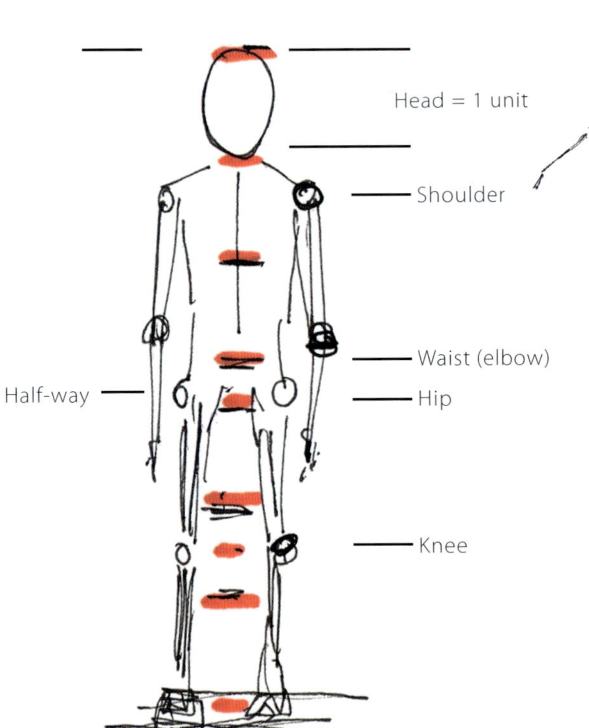

USING MEASUREMENT FOR PROPORTION

▲ *You need to start with a unit of measurement so you can compare relative proportions. I use the head for this; everyone's got one! The head goes into the torso just over twice. The hip to the knee equals one and a half heads. Then there is slightly less than this distance from the knee to the foot. This makes five and a bit 'heads' into the rest of the body. This is a generalization; it varies between five and six with most people. The main thing to watch out for is that you don't make the legs too short. People tend to do this because they assume that the waist is half-way up the body when half-way is (usually) just below the hip. Measure yourself and see!*

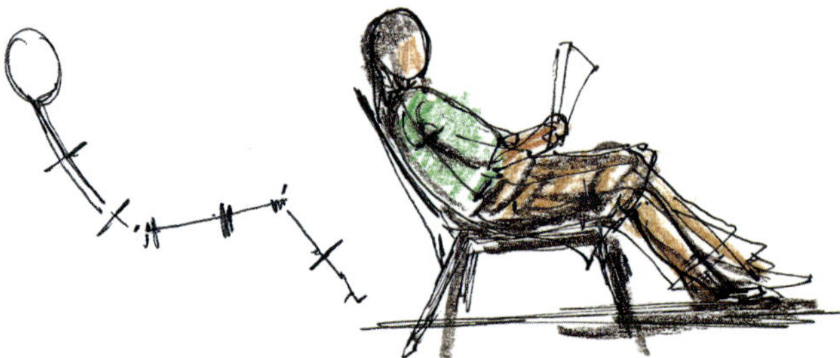

RECLINING FIGURE

▲ *A reclining person is measured in the same way. Draw guidelines in before building the figure out and adding colour; here I've used coloured pencil.*

Centre of gravity

USING THE CENTRE OF GRAVITY

▲ *Figures at work. If a person is pushing or pulling, then their centre of gravity tends to be in front of them (if they're pushing) or behind them (if pulling). Again, drawing the guidelines and measuring with the 'head' unit of measurement will give a good starting point.*

QUICK & CLEVER!

Why not practise drawing a real person? Get a friend and ask them to stand or sit still for you. Try to draw for a maximum of ten minutes at a time, otherwise you'll both get tired!

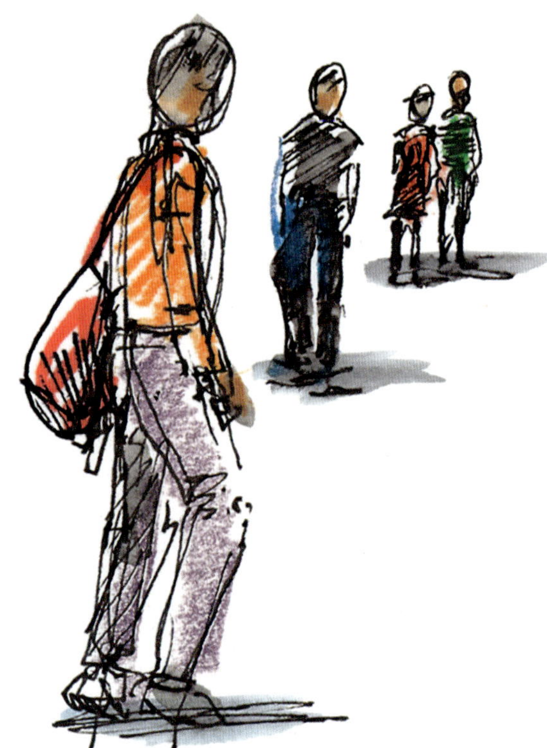

DISTANT FIGURES

▲ *We know that as objects get further away they appear smaller. People are no exception. The thing to observe is that, standing on a level area, figures appear to get smaller from the feet up; most people's heads remain more or less on a similar line.*

TECHNIQUE – FACIAL PROPORTIONS: A ROUGH GUIDE

As with the figure, these tips are for general guidance; there is no substitute for observation. The head can be divided into three, which fits most shapes of face. From the hairline or top of the forehead down to the eye is one-third, then to the base of the nose is two-thirds, and then down to the chin is the last third. When setting out the positions of the elements of the face, use faint guidelines in the usual way to fix the position of everything. The ear, for instance, goes from the eye to the bottom of the nose.

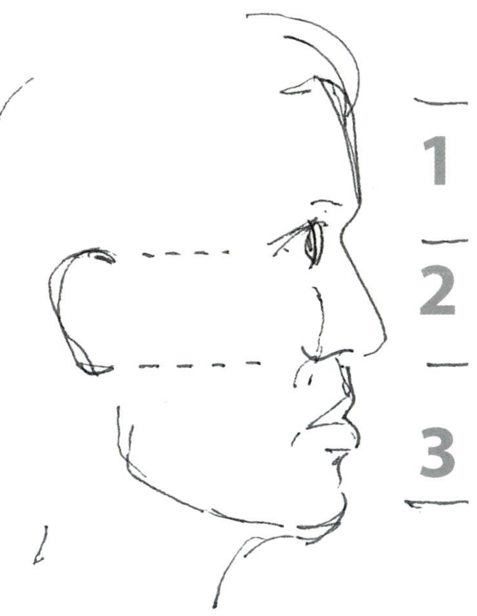

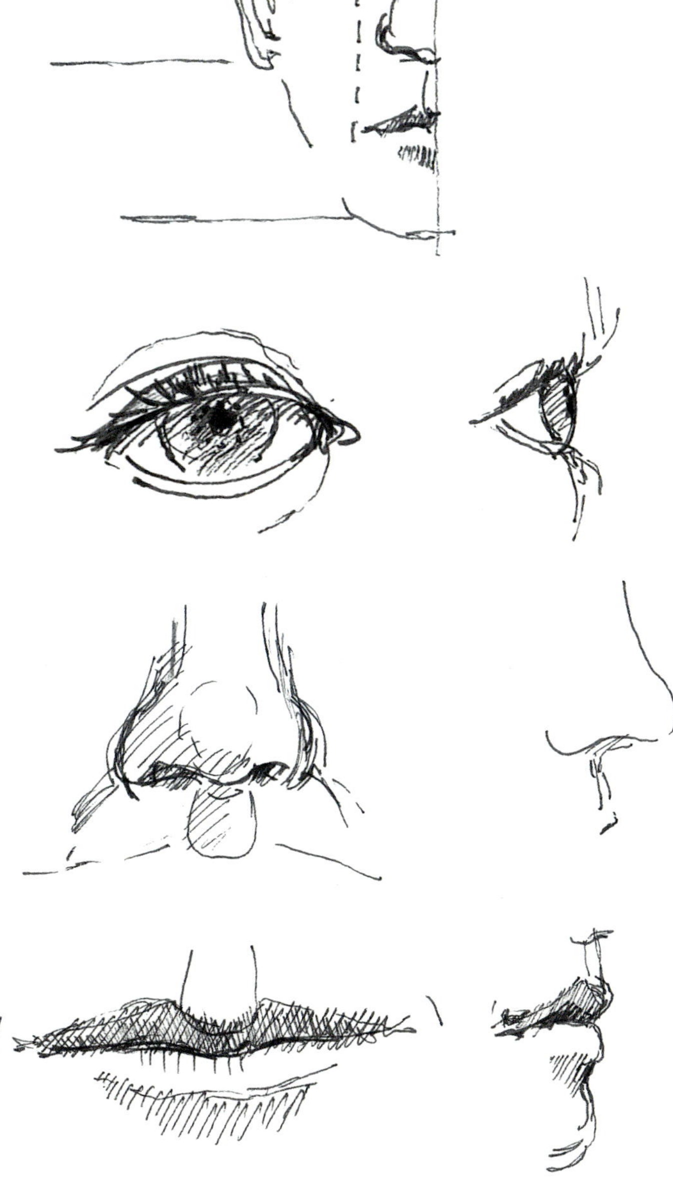

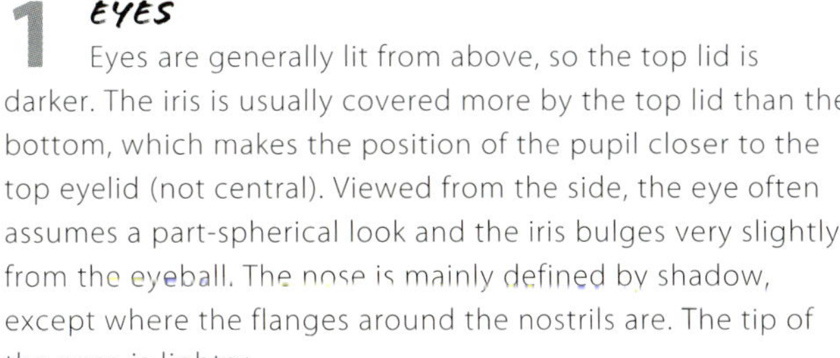

1 EYES

Eyes are generally lit from above, so the top lid is darker. The iris is usually covered more by the top lid than the bottom, which makes the position of the pupil closer to the top eyelid (not central). Viewed from the side, the eye often assumes a part-spherical look and the iris bulges very slightly from the eyeball. The nose is mainly defined by shadow, except where the flanges around the nostrils are. The tip of the nose is lighter.

2 NOSE

Nostrils are downward-facing, and so are visible only obliquely, never round. Running from outside the nostril are little creases that travel down towards the corner of the mouth. The nose, in side view, shows the underside of the nostril as a gentle curve, with a touch of shadow.

3 MOUTH

The mouth is usually darker on the top lip than the bottom, because the top lip is partly shielded from the light by its shape. The bottom lip is more full than the top, especially in women, and catches more light, which is emphasized by the shadow underneath. The corner of the mouth is usually quite close to being directly under the pupil of the eye. The shadow under the chin emphasizes its prominence, and is usually stronger in men than women.

TECHNIQUE – DRAWING FACIAL FEATURES

The best way to begin drawing portraits is to look at the features of the face in isolation, and practise getting their shapes right before combining them in a complete image. Look especially for the subtle tones around the nose and eyes, and down the side of the face.

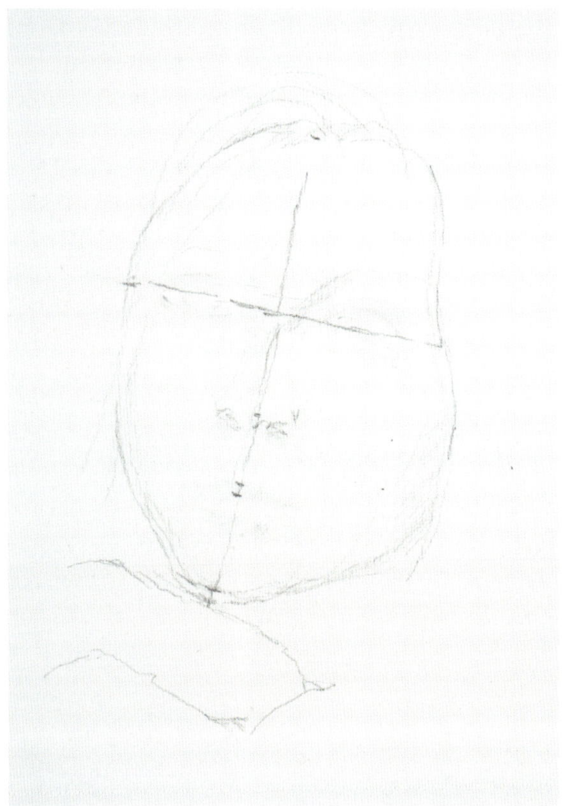

1 DRAW IN GUIDELINES WITH A PENCIL

The first thing to do when drawing the face is to establish faint guidelines. Drawing a centreline is a good place to start. Then add a crossline to indicate where the eyes will go. Most people hold their head slightly on one side, so remember to check if this is the case with your subject.

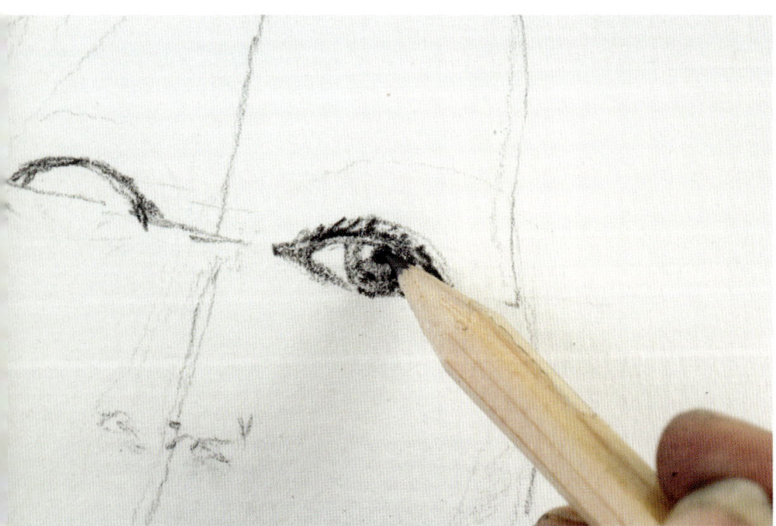

2 ADD EYE DETAIL

Eyes need to be observed carefully, making sure that the upper eyelid is darker than the lower. This is because the light usually comes from above and casts a shadow under the top lid. The pupil (the dark dot) isn't usually in the middle of the eye, but slightly higher. The coloured part of the eye (the iris) is also usually above centre.

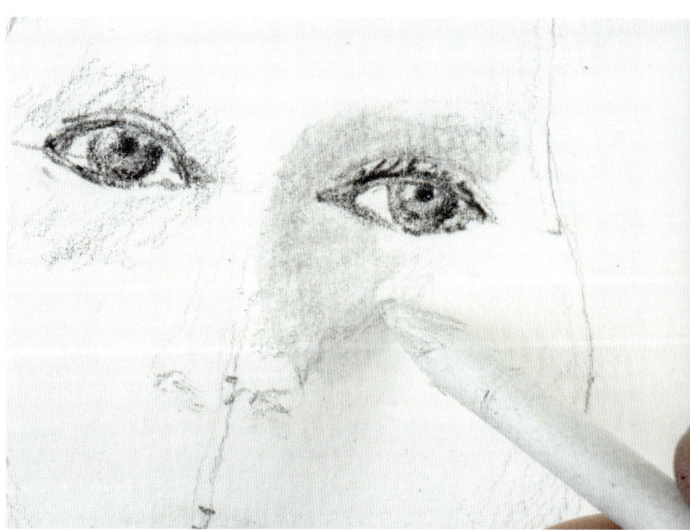

3 DEFINE THE NOSE

The eyes are recessed slightly, and the nose defined, simply by tone. The tone can be lightly hatched with line, or smudged on with graphite and a finger or torchon. Avoid drawing hard-edged lines to define the nose, and make sure that the nostrils aren't too round or too dark. There is usually more tone on one side of the face than the other.

4 DETAIL THE LIPS

The lips come mid-way between the nose and chin. The top lip, like the eyelid, is darker than the lower lip, for the same reason. To establish the lower lip without drawing a line around it, which never looks right, simply shade in some shadow under the lip to define the bottom edge. Put in the crease between the lips with a single line.

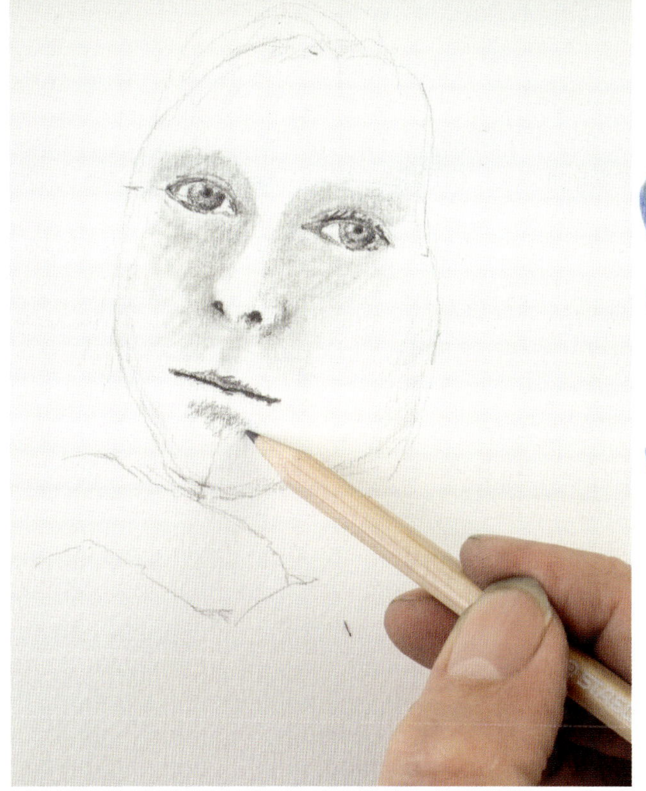

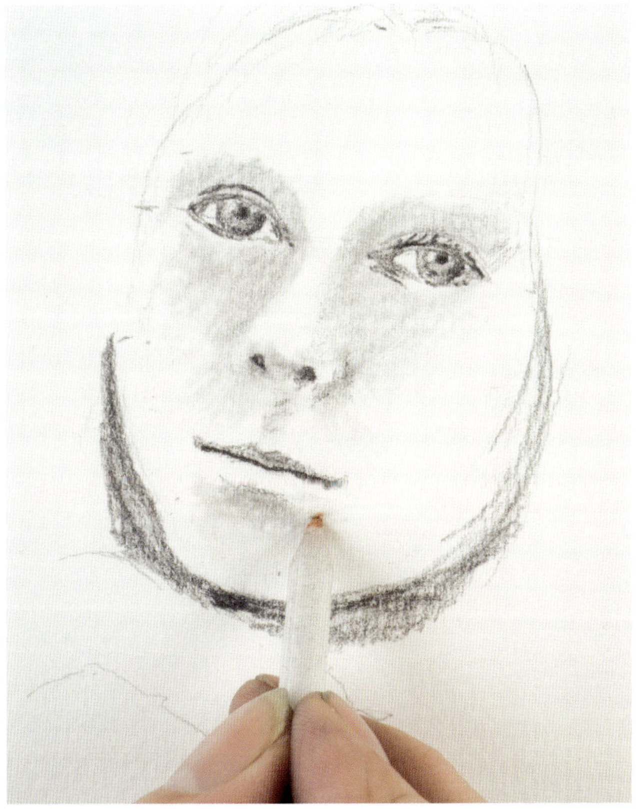

5 SHADOW THE CHIN

The chin is defined by shadow, again without a line. The darker the tone here, the more jutting the chin will look. The tone edge can be softened by rubbing with a finger or torchon, to give a soft, feminine appearance, or left hard for a more masculine look.

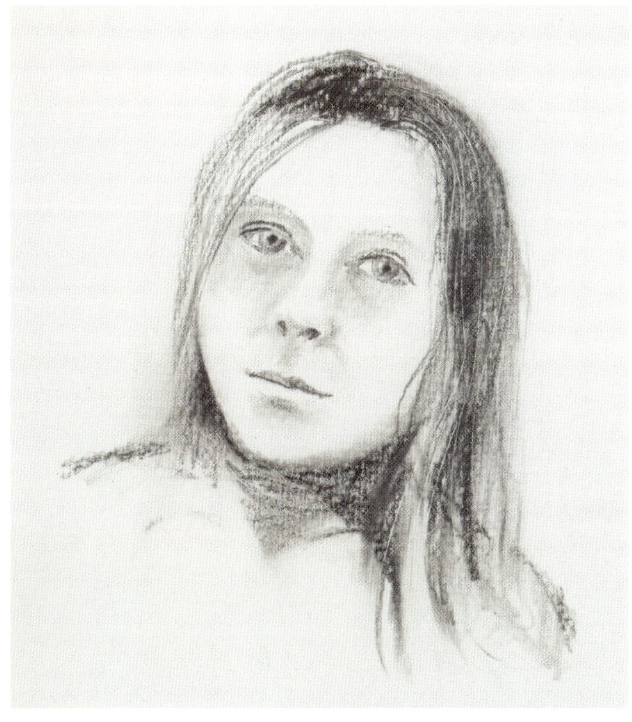

6 CREATE THE HAIR

Hair can be defined by incising lines with a cocktail stick, or drawn in flowing lines with a pencil. Some masses of hair can be quite dark in tone, even in blond hair. When drawing pencil portraits, the eraser can be used as a drawing tool to remove highlights like the tip of the nose, cheekbones and chin. In general, keep lines to a minimum and use gentle gradations of tone instead.

TECHNIQUE – TAKING YOUR PORTRAIT PHOTOS

Lighting is one of the most important, and most often overlooked, aspects of photographing for a portrait. In order to make tonal differences easy to see, the light should come partly from the front, and well to one side. This will make one side of the face darker than the other, which is a good start. A simple way of achieving this is to put the person near a window, looking slightly out of it. The natural light will accentuate the tones and give soft shadows, all of which help to define form.

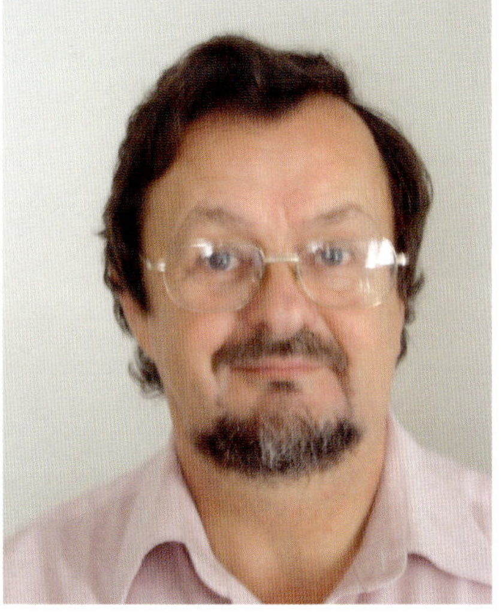

FULL-FACE

▲ *A full-face portrait like this is difficult to work from; it doesn't have much tone, and can appear flat. Even if lit from the side, there won't be much definition. Also, this photo would not be useful because camera shake has made a blurred image.*

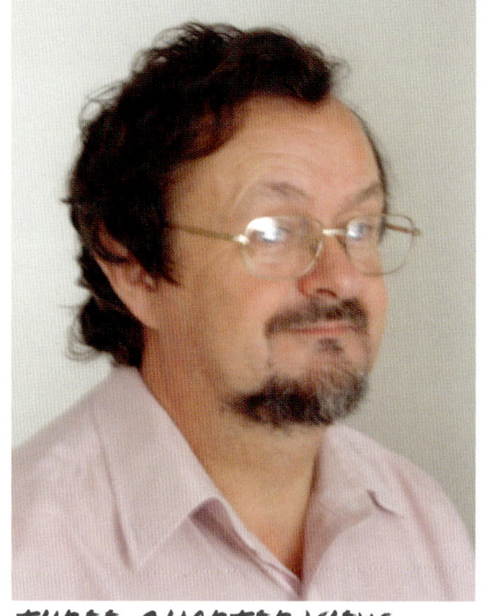

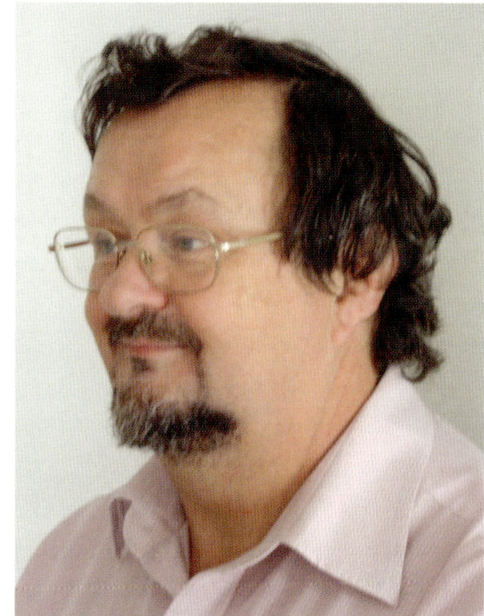

THREE-QUARTER VIEW

▲ *A three-quarter view is easier and, if lit from one side, can be the easiest way of getting started. One eye will look larger than the other because it's nearer, but it's best not to emphasize this too much. The tones and soft shadows help to define the form.*

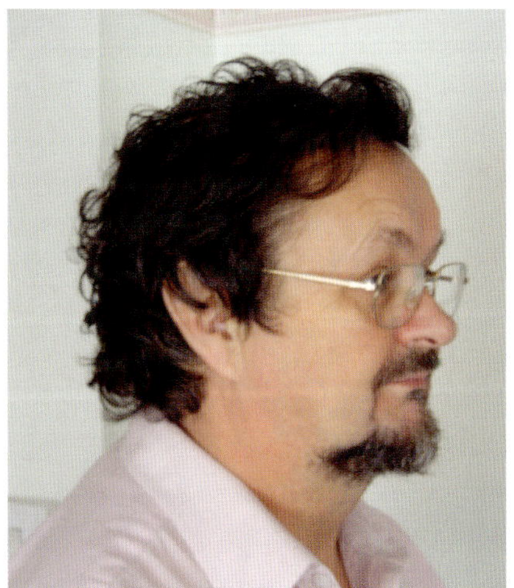

PROFILE

▲ *A profile can be an unusual portrait, and once was very popular. If photographed against a contrasting background, the effect can be used to make a good drawing. Notice that eyes and mouth, when viewed from the side, will be a different shape than from the front.*

QUICK & CLEVER!

When taking a photograph to work from, remember that a portrait will need only head and shoulders. Place your sitter against a plain background, and use a tripod to avoid blurry images. Flash tends to flatten tones, so use natural light only.

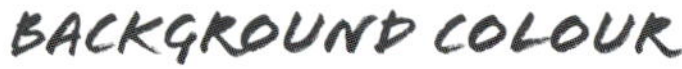

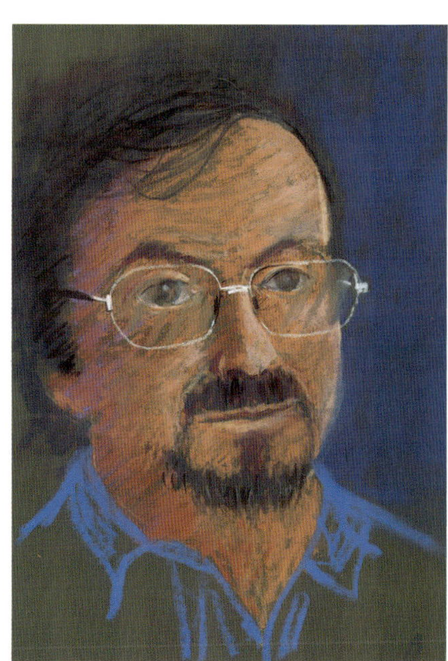

BACKGROUND COLOUR

▶ *Remember that the background colour for the drawing is your choice; you don't have to use the same colour as in the photograph.*

TECHNIQUE – PASTEL PENCIL TECHNIQUES

Flesh tones are usually quite similar to one another, and there often isn't a sudden jump from one tone to another. For that reason, portraits require some subtle techniques.

BLENDING

▶ *Blending is used to smooth the gradation from one tone or flesh colour to the next. With pastels and pastel pencils, though, it's always risky to blend too much; overdo it and 'blend' quickly becomes 'bland'. It's very easy to blend pastel pencils with a paper stump or finger.*

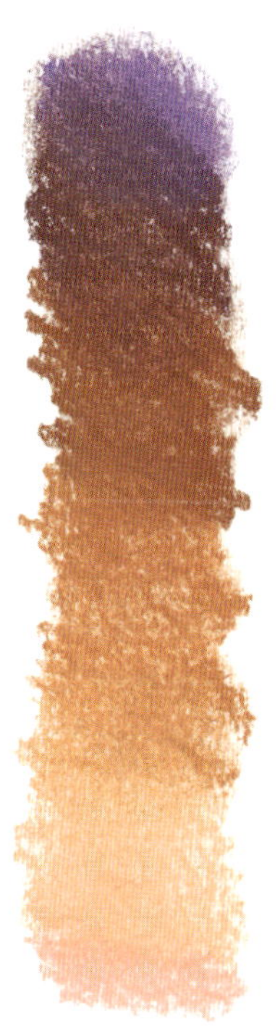

HARD LINES

▲ *Hard lines occur if the pressure is heavy, and don't have much use around the face except for the creases and folds. Lines that are deemed too heavy can be softened with a finger or stump.*

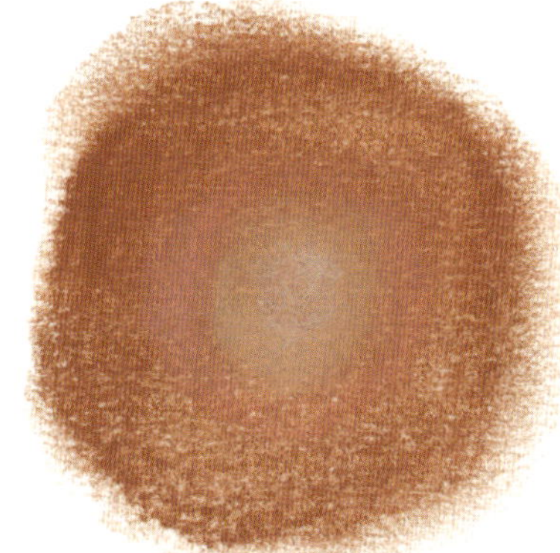

HIGHLIGHTS

▲ *Highlights are applied in the lightest of the flesh tones, when the portrait is nearing completion. Light touches on forehead, nose and chin will make these more prominent. Dark areas, on the other hand, will look receded, so jawlines and neck areas can be made darker and with cooler colours.*

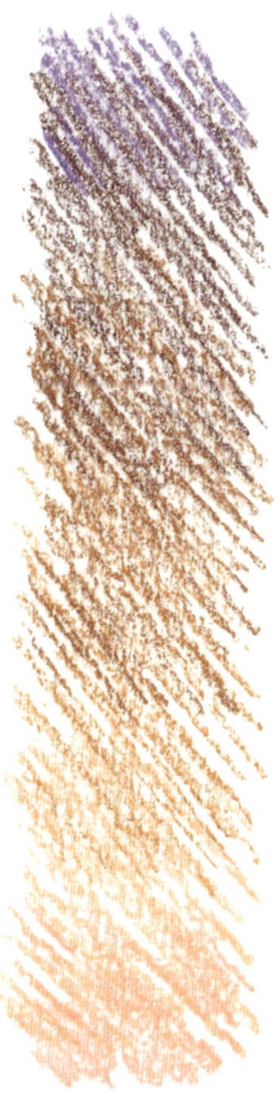

HATCHING

◀ *Hatching is very attractive on a portrait, especially if the lines are very fine and follow the curves of the face. To gradually move from one tone to another, overlap each shaded area with the next one, allowing the lines to merge.*

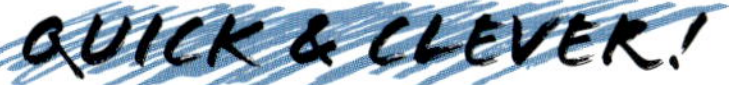

A torchon is a very useful tool for blending, but can sometimes be too hard or clumsy for fine detail work. Try using a cotton bud instead, with gentle pressure. If you save some pastel dust on a plate, the cotton bud can be used to apply colour as well.

QUICK & CLEVER DRAWING

PORTRAIT OF THE AUTHOR

This project, although it's a portrait of me, will teach you the processes you need for making a portrait of yourself. When you have practised on me, have a go at you! It will be easier if you make an enlarged copy of your portrait photo on photocopy paper, and then you can draw the centreline and guide marks as I have done here. By the way, don't worry if your attempt doesn't look much like me, I won't be offended. Honest!

1 INITIAL GUIDELINES With a Medium Terracotta pastel pencil, draw a centreline and guidelines onto the pastel paper. Use a pair of dividers to measure distances between the hairline, bridge and tip of the nose, mouth and chin. Mark these onto the centreline with pastel pencil. You can scale the size up from the photo by simply taking the measurement and doubling or trebling it.

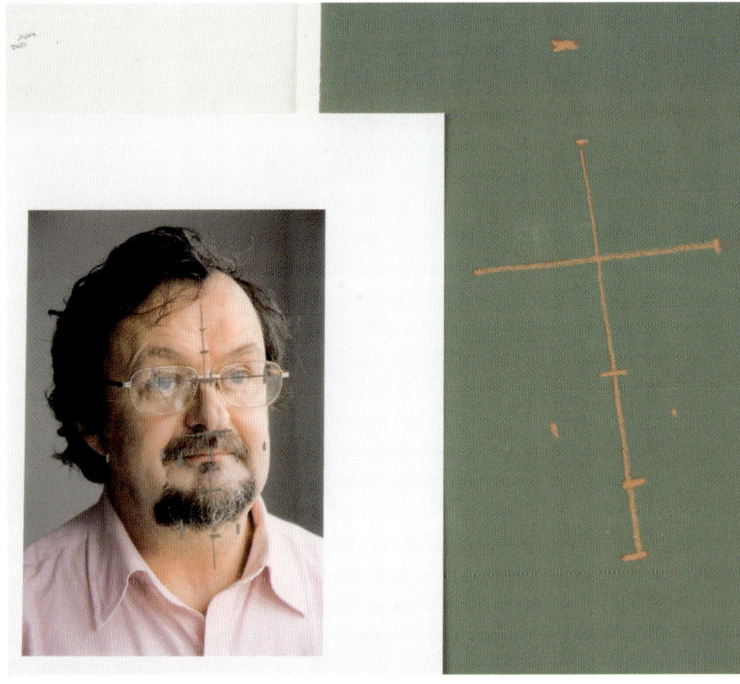

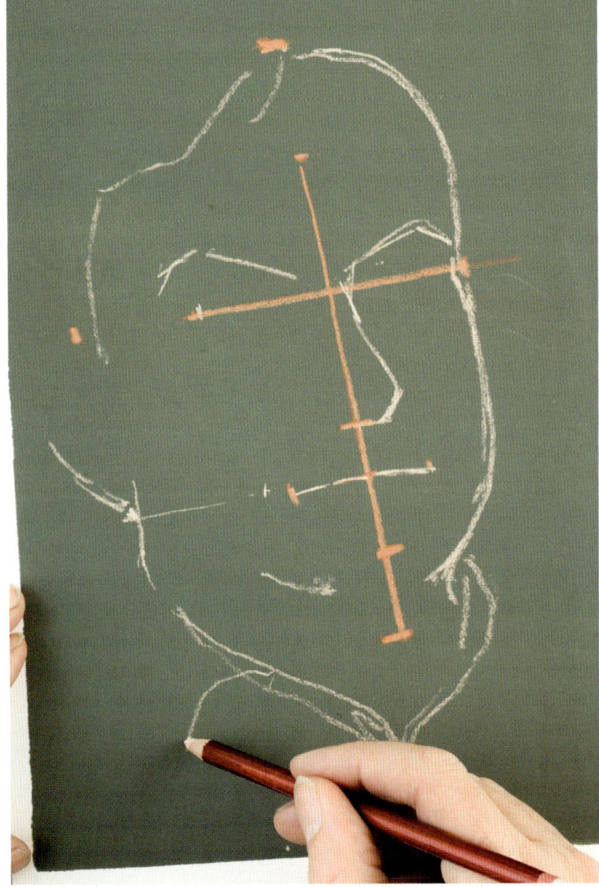

2 MEASURE DISTANCES With some guidelines in place, you can take other measurements, in the same way. Measure distances from the centreline to the side of the face and the ear, and make light marks. Define these guidelines in a Light Terracotta.

PROJECT 6

3 BLOCK IN

Next, shade around the left side of the face, the left of the nose and under the eyebrows with Dark Terracotta. Use light pressure and diagonal hatching. Don't get too neat and fussy at this stage! All you are doing is 'blocking in'.

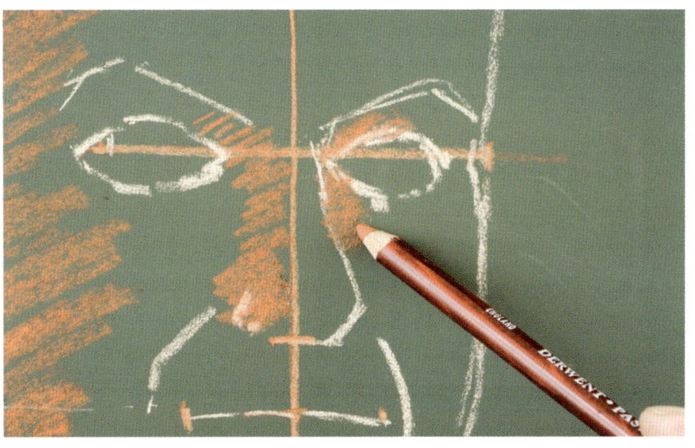

4 COVER REMAINING GUIDELINES

Use a Light Terracotta pastel pencil to block in the remaining areas, including the neck below the beard. Leave the beard and eyes. The aim is to cover the face with skin tones – light, mid and dark – without any detail or blending, except to blend away the remaining guidelines on the chin and under the nose with a torchon.

PROJECT 6

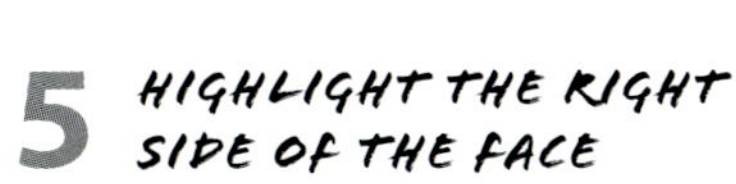

5 HIGHLIGHT THE RIGHT SIDE OF THE FACE

To indicate that the face is lit from the side, use a Spectrum Orange on the right of the face, including the right side of the cheek, nose, forehead and across the lower lip. Work this in on top of the Terracotta colour previously applied. You can apply some frown lines above the brow now as well (if you must!).

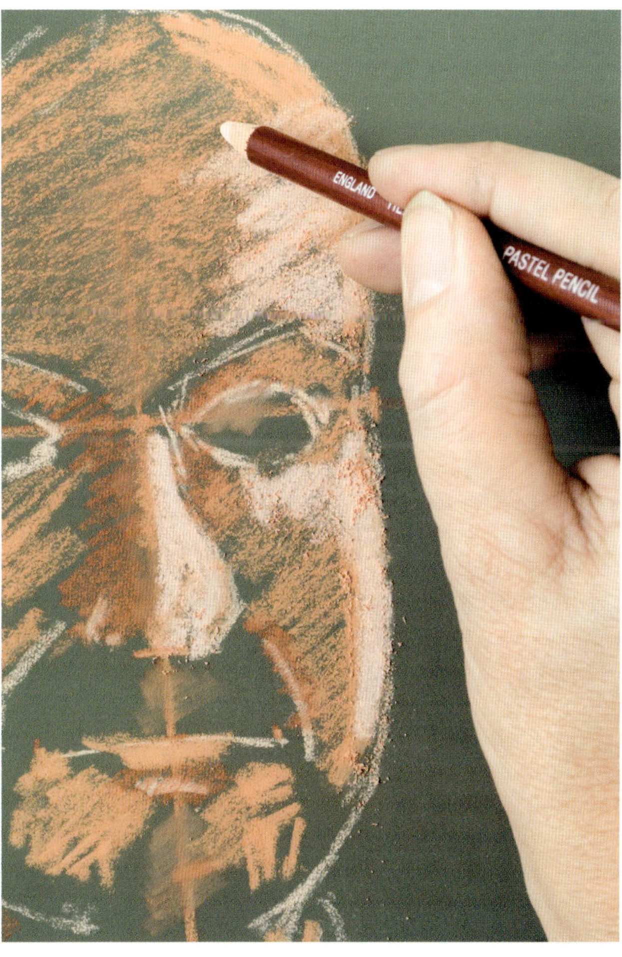

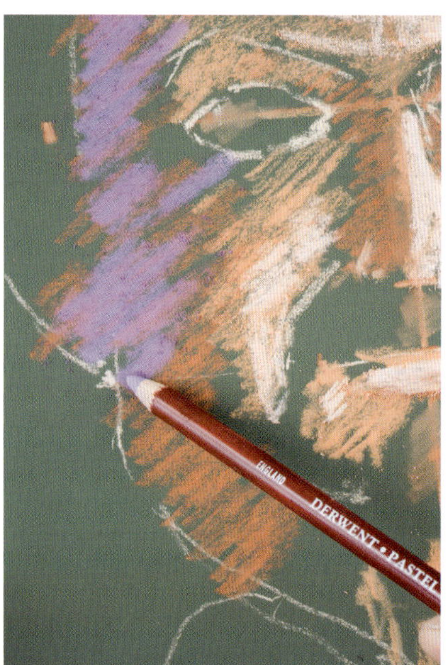

6 USE DARK VIOLET FOR THE SHADOW

Emphasize the shadow on the left side with a Dark Violet, working over the dark flesh tone already there. Keep the diagonal hatching method of applying the pastel pencil. This cool area will appear to recede when compared to the warm, light area.

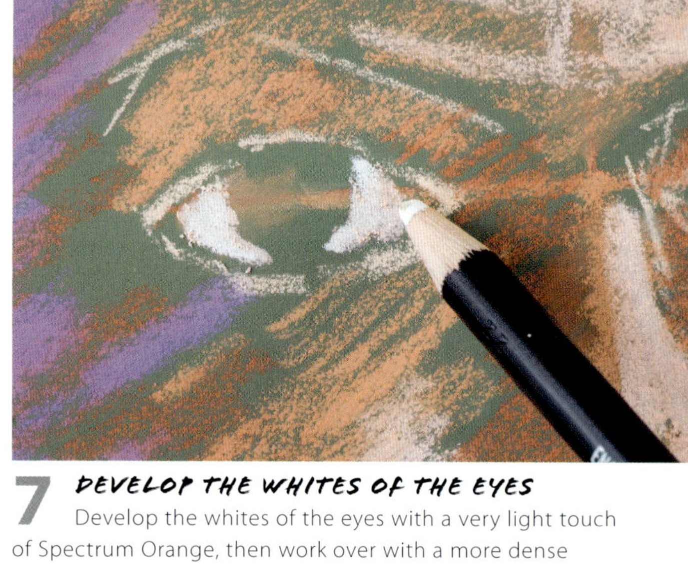

7 DEVELOP THE WHITES OF THE EYES

Develop the whites of the eyes with a very light touch of Spectrum Orange, then work over with a more dense application of White pastel pencil. Add deeper shadow under the top eyelid with Driftwood tinted charcoal.

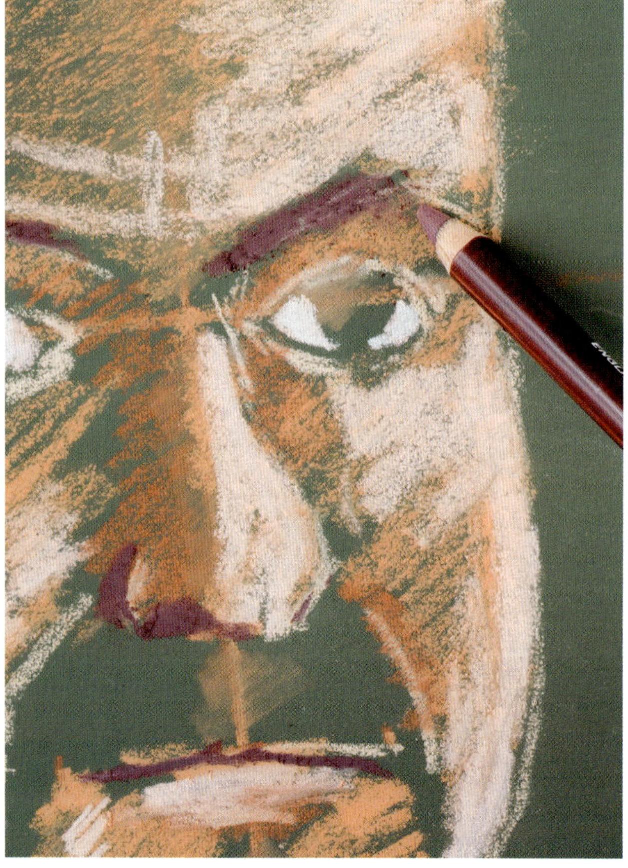

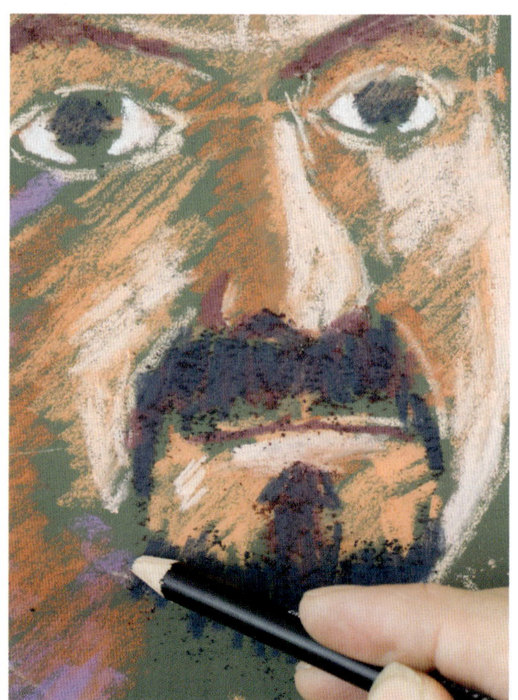

8 ENHANCE THE EYEBROWS

The darker areas under the eyebrows are enhanced next, using a Burnt Carmine pastel pencil. Use some of this colour on the area below the lower lip, defining the shape of the beard, and down the left side of the nose, including the nostril. Don't make the nostril too big!

9 ADD FACIAL HAIR

Use tinted charcoal Mountain Blue to give some colour to the iris of both eyes. This colour can also be added to the moustache and beard to deepen the colour. A thin line of Mountain Blue can be added to the underside of the upper eyelid to darken it, and to the nostril.

10 START THE HAIR

Establish the hair on the right with Mountain Blue, continuing this around the top of the forehead to the other side. Add some strands across the forehead in thin, curving lines; this was a bad hair day!

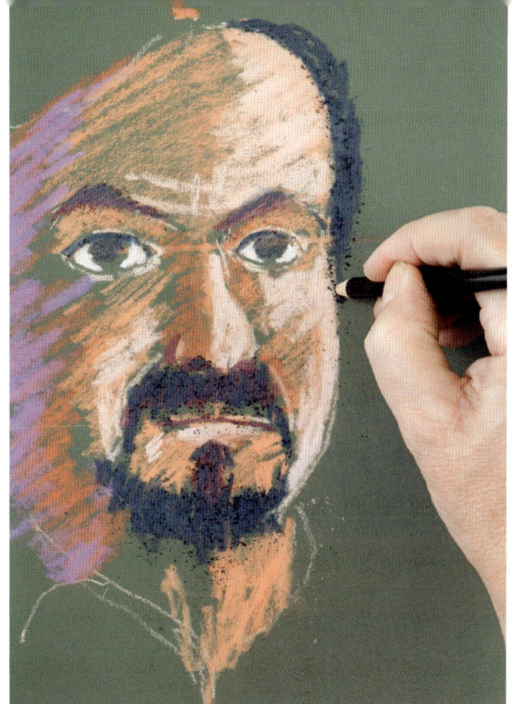

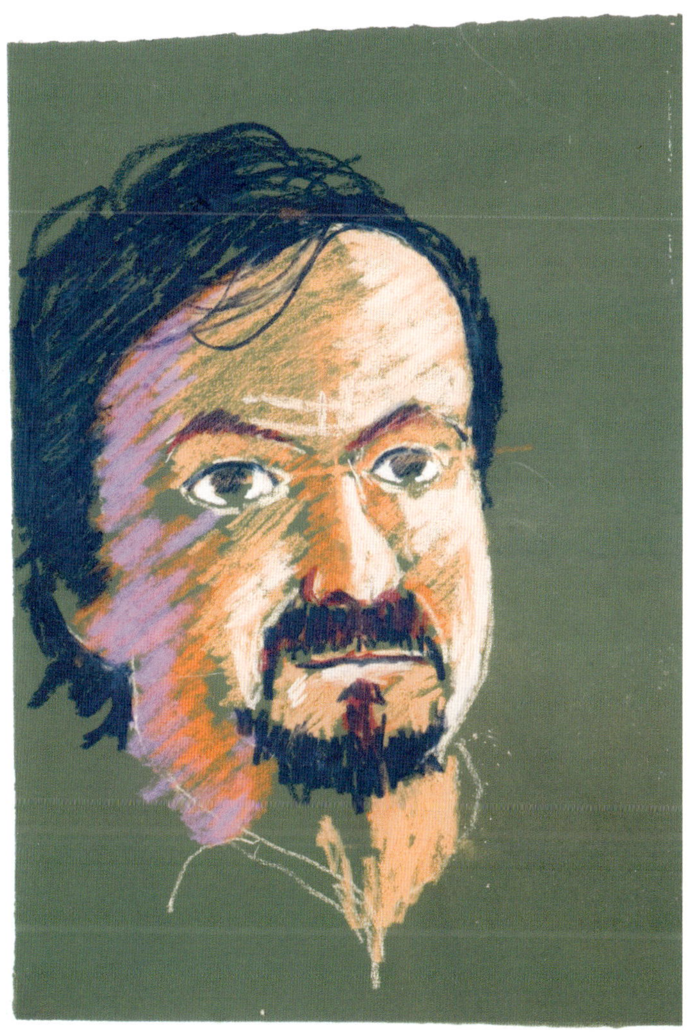

11 DON'T OVER-BLEND

So far the tones have been established and defined with bold, linear marks. Avoid the temptation to blend these strokes together as you go; an over-blended portrait can look very bland.

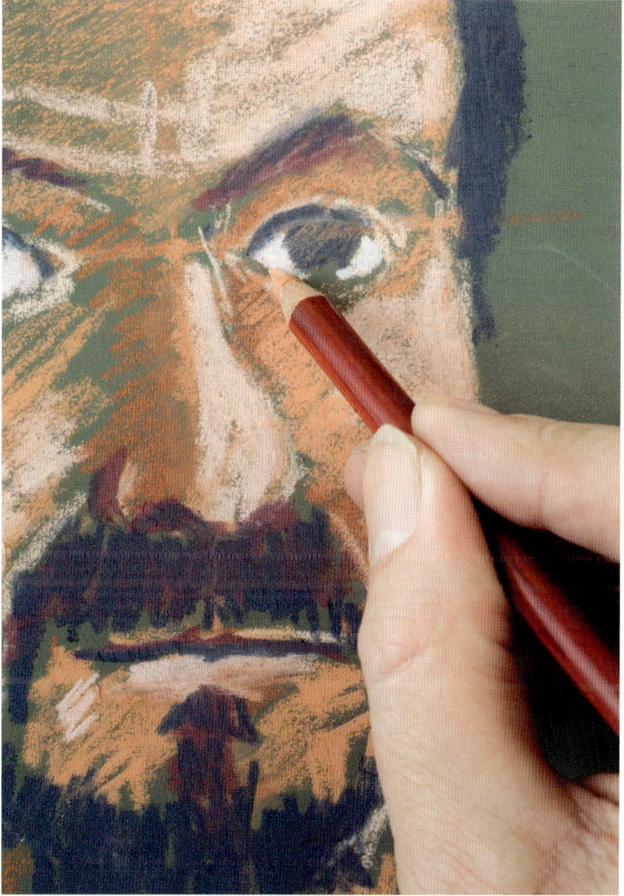

12 TONE TO DEFINE CONTOURS

Take a Medium Terracotta tinted charcoal and follow the contour of the lower eyelid, working around to smooth the area below the eye. Use the same colour to build the look of a crease under the nose, going around the moustache. Add the bottom of the earlobe. Also use this to fill in more solid colour on the forehead, cheeks and anywhere where there is too much of the paper showing. Use Dark Terracotta tinted charcoal for the neck below the beard.

PROJECT 6

13 USE LIGHT TERRACOTTA ON EYELID

With a Mid Grey tinted charcoal, add some shadow to the whites of each eye, under the upper eyelid. Then use Light Terracotta to add lights to the fold of skin on top of the upper eyelid.

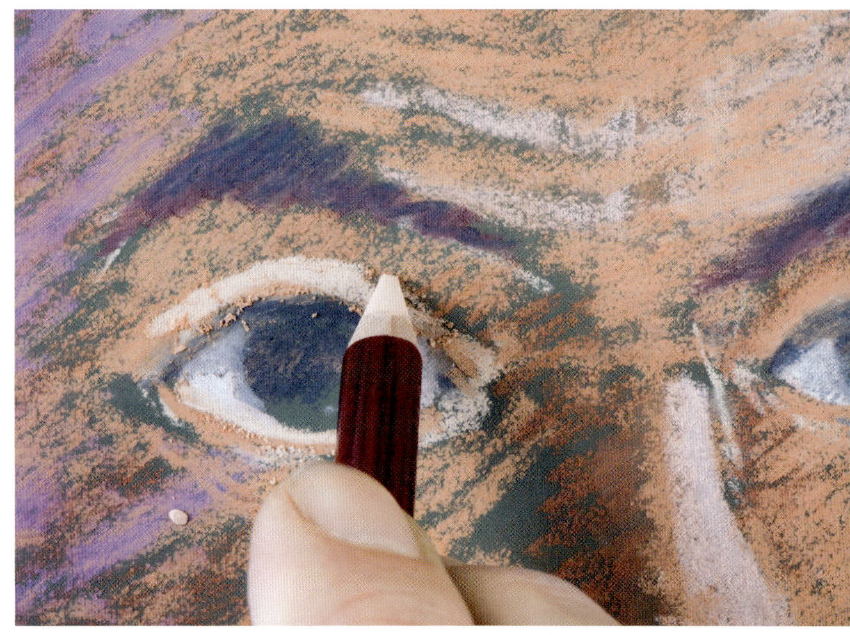

14 DEFINE THE EYE

Driftwood tinted charcoal, sharpened to a point, is used to finalize the dark of the upper eyelids. The same colour is used to put some streaks into the beard and moustache, and also some curved lines into the hair, above the hairline.

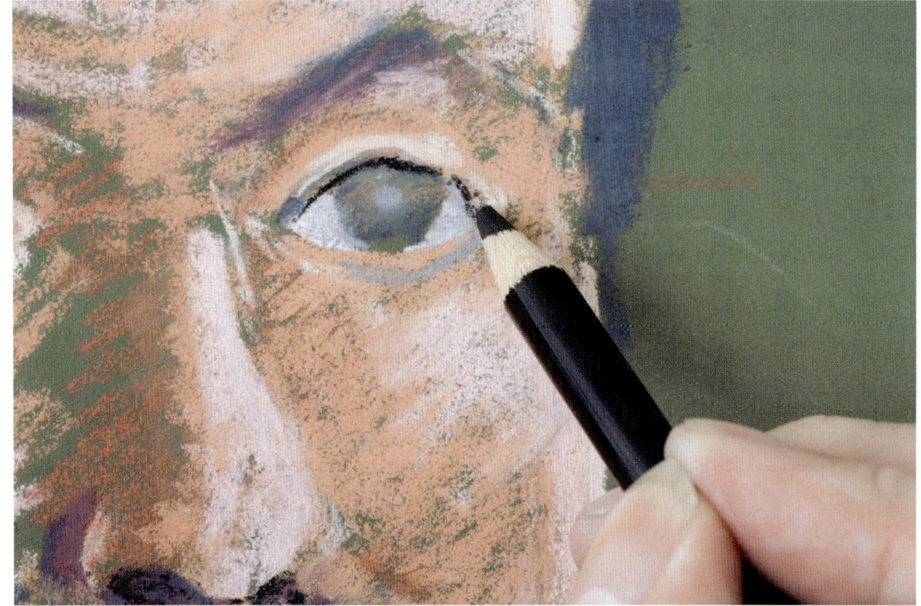

15 OUTLINE THE GLASSES

Use White pastel pencil to carefully draw in the spectacles (practise the shapes first on a separate piece of paper; they aren't as easy as they look!). Then take a Burnt Umber pastel pencil and add a few shadow lines on the rim. This will make the glasses look more solid.

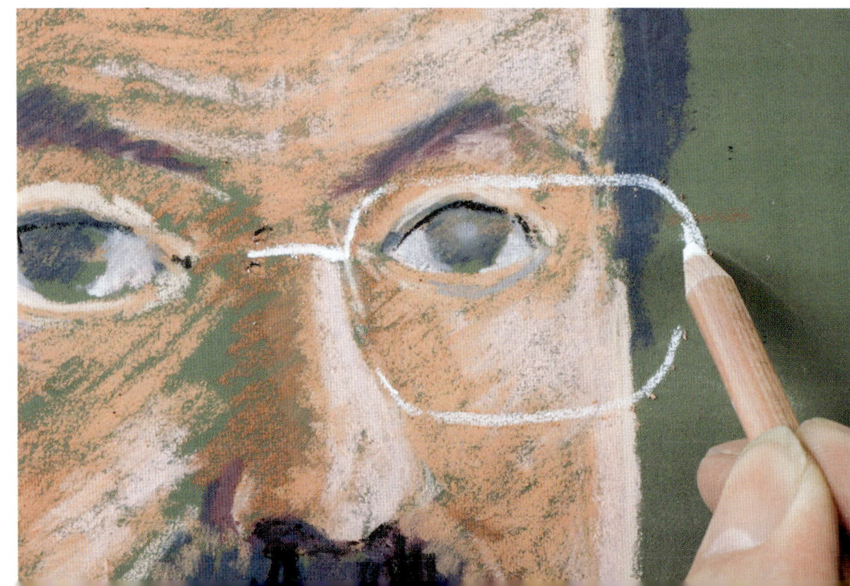

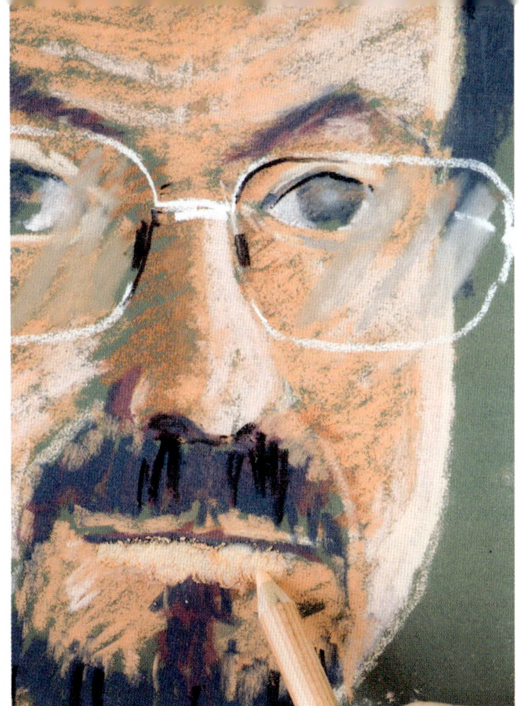

16 APPLY COLOUR TO LIP

Almost finished! Apply some colour onto the lower lip to enhance it, using a Peach pastel pencil, and work a Medium Terracotta tinted charcoal gently over the violet on the left, to make it less bright. Use the same colour to darken the left-hand side of the neck.

17 THE FINISHING TOUCH

To complete the portrait, add an Indigo hard pastel on the background down the right side of the face. If the shape of the cheek isn't quite right, you can use this dark colour to make minor adjustments. Use another hard pastel, Mid Blue, to sketch in the appearance of a shirt.

Now, sit back and admire your first portrait! As I said earlier, don't worry if it doesn't look like me; if it looks even slightly human, you're well on the way! So, how about another portrait? Of yourself, this time…

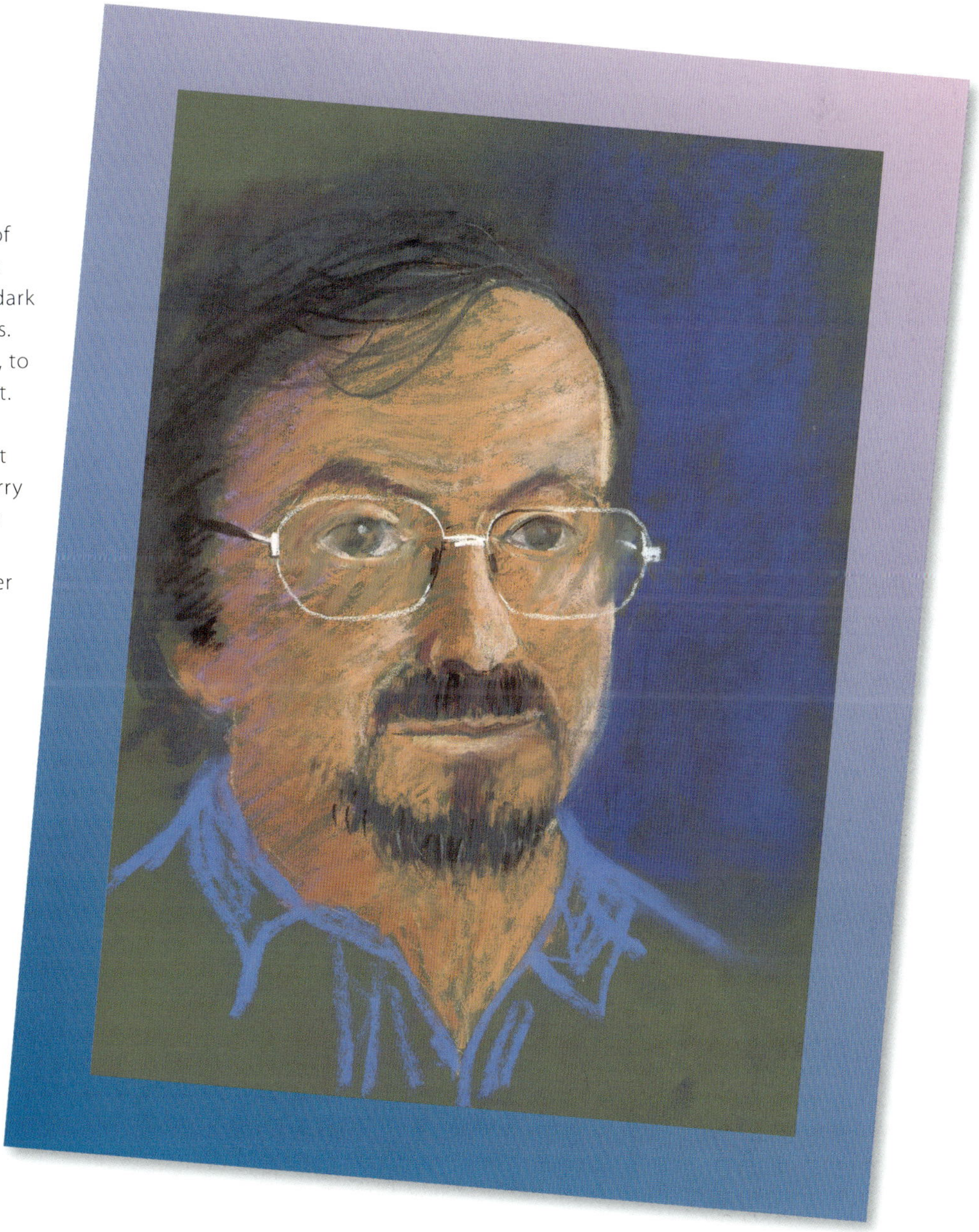

A FINAL WORD

I hope you have enjoyed reading this book and practising the techniques as much as I enjoyed writing it. Drawing can be a really expressive medium, and you will find that the more drawing you do the easier it becomes. Next time you go on holiday, who knows; you may well come back with holiday drawings instead of holiday photos. The main thing is to keep practising.

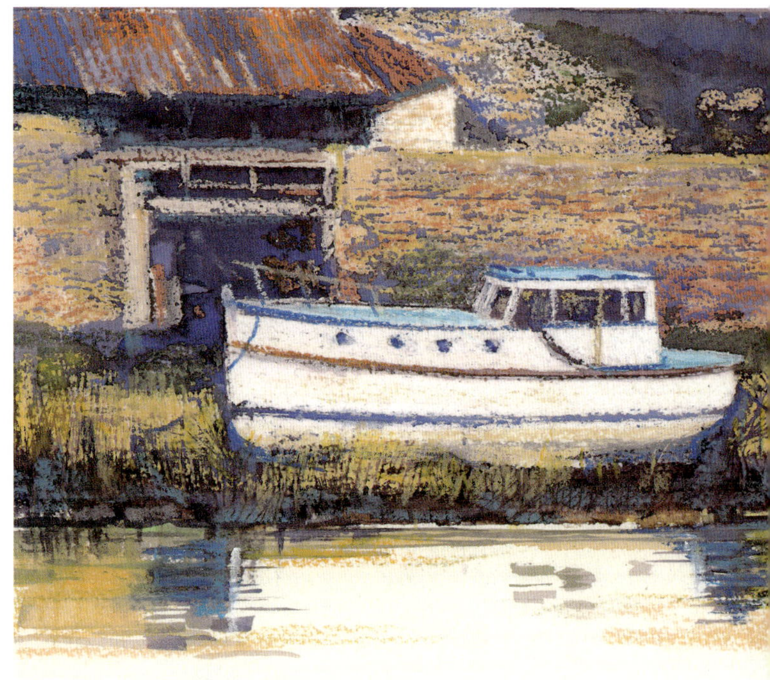

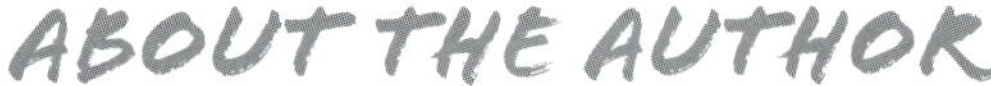

Michael Sanders studied graphic design and ceramics after leaving school, and has been involved in creative work ever since; his work is in collections worldwide. A qualified teacher, he conducts workshops and classes on drawing and painting, and runs painting holidays, where his infectious enthusiasm for all things artistic ensures that everyone has an enjoyable and productive time. Michael also holds a commercial pilot's licence, and when not involved in art he teaches aviation and pilots his own light aircraft.

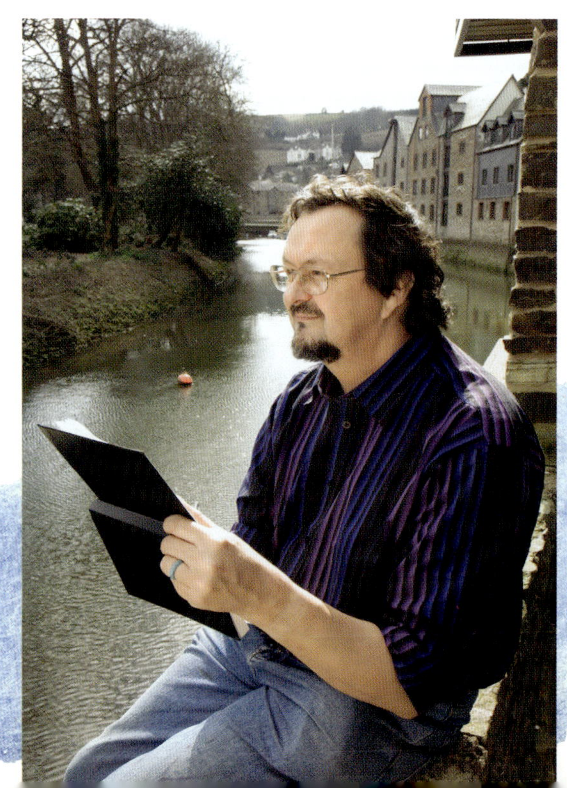

ACKNOWLEDGMENTS

I would like to thank Kim for being such a talented photographer and making our sessions relaxed and enjoyable; Freya for her enthusiasm for the book; and the design and editorial team at David and Charles for turning it into reality. Finally, a big thanks to anyone who has ever joined one of my classes with the words 'I can't draw'. That phrase has been responsible for the idea that became this book. I thank you all.

INDEX